Dreaming Blackness

Dreaming Blackness

*Black Nationalism and
African American
Public Opinion*

Melanye T. Price

NEW YORK UNIVERSITY PRESS

New York and London

NEW YORK UNIVERSITY PRESS
New York and London
www.nyupress.org

Library of Congress Cataloging-in-Publication Data

Price, Melanye T.
Dreaming blackness : black nationalism and African American public
opinion / Melanye T. Price.
p. cm.
Includes bibliographical references and index.
ISBN-13: 978-0-8147-6744-3 (cloth : alk. paper)
ISBN-10: 0-8147-6744-3 (cloth : alk. paper)
ISBN-13: 978-0-8147-6745-0 (pbk. : alk. paper)
ISBN-10: 0-8147-6745-1 (pbk. : alk. paper)
1. African Americans—Race identity. 2. Black nationalism—United
States. 3. African Americans—Attitudes. 4. Public opinion—United
States. I. Title.
E185.625.P74   2009
305.896'073—dc22   2009002433

New York University Press books are printed on acid-free paper, and
their binding materials are chosen for strength and durability. We
strive to use environmentally responsible suppliers and materials to
the greatest extent possible in publishing our books.

Manufactured in the United States of America
c   10 9 8 7 6 5 4 3 2 1
p   10 9 8 7 6 5 4 3 2 1

Dedicated to Sandra Faye Spates Price

Contents

Acknowledgments

This book would not have been possible without the help of wonderful teachers and mentors at The Ohio State University who trained and encouraged me. I am especially grateful for their support, insight, and patience. Paul Allen Beck gave me space to think through and explore ideas, the benefit of his expertise, and polite prodding in equal measure. He is a model scholar and teacher, and I can only hope to benefit from his example. William E. Nelson Jr. has been for me and for many other young black scholars a mentor, advocate, teacher, and continuous source of wisdom. He remains one of the most insightful people I know, and I am still awed by his ability to ask the hardest and most essential questions. At the last minute, Clarissa Rile Hayward stepped in and brought fresh ideas and eyes to a project that I had long labored over. No one gets through graduate school well without a supportive community of friends and scholars. I was very lucky to find both in the halls of my department. I am thankful to Valeria Sinclair-Chapman, Kathy L. Powers, Cynthia Duncan Joseph, Teresa Todd, Shelly Anderson, Javonne Paul Stewart, Khalilah Brown-Dean, Travis Simmons, Jessica Lavariega-Monforti, and Ray Block. I am also grateful to Racquel Greene, Melanie Arum, and Nicole Johnson. In this process they have become more than friends; they are collaborators, coauthors, and, most important, family. It is a community that I have found impossible to replicate in any other space.

My colleagues at Wesleyan University provided me with space, time, and advice about the best way to transform this project into a manuscript. I am thankful to John Finn, Marc Eisner, and Manolis Kaparakis, who offered helpful feedback at various stages of the manuscript. My Wesleyan family has been invaluable in keeping my sanity through this process. I am grateful for the support, encouragement, and friendship from my colleagues and their families—Gina Ulysse; Katja, Bo, Zenon, and Axel Kolcio; Renee, Cliff, Afia, and Nkosi Johnson-Thornton; Kate Rushin; Lorelle, Brian, and Elijah (Semley) Robinson; and the members of the

Administrators and Faculty of Color Alliance. Everyone should be lucky enough to have an office next to two of the greatest tech guys ever. John Hammond and Manolis Kaparakis aided greatly in technical support as well as laughter, lunch, and camaraderie. Kristen Olson provided comments and edits on early versions of the manuscript. There are two people at Wesleyan University who for reasons I still cannot quite explain have taken me into their hearts and been generous with their friendship. Tina Salafia and Janet Demicco have been my sanctuary when I have needed smiling faces and encouragement. For that I am forever in their debt, and they are forever in my heart. My transition from Ohio to Connecticut was also made easier by the arrival of the Brown-Dean family (Khalilah, William, and little Hayley), Shayla Nunally, and new friends like Kerry, Zoe, and Frankie Kincy, Catherine Johnson, and Erica Augustine.

I would also like to thank Ilene Kalish at NYU Press, who eagerly answered questions and offered advice while ensuring that this project moved along at a good pace. There were also anonymous reviewers whose insightful comments and criticisms pushed me to think through and clearly explain my arguments. All the reviewers provided pages of detailed comments about every aspect of the document, and as a result the manuscript was greatly enhanced. In addition to Ilene, her assistants—Gabrielle Begue and Aiden Amos—handled my day-to-day questions and offered friendly inquiries as to my progress. I could not have asked for a better team for my first book.

During the data collection process, Cynthia Duncan Joseph and Francisca Figueroa-Jackson stepped in at a crucial moment and helped me collect all the data I needed before I left for Connecticut. I have also been fortunate enough to present parts of this research here at Wesleyan, the University of Rochester, and Central Connecticut State University, as well as at professional conferences. It is my sincere hope that members of these various audiences will see great advances in the final product. Their comments and questions have been appreciated.

As I try to find my place in this profession, I have had the good fortune of seeking solace and advice from people who are making this journey with me and who I am proud to call colleagues and friends. They turned one miserable summer of AP grading into the best time I have ever had. Then and in subsequent summers I have fleshed out research ideas, critiqued others, discussed professional development, and become a better (and louder) card player. Wendy Smooth, Byron D'Andra Orey, Keesha Middlemass, Evelyn Simien, Menna Demessie, Randolph Burnside, Boris

Ricks, James Taylor, and Tiffany Howard have been invaluable in this process. I also have found that the advice of people who are where you want to be in your career is as useful as good research comments. Melissa Nobles talked me through the book publishing process and helped me make crucial decisions about the future of this manuscript. Developing these relationships has made conferences professionally and socially more fulfilling and provided honest and useful feedback at all times.

Before I began to formulate this research question, my interest in black people and their empowerment and politics was nurtured by my professors in the Benjamin Banneker Honors College at Prairie View A&M University. They saw my intellectual abilities and opened my eyes to academic and career opportunities that were beyond my horizon. My life is much better for it. Jewel Limar Prestage has ushered so many students through the graduate school process and given them the confidence to keep going despite the odds. I am so glad that she chose me to be one of them. How lucky I am to have met her when I was eighteen years old and have her say that I could be a college professor, a doctor, or anything else I wanted to be, and then equip me with the tools to actually do it. I am eternally grateful for the doors she has opened for me, phone calls made on my behalf, unexpected calls to assess my progress, encouragement to keep trying, and assurance to my family that I was on a good path. Mack and Barbara A. P. Jones helped provide a sound academic foundation to build on in graduate school. At a time when I was least confident in my abilities, Barbara Jones gave me helpful advice and loving encouragement that I still cherish to this day. Though we spent only one year in the same place, Lisa Aubrey had a profound impact on my interest in politics. She was an engaging teacher and has become a valued friend. My experience at Prairie View embodied what is best about historically black colleges, and that is their ability to see and help students to identify dreams larger than the ones they knew to have and provide them with the confidence and resources to attain them. At that small college forty-five miles northwest of Houston, I learned the value of intellectual curiosity, good mentoring, and true friendship. Though we have dispersed, I am still grateful to the friends I made there. Salina Gray, Rhoda (Robinson) Freelon, Byron Freelon, Kesha Willis Parker, and Juba Watts-Cain have been my long-distance support network and providers of vacation residences for more than a decade. Our friendship has been steadfast through time and distance. Hopefully, this book is tangible evidence that their investment in me was worth it.

Ten years ago, I sat in a red chair in an office in the polimetrics lab in OSU's political science department to talk to another graduate student that I barely knew. That student became the best friend I have ever had. At varying times, Gloria Jean Hampton has been my confidante, my copy editor, my reality check, and my traveling buddy, but at all times I am glad to say that she has been my true friend. She is one of the smartest and best-read people I know. Her unquenchable desire for knowledge and unyielding intellectual curiosity are both enviable and awe-inspiring. She has witnessed my highs and lows and still wants to be my friend, and my life is the better for it.

There is one person for whom the title of best friend is insufficient. We have been together since conception, which makes her my first and truest friend, my twin sister, Melynda Janea Price. We have always complemented each other in ways that I hope bring out the best in both of us. She is my courage when I am fearful, my sanity when I am off the chain, my confidence when I am doubtful, my champion when I am under siege, my buffer when I am in pain, and my ally against all foes. I only hope that I have been the same for her. She is the first person I want to tell my good news and the person who knows me best. I am so proud of her and all her accomplishments and greatly admire her intellect and loving spirit.

This book begins a new page (pun intended) for my entire family. This is the first book any of us has ever published, and we are all excited about it. In many ways it is a collective achievement because they are my constant source of support and inspiration. I would like acknowledge the love and encouragement of my sisters, Sandra Juanita Carr, Leslie Lorraine Maxie, Sharon Diane Price, and Melynda Janea Price. We are the five Price girls. You mess with one, you mess with us all. I know in all things they've got my back and I have theirs. My family is the center of my heart and the orbit on which my world revolves. I thank those watching over me: James Spates, Andrew Spates, Gladys Spann, Sonny Spates, Alvin Gordon, and Tony Bryant. For the million little ways they sustain me, I thank Mary Gordon, Joe Spates, Alex Spates, Lily Spates, Faye Spates, Joseph Carr I, Shawana Bailey, Joseph Carr II, Adrienne Carr, Alicia Carr, Leslie Carr, Melissa Maxie, Alex Maxie, Diana Carr, Desiree Carr, Myricle Gordon, Alexa Maxie, Mykala Gordon, Erica Gordon, Wanda Gordon, Katherine Ellzy, Gregory Sims, Breanna Allen, Krystal Stewart, Kamille Gordon, Cameron Ellzy, Patricia Bryant, Muriel Robertson, Steve Spann, Steve Spann Jr., Michelle Spates, Derrick Bryant, Adrian Anderson, Jackie Anderson, Joshua Anderson, Jonathon Anderson, Monique McCardell,

Nia McCardell, TJ McCardell, Tori McCardell, Jimmy Spates, Lynn Spates, Wanda Spates, Gail Spates, Kathy Spates, Nicole Spates, Gerald Spates, George Spates Jr., Janine Spates, Inez Lands, Nzinga Rideaux, Harrison Joseph, Sydney Joseph, Simone Joseph, the Costas, the Reisslands, the community of Holy Rosary Saint John Church, Lori Duron, Rebecca Duron, Dahlia Duron, Rahema and Sadie Watts, and Israel Hakim. Any names not mentioned here represent an accidental oversight and not a lack of true gratitude.

Finally, this book is appropriately dedicated to Sandra Fay Spates Price, mother of six, lifetime healer, world traveler, superior intellectual, sci-fi enthusiast, corny joke teller, visionary, and the best person I know. She is my real-life hero. Talk about making something out of nothing—she mastered it. She dreamed a future for herself and her children that went beyond the world she knew, and any achievements we have accomplished are to her great credit. She is the descendant of slaves, who raised herself and her children out of poverty and instilled in them the value of education. As a result, her children have earned three associate degrees, four (and counting) bachelor's degrees, one law degree, and three doctorate degrees. She is the matriarch of an unwieldy family, and we would be lost without her. Thanks, Mama.

Introduction

In the summer after I completed middle school, I got on a school bus everyday and traveled for an hour each way to one of the most prestigious private schools in Houston for a math and science program. During those rides, my friends and I traded stories, frustrations (of having to go to volunteer summer school), gossip, and music. On one of those many trips, my classmate Travis insisted that we all listen to his new rap tape, which he assured us would rock our worlds. The group, shouting over heavy bass lines and guitar licks, turned out to be Public Enemy, and *It Takes a Nation of Millions to Hold Us Back* was the album. It was the first time I had ever heard them, and I was overpowered by the bombardment of sound and concepts. As lead singer Chuck D forcefully expelled rhymes about Black Nationalism and community uplift in rapid-fire succession, I was struck by the power of the verses. Over the next few years, Public Enemy's albums served, for many young African Americans, as political courses composed of folk knowledge and black history with Chuck D cast as the primary instructor.[1] Through melodic prose and storytelling, Public Enemy introduced me to black intellectuals (Malcolm X, Marcus Garvey, Ida B. Wells), African American history (slavery and its consequences, lynching, racial profiling), and, most importantly, political empowerment strategies (community control of institutions, boycotts, riots, armed struggle, expatriation).

Public Enemy talked about black oppression, community solidarity, and the consequences of stark inequality—concepts that were, in many ways, embodied in the very endeavor we were engaged in that summer. Students in the program represented all sections of the city and every racial minority group; however, my particular bus shuttled poor and moderate-income black public school students from the southeast side to an affluent, white enclave on the west side. During that summer the veil of privilege parted, and we were allowed to temporarily exist in the world of elite education where secondary schools had entire science wings and not just two science labs. The juxtaposition was profound. We lived in the same city, shopped at the same malls, and watched the same movies as the private school students, yet we were clearly interlopers in their space, differentiated by race, class, and social position. Though I attended the program for three more summers, the feeling of trespassing in someone else's space and being permanently othered by race never subsided.

During that first summer, it was clear to everyone that we were outsiders, our phenotype immediately calling into question our membership. There were students of color who regularly attended the school, but as our numbers accumulated, their standing was rendered suspect as well. In the post–Civil Rights era, blacks have had a similar relationship with America. The black middle class is larger than ever, as a group blacks are more prosperous, and legal barriers to black political participation and racial integration have been largely removed; however, blacks' citizenship is still a negotiation in progress. Over and over, the country seems to engage in public debates about where African Americans fit into the political and social order. Discussions about whether stranded black Katrina evacuees should have been referred to as refugees and questions about Barack Obama's level of patriotism and his failure to wear an American flag pin on his suit coat are glaring examples of the nuanced ways that African Americans' right to American citizenship continues to be an unsettled question (and Obama now wears the pin). There are also less public examples of racial profiling, misread cultural cues, and racial distance that pollute interactions between blacks and whites. How, then, do black citizens make sense of their political world? Are they more inward-looking as a racial group because of shared history and experiences, or do they subscribe to America's melting-pot mythology?

When I was a graduate student, that summer school experience and my interest in Black Nationalism came full circle. I returned to a topic that had so engrossed me in my youth. During the course of collecting data, I had the wonderful opportunity to engage black citizens in spirited discussions about their politics using their own vernacular in guided conversations with their peers. As group members outlined their political beliefs and how those beliefs developed, I found myself creating a skeletal map of my own political development and noting when participants' experiences mirrored or differed from my own. It seemed that my experience was a small sampling of the kinds of experiences African Americans have long contemplated. Where they fit in American life, the oscillation between citizen and alien, the push and pull of patriotism and racism were just a few of the questions considered by members of these focus groups and African Americans as a racial group.

I was looking for answers to questions I had begun asking, implicitly, on those long, hot bus rides more than a decade earlier. At the most basic level, I was (and continue to be) interested in how citizens come to know what they know about politics and how they express those ideas through everyday talk. More concretely, I wanted to know how black people, given the calamitous history they have endured in their American sojourn, make sense of their political world. How did they come to grips with the complex bonds that tether them to this nation and its government? *Dreaming Blackness* diagrams the contemporary political landscape, especially as it relates to black Americans, and its impact on questions and data that inform this book. It also links conversations of focus group participants with a conversation that surely began in antebellum America, if not before. The members of the focus groups conducted in this project are trying to map a course for black empowerment or, in the words of Fredrick Douglass, deal with the "Negro problem." Just as David Walker and Martin Delaney offered their answers in the 1830s and Martin and Malcolm offered answers in the 1960s, these participants were contributing answers to that concurrently timeless and time-bound question of how (and to a lesser extent where) blacks can create a space for dignity, justice, and progress. With each era of renewed interest, Black Nationalism has interacted with the political landscape of its time—African enslavement, civil rights struggles, social conservatism, and multiculturalism. The organic narrative created by black citizens elucidates the political calculus used to make decisions about the impact of race and racism on their lives, the proper level of engagement in politics, trustworthiness of candidates, and reliability of media sources. The intent here is to create a narrative that highlights a particular ideological viewpoint through the characteristics of people who both incorporate and exclude it and to ultimately make arguments about difference and its meaning for contemporary politics.

The ideological focus of this project is Black Nationalism, which is one of the oldest and most enduring ideological constructs developed by African Americans to make sense of their social and political world.[2] Though there is some disagreement even among Black Nationalists about what it means to subscribe to this particular worldview, *Dreaming Blackness* suggests four principles around which all Black Nationalists coalesce. These principles are support for black self-determination through control of homogeneous black institutions, support for black economic and social independence in the form self-help programs, psychological and social disentanglement from whites and white supremacist notions of black inferiority, and support for a global or Pan-African view of the black community (Shabazz 1989a [1965], 38–41).

Dreaming Blackness examines the presence of Black Nationalism in post–Civil Rights America in several ways. First, it makes connections between ordinary black citizens' embrace or rejection of Black Nationalist principles and the intellectual writings of African American elites. There is considerable information about elite views of Black Nationalism; less is known, however, about how elite rhetoric translates and is appropriated by everyday citizens. Next, it examines differences between accepting and rejecting this ideological viewpoint. How do Black Nationalist principles shape and inform the way individuals characterize the nature of black politics and the way political scientists have traditionally studied black political behavior? Finally, it makes assertions about the connection between ideological thinking, opinion formation, and real politics. When and how does support for Black Nationalism impact attitudes toward government and political participation? Now, *Dreaming Blackness* turns to fleshing out the literature that informs and inspires the questions asked and answered here and by outlining the methodological approach employed.

Linked Fates and Disconnected Realities

Many black politics scholars, especially those working in the behavioralist tradition, have used the concept of linked fate as the primary explanation of group political cohesion.[3] Linked fate measures race consciousness and attachment by asking respondents whether or not they feel that their individual fate is tied to the collective fate of their racial group. Miller et al. (1981) distinguish between mere group identification and group consciousness and suggest that group identification has to do with perceived membership in a certain social category. Alternatively, group consciousness is a more politicized view of membership in a social group and relative social status of group members. They find that the existence of group consciousness increases political participation among some groups, specifically blacks and women.[4] Surveys show that blacks do see their lives as being tied to the destiny of other blacks. According to the 1984 National Black Election Study (NBES)—a survey series developed by the Program for Research on Black Americans at the Institute for Social

Research, University of Michigan—the overwhelming majority of African Americans had a strong identification with other blacks (approximately 75%). Tate (1993) points out that in the 1984 NBES "only two blacks out of the sample of 1,150 voluntarily told interviewers that they never think about their race" (25). Additionally, in 1996 nearly 86% of black respondents in the NBES believed they shared a common fate with other blacks (Tate 1996). We also know from anecdotal evidence (e.g., media coverage, influential autobiographies, public discourse) that African Americans tend to view their group affiliation and the historical relationship of that group to the larger white society as very important to their personal and political lives.[5]

Focusing on a shared fate does not explain intragroup differences, however. Blacks do exhibit policy differences.[6] For example, from the 1996 NBES data, we know that although 60% of blacks favor laws to protect homosexuals against job discrimination, nearly a third (26.9%) are opposed. Second, blacks are split almost evenly over the death penalty, with more in favor (47%) than opposed (40%). When questioned about perceived policy preferences on federal spending, 68% of respondents felt federal spending on health care should be increased as opposed to 27% who felt it should be decreased. Nearly the same number of blacks favored decreases in military and defense spending as favored an increase in spending. From these statistics we know that large numbers of blacks tend to agree, but we also see that a nontrivial number of blacks go against the majority opinion. *Dreaming Blackness* is an attempt to move beyond linked fate as a singular explanation of black political opinion to an appreciation for disagreement within the black community, especially over Black Nationalism's viability as a route to black empowerment.

This emphasis on linked fate and group behavior is also problematic because there are important conceptual holes. First, this link is not adequately problematized. Though we ask questions that measure perceived presence of a link between individuals and blacks as a group and whether respondents view that link as strong or weak, rarely are respondents asked about a third dimension of linked fate. This attachment can presumably be positive or negative, but it is unclear because surveys merely offer one or two closed-ended questions that simply measure the presence and degree of linked fate. Ostensibly, some individuals see that link as a tethered anchor around their proverbial political and social necks. For instance, this was seemingly demonstrated repeatedly by the development of a new memoir genre in the 1990s in which successful

African Americans discussed how negative perceptions of blacks were unfairly attached to them and the subsequent impact this had on their personal and professional lives.[7] Stephen Carter's *Reflections of an Affirmative Action Baby* (1991) suggested that being an African American and an intellectual placed him involuntarily into a box where others attached labels to what he should be and think as the token person of color. According to Carter, this was a truism for all black intellectuals who came of age under the shadow of affirmative action policies that positioned any meritorious achievements by "affirmative action babies" as ill-gotten. Carter offers:

> In the new rhetoric of affirmative action, it seems, the reason to seek out and hire or admit people of color is that one can have faith that their opinions, their perspective, will be different from the opinions and perspectives of people who are white—who evidently have a distinct set of views of their own. The unfortunate logical corollary is that if the perspectives a particular person of color can offer are not distinctive, if it is more like the "white" perspective than the "black" one then that person is not speaking in an authentically black voice—an accusation that has become all too common. (6)

Through this observation Carter seeks to diminish the impact of racial group membership on individual thought or at least de-emphasize the degree of difference that results from it.

Historically, this connection that blacks have to each other has been complicated and sometimes contentious. For participants in the Black Women's Club Movement, part of their racial uplift agenda included "lifting the burdens of 'ignorance and immorality'" from the lower ranks of the black community (Giddings 1984, 102). Alternatively, the fact that Black Nationalists have to work so diligently to re-create supporters' images of themselves and their racial group serves as an indication that connections among blacks are more complicated than has been suggested by the black politics literature. If this connection was perceived solely as positive, there would be no need to transform or reshape it in any way. These contentions and their political impact are fleshed out in much greater detail in chapter 4.

Next, our current understanding of linked fate is problematic because it is nonprescriptive. Attachment does not equal or even necessitate action.

Nor is there any logical behavioral end that results simply from feeling attached to other blacks. Does linked fate necessitate mass Democratic support? Does it increase voter apathy? Does it create a set of criteria for weighing candidates against each other?[8] In a recent study of Latinos in Los Angeles, Lisa Garcia Bedolla (2005) uses interview data to critique commonly held assumptions about racial group attachment. She finds that individual political outlook and behavior are shaped heavily by whether Latinos felt positively or negatively about their racial group attachment. Further, she argues that measures of perceptions of social stigma should be analyzed in conjunction with racial group attachment because of its powerful impact on the individual political calculus. Hence, when scholars focus on cohesive behaviors such as bloc voting and party affiliation, the presence of linked fate serves as an excellent explanation for why this occurs. But it does little to explain examples of black actors behaving out of sync with each other.

So how does linked fate relate to Black Nationalism? Focusing on the "groupness" of blacks is the scaffolding upon which decision making is layered for blacks who acknowledge their membership in that group. Any time individuals make normative statements about appropriate black behavior in a possessive manner, linked fate is invoked. It is omnipresent. While some blacks might have a strong desire for racial categorizations of any kind to be rendered useless, Black Nationalists see their racial group affiliation as the filter through which all issues are sorted. But it is not that easy because for many African Americans their connection to other blacks has been both a tethered anchored and a vital lifeline—often separately and sometimes simultaneously. So as the defining process begins, and throughout this project, the presence of linked fate viewed as a constant. However, how that connection is shaped, adjusted, hidden, emphasized, and otherwise manipulated will be analyzed.

Origins of a Racialized Ideology

Individuals who subscribe to and reject Black Nationalist beliefs have adopted principles and mobilization strategies that are rooted in the history of African American people. They recognize the historically contentious relationship between African Americans and the political system and the resulting obstacles across generations. The differences emerge between Black Nationalists and other African Americans when examining their ultimate definitions of African American empowerment and the "reper-toires of contention" that result.[9] Scholars have focused on popular in-tegration efforts of the abolitionists and participants in the civil rights movement, for example, yet they have placed little emphasis on Black Na-tionalist movements such as maroon communities during slavery (Blass-ingame 1979) or subsequent separatist movements up to contemporary organizations like the Republic of New Afrika and the Nation of Islam (Allen 1998; Essien-Udom 1962).

With the approaching abolition of slavery and the eventual deliv-ery of the Emancipation Proclamation, blacks and whites alike had to decide what should be done with the newly freed blacks. After many years of antislavery and Integrationist activism, Frederick Douglass, writing in 1894, suggested that the "so-called, mis-called, Negro prob-lem is one of the most important and urgent subjects that can now engage public attention" (1996 [1984], 340). Inherently assumed and often overtly stated in the proposals of racial segregation offered to these new citizens of the United States was the belief that blacks were inferior or nonhuman (Franklin 1992). Blacks and some whites agreed that slavery and oppression of blacks were morally wrong and liabili-ties to U.S. national interests. However, that initial agreement yielded divergent strategies. A popular remedy during the Reconstruction era was the colonization or mass emigration of blacks to various locations (Carlisle 1975). Only a small number of blacks were ever successfully relocated to other countries and western territories, and it became apparent that solving racial tensions would entail more than just re-moving blacks to some other place. These efforts failed for a myriad of reasons. First, and probably most important, many blacks did not want to leave. Their "Africanness" had been systematically eliminated, and the only connection the vast majority had to any nation was their connection to the United States. Additionally, other countries did not want to take them. Sympathy for their plight was not an invitation to harbor people who were largely uneducated and impoverished (Good-man 1998). The recognition of this resulted in two major strategies—to integrate the newly emancipated by incorporating them as equal citizens or to keep them permanently separated from the full rights and benefits available through unabridged opportunity. These strate-gies have both competed and overlapped at various times and during various periods in history. Lewis and Hill (1956) suggest that blacks must ask themselves:

Which represents the greater "need" for my services, blazing the trail and expanding opportunities for other Negroes in an integrated set-up or the continuing demand for new and more talent in the Negro community from which I have come? And which course offers greater rewards—psychologically or materially? (123)

Michael Dawson (2001, 15–23) outlines six ideological categories that capture the roots of African American ideology. The first ideology is Radical Egalitarianism, which simultaneously criticizes and endorses American democracy. Second, Disillusioned Liberalism is similar to the previous ideology in that adherents still embrace the principles of American democracy, but they also believe that "America is fundamentally racist." A third ideological group, Black Marxism, "adapts the tenets of Marxism to the situation of African Americans" so that the capitalist critique is coupled with beliefs about the centrality of race and spirituality. Black Conservatism represents the fourth category and emphasizes "reliance on self-help, an attack on the state as a set of institutions that retard societal progress in general and black progress in particular, and belief in the antidiscriminatory aspects of markets." Fifth, Black Feminism is a mix of traditional feminist ideology and community focus. In this case black women emphasize their gender and racial identities as inextricably intertwined. The last category Dawson identifies is Black Nationalism. This ideological category's "core concepts include support for African American autonomy and various degrees of cultural, social, economic and political separation from white America." Dawson's categories are quite extensive. My project is complementary to Dawson's efforts. Rather than attempting to corral all of these ideological constructs to explain the entire African American political constellation, *Dreaming Blackness* takes one ideological viewpoint—Black Nationalism—and fully explores what it means to accept and incorporate that viewpoint into a cohesive belief system and use that belief system to make prescriptions for the black community.

Why Black Nationalism?

Given the universe of ideologies employed by blacks, it is important to outline the reasons for focusing on this particular ideology. Does it deserve a more important status than other ideological strains within the African American community? There are several justifications for why examining the presence of Black Nationalism in the black public is particularly helpful. First, though there is minimal support for complete withdrawal of African Americans from American society, there is wide support among the mass public for more moderate tenets of Black Nationalism. Data from the 1996 National Black Election Study reveal that one-fifth of the respondents supported the idea of black children attending Afrocentric schools, and more than three-fifths believed that blacks should shop in black-owned stores whenever possible. This suggests that there are a nontrivial number of respondents who support these tenets of Black Nationalism. Alternatively, just over 10% of respondents are willing to unconditionally support black candidates and even fewer agree that blacks should have nothing to do with whites if they can help it. A cursory look at these data would suggest that Black Nationalist views are supported by only a small minority of individuals in the African American community, but when amplified with focus group data and accounting for the impact of the race of the interviewer, the story changes significantly. Additionally, Cohen's (1999) work on advanced and secondary marginalization suggests that attempting to understand black politics from the perspective of in-group minorities is quite useful in articulating the manner in which the priorities of some subsets of a racial group are privileged over others. In so doing, we are able to understand and articulate black politics as a robust set of experiences rather than as a static set of monolithic issues. Adolph Reed (2002) argues that this consistent focus on blacks as a "corporate racial entity" poses problems for the black politics subfield because

> by vesting [a fixed racial identity that exists in greater or lesser degrees] with the appearance of a settled finding of social science, the interaction of unexamined ideology and approach to inquiry in this case buttresses the perception of black interests as given and unproblematic. (28–29)

Second, Black Nationalism has served as the ideological alter ego and sparring partner of most efforts to advocate for racial integration. At every historical moment that one highlights, there are subsets of the black population simultaneously lobbying for Integrationist and Black Nationalist goals. Harold Cruse, in his influential book, *The Crisis of the Negro Intellectual* (1967), suggests that African American leaders fall into two ideological camps; they are Integrationists or Black Nationalists, with varying degrees of adherence within each category.[10] Accordingly, this ideological debate has polarized elite discourse related to the appropriate political strategy for African American empowerment since the arrival of enslaved Africans in the Americas. In fact, Cruse suggests and Henderson has empirically demonstrated that these ideologies have a cyclical relationship in which one ideology is dominant and the other subordinate at various periods in history.

If Cruse's pendulum thesis bears out both theoretically and empirically, then examining Black Nationalism in both its dominant and subordinate periods is particularly important to get a clear picture of members of this ideological subgroup. This is also necessary, since a whole host of factors differentiate individuals who support Black Nationalist principles when this ideological viewpoint is popular and championed by leaders and organizations within the racial community and those individuals who remain supportive or take on a Black Nationalist stance when other ideological views dominate. It is instructive here to look at the work of Rupp and Taylor (1987), who have done extensive research on what happened to the American Women's Movement between the most popular waves of feminist activism. They successfully outline the manner in which core activists and ardent believers maintained scaled-back organizations and continued to engage in advocacy for women between the first and second waves of feminism. Additionally, Taylor (1989) uses the Women's Movement as evidence of how social and other ideological movements are dynamic processes rather than disconnected or discrete. Thus, there are times when the political opportunity structure is conducive to active protest and other times when movement activists are absorbed into an abeyance structure (i.e., smaller organizational structures or a cadre of activists without a mass base). This may also be the case for ideologies that serve as the foundation for social movement development. When Rupp and Taylor's findings are coupled with arguments made by Henderson and Cruse, the importance of the analysis in this book is bolstered because it tells us about ideological opinion and its impact on ideological minorities.

In many ways Black Nationalism represents the "little engine that could" of black political ideologies. Despite the fact that scholars almost unanimously agree that it has existed as an organized political worldview as long as any Integrationist efforts, Black Nationalism receives substantially less scholarly focus in political science. Less scholarship has resulted in less clarity of the mechanism and sources of Black Nationalist subscription and rejection. Thus, leaders and laypeople can rely only on anecdotal evidence and conjecture. This led Hanes Walton (1985) to note that few scholars "have bothered to analyze the role that Black Nationalism plays in black politics or how it translates itself into political action in the black community" (29). Additionally, Marable (1985) asserted that Black Nationalism, though a "logical manifestation of the political, ideological, cultural, and economic development of people of African descent," "has never been the central focus of black political practice and social thought" (66). Marable's claim illuminates the dearth of attention that has been paid to this ideological viewpoint. Recently, a few political science scholars have turned to the study of black political ideologies and their impact on the opinions of ordinary citizens (Harris-Lacewell 2004; Brown and Shaw 2002, Davis and Brown 2002, Dawson 2001). This project continues in that vein by using a singular ideology—Black Nationalism—to make claims about how African American political thought is ingrained in and employed by everyday citizens. Additionally, it responds to Walton's (1985) contention that a simple reliance on a single methodological approach can provide only a limited portrait of black politics because it ignores the political context.

Last, political behavior cannot and should not be properly understood without taking into account "the political environment (a particular time period and a particular place) in which [political behavior] occurs" (Walton 1997, 7). This suggests that even timeworn narratives (both social and political) can take on altered meaning as the context in which they are employed is amended. During previous periods of heightened Black Nationalism, the political context was quite different. In the last twenty years, more blacks have moved into the middle class than in any period in history (Patillo-McCoy 1999). However, while many blacks have seen great economic gains, scholars have pointed to a growing group of African Americans who are more entrenched in cyclical poverty and disaffected by the political process (Wilson 1999, 1997, 1978; Cohen and Dawson 1993). These simultaneous trends have led to some disconnect between wealthy and poor blacks. Indeed, Hochschild, in *Facing Up to the American Dream* (1995), suggests, "Most recognize that the gap in living standards between rich and poor African Americans is increasing; many think successful blacks do too little for the poor; many fear, perhaps as a consequence, that the values of middle-class and poor blacks are also diverging" (125). Undeniably, class differences among blacks were less pronounced prior to the Civil Rights Movement of the 1960s. Racist housing practices and segregation laws resulted in most blacks living in close proximity to one another despite class differences; this is no longer the case. Racial residential segregation is still quite common, but now African American neighborhoods are also segregated along distinct class lines (Massey and Denton 1993; Patillo-McCoy 1999). The problem goes beyond class differences. In the absence of overtly antiblack legislation and policies, racism in the post–Civil Rights context has acquired an amorphous nature that is difficult to define, to litigate, and often to defend against. Robert Smith (1995) characterizes it as having a "now you see it, now you don't quality." Political psychologists have been engaged in a debate over the changing nature of racism that has now spanned several decades.[11] They all generally agree that fewer whites are willing to express a belief in black inferiority and other antiblack sentiments in survey data (Kinder and Sanders 1996; Sniderman and Piazza 1993). However, very few African Americans would be willing to say that because whites no longer express them that these sentiments are now obsolete.[12] Thus, combating or even creating strategies to counteract the effects of racism is a daunting and unenviable task. So how does Black Nationalism, which sees the black Diaspora and white America as separately unified and oppositional groups, counteract racism and white supremacy? The former mobilizes citizens around shared experiences of racial oppression, and the latter around white supremacist notions of black inferiority.

But *Dreaming Blackness* explores more than how Black Nationalists deal with the countervailing and enduring themes of white racism and black empowerment. African American elites, who both support and reject major Black Nationalist tenets, have gone a long way in terms of outlining important theoretical positions and policy solutions. We know much less about the nature and degree of support this ideological category can boast among ordinary citizens. In the post–Civil Rights era, factors that might encourage (or discourage) African Americans' rejection of the American component of their identity are more fluid and thus potentially more difficult for ordinary citizens to define and digest. *Dreaming Blackness* uses the conversations and policy preferences of everyday citizens to understand how, in this new political and racial climate, Black Nationalist principles take hold in the minds and actions of citizens.

Methodological Approach

This project involves some exploratory analysis, so it is important to utilize multiple methodological approaches (in the form of survey and focus group analyses) to draw sound conclusions about the role ideology plays in African American opinion formation. Because survey research in black politics is relatively limited, we are not able to give in-depth attention to every aspect of African American politics.[13] Much of the attention to ideology went into explaining the continuity (and some might say ideological monopoly) of liberal policy adherence and Democratic Party loyalty.[14] When attempting to move beyond traditional liberal conservative ideology to ideologies specific to racial minorities, the picture we get is not nearly as clear and robust. Thus, analysis of survey results represents only one way of understanding the importance and dynamism of Black Nationalism as a tool for African American decision making. In conjunction with other empirical tools, we can get a more comprehensive view of Black Nationalist adherence.

I employ focus group analysis to supply the breadth needed to gain a fuller understanding of the role this ideology plays in African American political decision making. Although most discussions surrounding the relationship between focus groups and surveys emphasize the usefulness of focus groups in the question formation stage, there is some evidence that focus groups augment exploratory analysis of quantitative data. They allow scholars to understand whether the questions they are asking have the desired meaning or elicit results that inform their research. Also, focus groups provide a broad universe of thoughts that contribute to the formulation of respondents' answers. Additionally, they enable one to see how citizens devise opinions on their own terms. Moreover, we are able to get some sense of motivations and judgmental calculus rather than mere agreement or disagreement with preset questions (Morgan 1997).

This type of analysis is especially important here because focus groups are a useful way to experience dialogue. It serves as a first step in understanding and categorizing important concepts used in social interactions, which include many spheres but especially political interactions. Focus groups offer researchers the chance to hear and analyze how ordinary citizens conceptualize, express, and activate their political opinions. Thus, focus group analysis becomes an important precursor to question formulation, in the sense that it allows scholars to create questions that are in the appropriate jargon and that are relevant to the actual interest of the citizenry. Also, focus groups are important because they go beyond just interacting with the interviewer in a one-on-one process in which the conversation is constrained by the thoughts and attention spans of two participants. With the introduction of other members, the qualitative research process becomes multilayered and a more nuanced experience than simple one-on-one interviews. Last, it is also a process in which single interviewer effects can be overcome and real-world information gathering and opinion formation processes are simulated. The data accumulation process, like the political process, is based on group interactions and discussions, complicated by interconnected (and often nonpolitical) topics and random distractions, and highly dependent on the actors who are participating at any given point. Hence, for this project, which is arguing that the way in which blacks conceptualize and attempt personal and community uplift ultimately impacts both individual opinion and collective racial goals, one must talk directly to ordinary citizens.

The data for this book stem from a series of focused group discussions that were conducted with a total of thirty-two participants. These groups were composed of adults who self-identified as black or African American, and all took place over a two-week period during the summer of 2002 in Columbus, Ohio. Following the model provided by Gamson (1992) in *Talking Politics* and other projects, these were peer discussion groups in which contact was made with one person, and she was asked to invite friends, families, neighbors, coworkers, and so forth, into her home for a discussion about blacks and politics. The initial contacts were recruited in several ways. First, employees of community centers in predominantly black neighborhoods were asked to recruit from the centers' client pool. For instance, in one group, students from GED classes, soup kitchen workers, neighborhood activists, and the director of an after-school program were all recruited by a GED program director.[15] Participants were also recruited through a summer program for minority undergraduate students at Ohio State, a neighborhood improvement association, and a natural hair salon. During each session, all participants were offered a small prize for participation and entered into a raffle for one large prize. Each session lasted about two hours.[16]

The second half of *Dreaming Blackness* investigates Black Nationalism through analysis of the NBES data. Using items from the 1996 NBES, I constructed an additive index to measure adherence and rejection of Black Nationalism. First, this measure is used to construct a portrait of members of the African American community who either accept or reject Black Nationalist beliefs. This entails examining the index in relation to traditional measures of liberalism and conservatism, party affiliation, linked fate and various sociodemographic and socioeconomic factors. Second, this measure is used to predict African American political behavior and preferences. While the available questions are somewhat limited in scope, they provide some insight into whether or not elite discourse surrounding this ideology translates into mass acceptance. Additionally, it allows me to use available quantitative data to study blacks—a group that has been limited by few data sets that include a large number of respondents and cover a diversity of topics.

Chapter Outline

Dreaming Blackness follows a fairly simple outline. The first chapter provides a historical overview of this ideological position and defines the central tenets of Black Nationalism. It also offers various reasons why black leaders and citizens might be reluctant to embrace this ideological viewpoint. This is accomplished by presenting a thorough explication of the major intellectual writings and speeches that champion and oppose Black Nationalism as an appropriate path to black empowerment.

Chapter 2 uses focus group data to explore the thinking of ordinary African Americans in relation to Black Nationalism. This chapter is an outgrowth of the standard opening discussion of two iconic African Americans—Martin Luther King and Malcolm X. The discussions started with these leaders because they resonate, are identifiable across generations, and represent alternative approaches to "black problems." Oppositional portrayals and popular discussions surrounding these two men have framed Malcolm X as the revolutionary, self-reliant leader and King as more capitulating and accommodating. I hypothesized that starting a discussion about support for Black Nationalism in this way would invoke this dichotomy among participants and prime them for more ideological thinking. From there, the chapter quickly moves to a discussion of how participants view the current American political landscape.

Chapter 3, "Rights and Resistance: Mapping the Terrain of Black Nationalist Adherence," moves beyond assessments of community and national problems to examine how subscription to and rejection of Black Nationalism are articulated by group participants. It lays out a typology of Black Nationalist adherence, those who moderately accept the tenets of Black Nationalism and those who reject it outright. It outlines seven major issue attitudes that shape participants' ideological outlook. The first two components examined are how participants construct their own identities and whether or not their social outlook is group based or individualistic. Next, it examines problem perceptions and explanations of their origins by examining whether or not participants engage in system blame or black blame, and who becomes the causal target of those problems. This particular finding is so consistent throughout the groups that it will be discussed in greater depth in the next chapter. Additionally, it examines three attitude positions related to whites—white affect, racial designation assigned to government actors and institutions, and the motivation of white actors. Finally, it examines whether Black Nationalists are more likely to make direct or indirect references to experiences of racism.

As chapter 3 demonstrates, blame serves as a powerful determinant of racial and ideological outlook. Therefore, chapter 4 takes up the question of who is responsible. In all the discussion groups, blame is assigned to a particular target, and as the targets differ, so do the evaluations of consequences. Much of the blame is attributed to two primary sources—either the black community itself (black blame) or a dysfunctional political system (system blame). Thus, chapter 4 looks at the systematic employment of blame and its impact on support for Black Nationalist ideology and strategies.

Chapter 5 turns away from the focus group data to flesh out comparisons between findings in the previous chapters and those drawn from a large national sample. This chapter begins by creating and validating a Black Nationalist Index that measures adherence to major principles of Black Nationalism. Once the measure is established, the chapter moves to an assessment of how various discrete demographic categories (e.g., age, gender, income class, education) and important sociopolitical variables (e.g., linked fate, church attendance) array themselves across the Black Nationalist Index. This chapter offers a statistical examination of the variables that significantly predict respondents' inclination toward Black Nationalist beliefs and a closer analysis of race of the interviewer effects found throughout this analysis.

Chapter 6 compares attitudinal and behavioral characteristics developed from the focus group discussion to similar measures in the larger sample. The chapter examines subscription to Black Nationalism's impact on political trust and efficacy, support for government efforts and civil rights policy, support for an autonomous black third party, and level of political participation. It assesses the manner in which support for Black Nationalism systematically and significantly impacts important political variables. It finds that increased support for Black Nationalism has a profoundly negative impact on political efficacy. Additionally, it significantly predicts support for a black third party.

Just as this book began with the opening exercise of the focus group discussion, chapter 7 moves toward a conclusion of the data analysis by reporting findings from the closing exercise of those same discussions. This exercise, which I called "Dreaming Blackness," was intended as a way to get participants to really think about and focus on the notion of a self-determining black nation. They were probed to talk aloud about an all-black America, which did not require rejection of underlying principles of American democracy or any of its social and political traditions. They merely had to talk about what it would mean if that political structure was led, governed, and inhabited solely by African Americans. Complete and total separation is, for some, the most difficult and most extreme measure blacks could take to solve race problems. In the course of these focus group discussions, interestingly, no one ever actually proposed this as a personal strategy. Of course, there were participants who were vehemently opposed to the idea, some who supported the idea wholeheartedly, and others whose views were muddier.

The final chapter uses recent political events to provide a context in which arguments about the continued support and utility of Black Nationalism in post–civil rights America. From there it moves on to a discussion of major findings and their meanings for the entire African American community, its politics, and American politics writ large. It discusses the need for more research exploring how difference informs and shapes the everyday political lives of black citizens and how those experiences shape opinion formation, levels of leadership and policy support, and ultimately mobilization and action. The prescription for a focus on difference is important in terms of not only opinion difference but also methodological difference. Using both surveys and focus groups yields a multilayered view of African American opinion. It offers one possible road map for the kinds of questions black politics scholars should ask black respondents in surveys with a large number of respondents and whether we should take extra care to make sure that those surveys are fielded by more black interviewers.

1

Reconciling Race and Nation

Black Nationalism and African American Political Opinion

Black Nationalism as an ideology is a race-centered, self-deterministic view of black politics. As Malcolm X (Shabazz 1989b [1965]) succinctly states, "The political philosophy of black nationalism means that the black man should control the politics and the politicians in his own community; no more." In *Dreaming Blackness,* one is categorized as Black Nationalist based on support for four principles that buttress all support for Black Nationalism. First, all Black Nationalists support black self-determination. For them it is vital that African Americans be able to exert control over the institutions that define their world. Some Black Nationalists have asserted that this can happen only through self-governance of a black nation; others emphasize having control over community institutions with which African Americans interact daily (e.g., schools, businesses). Second, a self-determining black community is also one that has a clear plan for independence and self-sustenance by virtue of its own financial, political, and intellectual resources in the form of self-help programs. Third, there is consensus that blacks must sever any ties with whites that foster notions of black inferiority and white superiority. The impact of slavery and other forms of oppression on whites' images of blacks and blacks' images of themselves has resulted in an entrenched American belief in black inferiority. Hence, African Americans should be cautious of (if not totally avoid) whites. Last, there is a focus on fostering a global view of black oppression that connects African American oppression to that of people of African descent cross-nationally. This entails fostering a Pan-African identity in which the liberation of all African descendants from oppression is interdependent.

Noted scholar August Meier (1991) has argued that during Reconstruction and beyond, "the continued hostility of whites, particularly in the

*August Meier

South, encouraged attitudes favoring separatism" (12). Meier notes that this is true for a wide cross section of African Americans, even those who were not completely sold on Black Nationalism. However, this is not to suggest that Black Nationalist ideology is inherently reactionary. Supporters of Black Nationalism simply seek to follow the edict of Ture and Hamilton (1992) for the black community "to redefine itself, set forth new values and goals, and organize around them" (32). Similarly, Karenga (1993) suggests, after arguing that Black Nationalism results from the unique historical experiences of African Americans, that "[blacks] should therefore unite in order to gain the structural capacity to define, defend and develop their interests" (334). In Rodney Carlisle's (1975) view, "Black Nationalism opposes [and some might say exposes][1] the myths of American life because it presumes a black nation unassimilated along side the American nation" (4).[2] Nationalism stresses black self-help mostly through black organizations, psychological and social disentanglement from whites, and a Pan-Africanist identity (Henderson 2000). Its development is divided into two historical periods: the classical period that stretches from the American Revolution to Marcus Garvey, and the modern era from Marcus Garvey to contemporary times. The division should not be seen as overly rigid and discrete. Rather, it represents shifts from elite-based to mass-based movements and from predominant emphasis on emigration to a more expansive view of independence.

Wilson Jeremiah Moses (1996) argues that the classical Black Nationalism period that spanned the 1800s to the 1920s emphasized and worked toward the development of a black nation-state. These efforts represented "a desire for independence and a determination to demonstrate the ability of black people to establish a republican form of government" (2). David Walker, in his famous *Appeal to the Coloured Citizens of the World*, written in four parts between 1785 and 1830, offered clear expressions of a Black Nationalist ideology. In this appeal Walker initiated a call for the establishment of a black nation that would echo throughout history. Walker asserted that "our sufferings will come to an end, in spite of all Americans this side of eternity. Then we will want all the learnings and talents among ourselves, and perhaps more to govern ourselves."[3] Viewed as the ultimate practice of self-determination, some Black Nationalists have repeated Walker's endorsement of black Zionism. Often framed in biblical allegories such as liberating the Hebrews from Egyptian slavery (Delany 1996 [1852]; 1996 [1861]), emigration efforts have frequently focused on Africa as the ancestral homeland of formerly enslaved blacks, but there have also

*Ture & Hamilton / Karenga

been proposals for both resettlement in South America and the creation of a black homeland within the U.S. borders. In the "Official Report of the Niger Valley Exploring Party," Martin Delany outlined the needs of blacks in America and the vast resources potentially available to them on the African continent. He also noted the strong potential for alliances between returning Africans and those already residing on the continent. Beyond debates over the appropriate destination, Black Nationalists were fully in support of the goal of emigration. However, these early efforts at emigration were almost exclusively the adventurous undertakings of well-educated and well-to-do blacks who participated in various conventions. There is no evidence or even suggestion of widespread support.

Marcus Garvey and the Universal Negro Improvement Association (UNIA) represent one of the most successful Black Nationalist mobilizing efforts and the first capable of making a claim of mass support from ordinary citizens. At its height from 1917 to the late 1920s, the UNIA boasted multiple chapters in more than thirty states and dozens of countries (Sewell 1990). During Garvey's heyday, he and the UNIA were able to amass significant support for the "Back to Africa" campaign and the Black Star Line of steamships. Additionally, they "sponsored colonial expeditions to Liberia, staged annual international conventions, inspired businesses, endorsed political candidates, fostered black history and culture, and organized thousands" (Stein 1986, 1). His efforts sought the development of black nationhood and an increased African identity, simultaneously. For him, there was no debate; all black people were connected as "free citizens of Africa, the Motherland of all Negroes" (Garvey 1997 [1920], 26). So, there was no doubt about the appropriate space for relocation for blacks—the African continent.

Garvey's mass support for Black Nationalism and African resettlement has historically gone unmatched. Smaller pushes for the establishment of a black nation have reared their heads more recently. One such effort during the Black Power era was led by an organization called the Republic of New Africa, which called for the United States to relinquish five southern (and most densely black) states and pay reparations for slavery.[4] Other examples might also includes efforts to create what can cautiously be described as modern-day maroon communities that inhabit small self-determining and self-governing jurisdictions within the United States. For instance, for the last thirty-five years, a group has maintained the Oyotunji African Village in Sheldon, South Carolina.[5] In their own explanation of their struggle, they link themselves and their goals directly to the work of

Martin Delany and his Niger Valley Expedition. Additionally, the Shrine of the Black Madonna Pan African Orthodox Church runs a 2,700-acre farm and retreat center on the Georgia–South Carolina border that members believe will not only produce agricultural resources but also "represents an opportunity for Black People to realize GOD's will—to live as a self-determined People of God."[6]

For proponents of Black Nationalism, independence is a process by which blacks shed the indoctrination of black inferiority inherent in American society. Because African descendants initially arrived in the United States designated as chattel rather than fully human citizens and that legacy continued for centuries afterward, whites and some blacks see blacks as a group that should be kept in permanent servitude. In order for blacks to embrace independence, they had to rid themselves of any beliefs in white superiority and black inferiority. In 1833, Maria Stewart, though not strictly a Black Nationalist, cogently outlined the process that many Black Nationalists felt blacks had been subjected to in America. She asserted: "The unfriendly whites . . . stole our fathers from their peaceful and quiet dwellings, and brought them hither, and made bond-men and bond-women of them and their little ones; they have obliged our brethren to labor, kept them in utter ignorance, nourished them in vice, and raised them in degradation" (Stewart 1996 [1833], 98). Stewart went on to express incredulity at the fact that after everything whites had done to blacks, they were still unwilling to see blacks as fit for American citizenship and equality. Shortly after the passage of the Fugitive Slave Act of 1850, Martin Delany asserted that the very laws of America "stamp [blacks] with inferiority." Further, whites had "despoiled" and "corrupted" blacks and left them "broken people."[7] Thus, from the early phases of Black Nationalism's development, a major project of ideological adherents has been severing black social and psychological dependence on whites.

Though most early Black Nationalists defined this separation as possible only through emigration, activists and scholars have employed a more expansive meaning of separation to include economic and political independence within the American political context. African Americans needed to develop businesses, institutions, and organizations to sustain their community. For instance, another example of attempts to foster independent social and economic independence included the "Buy Black" campaign championed by Carlos Cooks in the 1940s and 1950s. Cooks believed this campaign would "make the black community behave like the other racial and ethnic groups. It will have blacks own and control the businesses in

black neighborhoods" (Cooks 1977 [1955], 89). The economic independence principle has been lived out quite successfully by religious Black
Nationalists such as the Nation of Islam and the Shrine of the Black Madonna, both of which promote the development of independent businesses
to their members and have collectively, as organizations, engaged in en-
trepreneurial development. Black independence also includes community
control of schools and other institutions that serve as socializing agents for
children and adults alike. During the Black Power era, for instance, Black
Panthers developed social programs—including free clinics, clothing and
food drives, and free breakfast programs—as a key to recruitment and social change. Abron (1998) suggests that these programs "provide a model
of community self-help" that was needed then and is still relevant today.

For Black Nationalists, self-reliance is based on more than social and
economic independence. It is a broader sense of independence that allows
blacks to choose any desired course for themselves, including the ability
to defend themselves from white oppression through armed resistance
and self-defense. This became particularly important in the Civil Rights
era, when violence against blacks was both ramped up and widely pub-
licized. These events served as both recent historical memory and fuel to
the burgeoning Black Power movement. Support for nonviolence was a
point of departure for increasingly radical activists engaged in social protest in the South during the late sixties. Activists like Kwame Ture (aka
Stokely Carmichael) and Robert Williams took issue with activists who
were wedded to Integrationist and nonviolent strategies despite the continued and escalating violence against black people (Tyson 1999).

In the modern era of Black Nationalism, the expansion of the meaning of independence has also elicited increased cultural production in the
form of "authentic" black rituals and traditions, education about black history in America and abroad, and strengthening the connections to a glorious African past. For Garvey's UNIA and Elijah Muhammad's Nation of
Islam, this involved high pageantry, rigid moral norms, and the development of new cultural products (Garvey 1997 [1920]; Stein 1986; Muhammad 1965). Parades and conventions brought widespread exposure and allowed for the recruitment of a more populist or grassroots membership,
while the UNIA's national newspaper, the *Negro World,* and the Nation of
Islam's weekly meetings provided a forum for mass education. Through
these networks, blacks learned histories that exposed them to the contributions of African Americans to American history, as well as mythical
narratives about the origins of racial divisions and social structures. Many

of these narratives were aimed at reclaiming or embracing a long-lost African past in which blacks were noble and dignified, black men were strong leaders, and black families were functional.

Breaking away from whites and their skewed view of blacks leaves a void for what identity African Americans should embrace. Although one could argue that African Americans had ably created a hybridized culture that was both American and African, for Black Nationalists, Africa has historically been the focus of identity-building primarily because of ancestral connections to the continent.[8] The look "back to Africa" has been couched in various narratives, however, simultaneously a source of pride and shame. Early Nationalists, in particular, really saw Africa through a Western hegemonic lens. Africa was a place to be civilized by their newly returning descendants. Henry Highland Garnet saw Africa as a place "to be redeemed by Christian civilization," and that would be achieved by the "voluntary emigration of enterprising colored people" (Moses 1996, 142). Garnet and many other Black Nationalists of the time viewed Africa as a place worthy of pity and prayer, but not really habitable without an enormous amount of activity and ingenuity on the part of returning blacks. References to the continent were often gloomy characterizations such as "outraged shores," "Africa's agony," and "the injured country." Their view of Africa was overly simplistic, judgmental, and one-dimensional. This was true despite their longing for reconnection and resettlement.

This simple hegemonic view of the African continent continued in the modern era of Black Nationalism. Though the perception of Africa as an uncivilized outpost subsided somewhat, in terms of political and social outlook, Black Nationalists in America largely saw it as a geographic blob of resources and political alliances. Thus, Garvey can proclaim in his "Declaration of Rights of the Negro Peoples of the World" that the UNIA believed "in the freedom of Africa for the Negro people of the world, and by the principle of Europe for the Europeans and Asia for the Asiatics; we also demand Africa for the Africans at home and abroad" (Garvey 1997 [1920], 22). This push for return to Africa, though not as imperialistic as that of previous Black Nationalists, is rendered a natural phenomenon that is both noncomplex and predestined. The difficulties that must be overcome lie in the ability to mobilize and persuade Africans throughout the Diaspora that return is necessary and then to gather the material means to return.

As the politics on the continent evolved after World War II and independence spread, the relationship between blacks in the Diaspora and on the African continent can be more appropriately characterized as bilateral and interactive than in previous periods. Probably the most vivid example of this is Malcolm X's travels in West Africa and the Middle East and his relationships with Kwame Nkrumah (Shabazz 1992 [1962]; 1989a [1965]).[9] Malcolm X uses those experiences to articulate an internationalist view of Black Nationalism with Africa as a free agent rather than a fixed object. When Malcolm X sets out the structure and purpose of his Organization of African Unity in his "After the Bombing Speech" in 1965, he relates how his travels and meetings with Africans, Arabs, and black American expatriates have shaped his belief in the value of and mobilization effort toward forming a Diasporic coalition (Shabazz 1989a [1965]). In that way, he extends the anti-imperialist and Pan-African work of DuBois (1995 [1922]), who suggested in an editor's note in *Crisis* that West Indians and American Negroes "have no more right to administer Africa for the native Africans than native Africans have to administer America" (661). Additionally, in the Black Power era, Black Nationalism in America was influenced and somewhat reshaped by African nationalist intellectuals. The writings of Frantz Fanon (1982 [1967]; 1963), for instance, served as important guiding texts for organizations such as the Panthers and the Black Liberation Army. Additionally, many of these new revolutionaries ended up seeking counsel and refuge in burgeoning independent African nations after fleeing the United States.

In the contemporary context, the role of Africa in Black Nationalist America has been as an alternative cultural home and source of opposition to Western values. This has played itself out particularly in the development and popularity of pedagogical frameworks such as Afrocentricism and new cultural traditions such as Kwanzaa. Molefi Asante's book *The Afrocentric Idea* (1998) serves as the guiding text for this paradigmatic outlook. Asante defines Afrocentricity as a perspective that places "African ideals at the center of any analysis that involves African culture and behavior" (2). In this process, "African" values rather than European norms and values become the standard for critically examining all aspects of black life such as educational institutional structure and curriculum. Additionally, Kwanzaa, a holiday created by Black Nationalist leader Maulana Karenga, is widely celebrated in African American communities (Karenga 1996).

In the seventies Carlisle (1975) argued that the most recent revival of Black Nationalism served as a reaction to "disillusionment" with whites and slow progress in improving race relations. During this time of increased African independence from Europe, African leaders began to employ the philosophies of black scholars like DuBois and Washington.

Additionally, frustrated supporters of integration efforts by the Civil Rights Movement (e.g., Kwame Ture and other members of the Student Non-Violent Coordinating Committee [SNCC]) began a renewed call for blacks to withdraw from the American political system and make changes within their own community structures and institutions.[10] Nationalism looks inward as a community to find solutions to black problems through internal resources. Brooks (1996) suggests that racial separation (whether limited or total) is juxtaposed with racial segregation, the latter of which is achieved by external imposition and coercion. It is also important to note that, at various points in history, African American leaders have adopted separatism as a temporary strategy before integration. This was predominant in the period from emancipation to the early part of the last century, when some black leaders argued for internal education and skill-building before integrating into the larger society. For instance, Frederick Douglass supported temporary segregation of certain institutions as a first step to eventual integration (McGary 1999). Additionally, Booker T. Washington (1968) believed that there needed to be concerted efforts by blacks to become "upstanding" and "worthy" members of the American community before they could be fully accepted by whites and able to contribute to American advancement. Policy preferences of this group would focus on those issues that are aimed at more community control and self-determining initiatives for African Americans. These kinds of initiatives would include community control of schools, cooperative economic efforts such as support of black-owned businesses, and efforts to transform African America's individual and group self-image through increased awareness of black American and African history.

Rejecting Nationalist Notions

By no means has Black Nationalism been the only ideological position taken by black elites or the masses. Previously, I referenced Dawson's offerings of six categories. Many blacks have been much more reluctant to reject the optimism of a more equitable and tolerant political climate within the structure of the American political system. The earlier quoted passage from Maria Stewart described her view of what white Americans had done to blacks and the impact of these actions on black people, but ultimately she went on to fervently declare that she would not allow that to drive her to a "strange land" by exclaiming that "before I go, the bayonet shall pierce me through" (Moses 1996, 98). The ability to rehabilitate and maintain connections to the American political system was fervently and eloquently championed among the mass public by Martin Luther King Jr.; however, earlier than the Civil Rights Movement, many African American leaders and organizations held to the same beliefs (King 1986c). For instance, Frederick Douglass made the full incorporation of blacks into American society his lifework. He suggested that America could not reach its full potential until it granted full citizenship rights to its most marginalized and oppressed groups. Speaking directly to the rampant lynching taking place in the South and more broadly to how to solve the "Negro problem," Douglass (1996 [1894], 366) urged white Americans, especially those in power, to "put away your race prejudice. Banish the idea that one class must rule over another. Recognize the fact that the rights of the humblest citizens are worthy of protection as are those of the highest."

In the foreword of a special issue of the *Annals of the American Academy of Political and Social Science* in 1956 that examined the possibility of full integration of blacks into American society, the editor, Ira De A. Reid, defines racial integration as "the situation and the process which exists when men in society are breaking down such barriers while moving toward the full acceptance of all people without reference to their racial, religious or ethnic differences. It is the process of achieving full equality of status conditions" (ix). A decade later Oscar Handlin (1965, 661) defined this method of racial integration through a lens based less on acceptance and more on an ethnic politics model "in which individuals of each racial or ethnic group are randomly distributed through the society so that every realm of activity contains a representative cross section of the population." One calls for disregarding or ignoring racial and other categorizations in an effort to alleviate racial inequality; the other focuses more on a conscious distribution of specific groups across social and political arenas. Agreeing with the former proposition, Douglass's goal was to wholly assimilate blacks into American society; therefore, race was "legally, morally and socially irrelevant" (McGary 1999, 50). In contrast, not all supporters of full integration see race as irrelevant. Many blacks are aware that, although racism is often experienced on an individual and personal level, blacks, as a group, have been an enduring and frequent target of white American ire. Therefore, implicitly, all African American political efforts are group-centered efforts to change the status of blacks. Ideally, however, the natural end of a more integrated America would be the diminished importance of race in the American psyche.

Those who both reject Black Nationalist tenets and seek to reshape the nature of their relationship with the American political system adhere to a guiding principle that calls for America to live up to its expressed ideals of having a society in which people are judged by "the content of their character." Myrdal (1962, 4) suggests that this belief is based on "ideals of the essential dignity of the individual human being, of the fundamental equality of all, and of certain inalienable rights to freedom, justice and fair opportunity." King believed black Americans should seek and would be able to have full citizenship rights. Echoing the earlier ideas of Douglass, King (1986a, 211) cautioned, "If we are to implement the American dream we must get rid of the notion once and for all that there are superior and inferior races." King's beliefs were essentially two-pronged. First, blacks would gain their rights by appealing to the moral dissonance of whites. Implicit in his assertion is the idea that one must simply expose whites to the plight of blacks and they would change. The treatment blacks had received at the hands of whites would weigh too heavily on white consciences, and whites would not prevent the integration process initiated by blacks because "In their relation to Negroes, white people discovered that they rejected the very center of their own ethical profession. They could not face the triumph of their lesser instincts and simultaneously have peace within" (1986d, 75). In King's estimation, whites had rationalized their treatment of blacks by adopting a belief in black inferiority. Once this belief was shattered through peaceful demonstrations, whites would have to contend with their own conscience and with the demands of blacks. This led to the second part of King's strategy: blacks would adopt the tactic of nonviolent direct action. Following the Gandhian model, blacks would enact political change by taking the moral high ground. King (1986b) suggests that black protesters

> do not seek to defeat or humiliate the opponent, but to win his friendship and understanding. The nonviolent resister must often voice his protests through noncooperation or boycotts, but he realizes that noncooperation and boycotts are not the ends themselves; they are the means to awaken the end of moral shame within the opponent. The end is redemption and reconciliation. (86–87)

King went on to suggest that this process is necessary for "the creation of the beloved community," which he saw as "an interracial society based on freedom for all."

For King and others, African Americans must recognize their importance and not abandon a nation and associated rights they have earned by contributing to the nation-building process. DuBois (1995 [1903]) in his earlier works suggested that American blacks should work to gain their civil rights through planned campaigns and multiracial coalitions.[11] Additionally, Booker T. Washington insisted on "inter-racial harmony and white good will as prerequisites for Negro advancement" (Meier 1991). Thus, those who reject Black Nationalism's more separate and self-deterministic approach are basically seeking equal access to American institutions, which would allow them equal opportunity to pursue the vision of the framers. However, the situation is more complicated when determining potential political goals because its proponents emphasize alternative or competing identities rather than a singular racial filter and stress individual effort as a mechanism for change. This leads them to take factors other than racial group membership and uplift into consideration when making political judgments.

Ultimately, individuals adhere to ideologies to varying degrees. Indeed, many individuals may find some middle ground by accepting some Black Nationalist tenets without fully embracing all of them. For instance, scholars such as V. P. Franklin (1992) have argued that whether pushing for assimilation into the mainstream or the creation of a black nation, the spirit of self-determination has been a recurring theme for all black leaders. This is true even for those leaders who historically have been portrayed as diametrically opposed philosophically (e.g., W. E. B. DuBois and Booker T. Washington, and Martin Luther King and Malcolm X). Additionally, Brooks (1996) has proposed a strategy that seeks to merge Black Nationalism with more reformist strategies through an idea that he calls "limited separation." Brooks defines limited separation as "a voluntary racial isolation that serves to support and nurture individuals within the group without unnecessarily trammeling the interests of other individuals or groups" (190). He suggests that this may be the best strategy because integration has failed and many of the tenets of Black Nationalism are unrealistic. Brooks suggests five reasons that explain the failure of racial integration: (1) it has never been fully instituted, (2) it does not change personal prejudices, (3) civil rights relies on coercion, and "coerced equality is a lesser quality equality," (4) resources and a strong community have descended into urban decay, and (5) white racism and its agents have thwarted attempts. Additionally, total separation suffers because of "the tendency to romanticize 'blackness' to believe that anything authentically black . . . is better for African Americans than anything white or European" (123).

We also know that intellectuals who embrace a particular strategy over time may modify original beliefs. For instance, DuBois was a staunch supporter of racial integration in his early life, but he ultimately rejected racial integration as a viable option for African Americans. Additionally, former Black Panther Eldridge Cleaver went from supporting the overthrow of the American government and calling for blacks to govern themselves to running for office as a conservative Republican. There is no reason to suggest that individuals will not do the same. Beyond individual changes, changes in the socioeconomic status of African Americans as a group may also lead to movement from one position to another. Recent studies suggest blacks in the upper income brackets are becoming increasingly different from their poorer counterparts in ways that are potentially very important to their political decisions and policy preferences.[12]

Conclusion

This chapter serves to ground this discussion in its proper historical context. It suggests that, although *Dreaming Blackness* is looking at a specific historical moment, the ideas and principles that inform Black Nationalist subscription have been an enduring presence in African American politics. This chapter relies on writings by noted scholars who study Black Nationalism. More important, it relies on original texts in the form of speeches and writings of major Black Nationalist figures. This establishes the intellectual and ideological stamina and, to some extent, elasticity of Black Nationalism as a guiding principle for African American proponents. In the next chapter, the stage is set for the social and political context in which focus group participants and survey respondents interrogate events (historical and contemporary), ideas, leaders, and beliefs that ultimately help form participants' ideological views.

2

Beyond Martin and Malcolm

Ordinary Citizens Talk about the Civil Rights Legacy and Community Problems

Fairview Pines

Fairview Pines is a lot like many other neighborhoods in urban America. It is an enclave of middle-class blacks in the central city who have managed to eke out a few fragile blocks of manicured lawns, minivans, and community pride. Walk more than four or five blocks in any direction and you are squarely among the urban poor—entrenched, disconnected, and often undesirable as neighbors. Over the years and across geographic space, neighborhoods like Fairview Pines have been referred to as "Sugar Hill," "Black Beverly Hills," and many other names that denote their wealth and separateness from both poor blacks and the residents' white economic peers. Fairview Pines is seen as fragile by both its residents and outsiders. Residents are aware that the demand for properties near central business districts with historic accoutrements is at record levels, and one death or divorce could start a course of gentrification in which they will be pushed out. Their concerns are twofold. First, there is a sense of entitlement. Many have maintained residence in these areas despite urban riots in the 1960s and 1970s, crack in the 1980s, and gangs in the 1990s; thus, they deserve special consideration for their perseverance. Additionally, they have a desire to be near their racial community; residents want proximity without being forced to bear the costs of typical urban life. These residents are doubly impacted by the issues described in Massey and Denton's *American Apartheid*—wealthy enough to afford the American dream of home ownership and black enough to not be welcomed in neighborhoods they can financially afford. Yet they are middle-class enough to bear some resentment toward the poor blacks who surround them. Thus, these residents are expected to offer cautious sentiments about the current state of the black community and solutions to its persistent problems.

There is a desire for blacks, in general, and the black poor, especially, to get their collective acts together. One resident offers,

> I want us [black people] to have political power. I want us to have economic power. . . . There's a place for, you know, lower-class blacks, and I want to see a little bit of that. I don't mind people who are poor. I just don't want to see them bring the drugs, the guns, and the alcohol and the violence.

Ohio State University

The following scene has become more familiar across college campuses as the gap has widened between black men and black women receiving college degrees.[1] A group of young black women have assembled to discuss all things black—romantic relationships, hair, and films. The purpose of this gathering is a little different, however, because the meeting was convened to participate in a focus group about the state of black politics. While they wait for the discussion to start, various issues come up—paychecks, fashion, cookouts—it is summer after all. When the formal discussion begins, they sit up straight, prepared for a serious conversation. They, in many ways, embody the questions asked in this book. They are at once burgeoning elites and the daughters of the Civil Rights Movement's greatest beneficiaries—soon to be college-educated and thus soon to be middle-class. These women are aware of this, and as expected from individuals involved in career preparation, they are consumed by the idea of making the necessary moves so that their education will pay off. They have come of age in the era of hip-hop, gangsta films, and Krispy Kreme doughnuts; the Civil Rights Movement now represents the lived experience of their grandparents. They often refer to themselves as people of color and casually use the terminology of the multiculturalism movement in higher education. This results in less of a focus on the individual struggle of African Americans and more on individual interactions with the system or the abstract plight of an amorphous group of people of color. What about "their people," "their community," and its politics? One woman explains:

> That's just a beginning of the whole idea of what is race and what is racism and what does it mean to be black and what does it mean to be black in America . . . and who is really holding you back is what it

gets to . . . and, I mean, the worst enemy that anybody can ever have is themselves. I mean, you can be your own worst enemy. You can be that exact same person that pushes yourself forward. You can be the exact same person that holds yourself back, and so I think it kind of gets into the concept or the frame of mind that it's not necessarily me being black against this white America or landscape of white people. It's more of me against the world and it's about me putting myself ahead of everybody else and ahead of everything else regardless of what I look like. It's what can I do.

North End Community Center

The difficulty in getting volunteers to sign up in a center with so many services becomes apparent immediately. The center includes a food pantry, a GED program, a soup kitchen, and several other programs, all running simultaneously. The director of the GED program promised to recruit participants, but no one seems to have heard of me or this discussion group. As participants are slowly recruited by another worker in the center, the group starts to take form. Its members are reluctant at first to offer their opinions. In this building, they are used to being asked questions about their eligibility for government programs and other assistance. However, this is an unusual setup, and talking about politics does not make it easier. As the volunteers begin to warm up, various themes emerge that evoke laughter, sadness, and inspiration. Some are engaged in the activity of personal improvement or they would not be in this center that houses various social service agencies under one roof. Others are engaged in the project of collective uplift as the providers of the social services. Some are doing both, simultaneously. Their words are tinged with nostalgia for a glorious past of a cohesive black community and desperate hope that the future will bring better personal and community fortunes. Like the Fairview Pines residents with whom they share geographic borders, they are wary of both blacks and whites, but not because of the need to maintain or diminish class boundaries. They are aware of the importance of being equipped to navigate a complex racial and economic world. While discussing intraracial and interracial interactions, a neighborhood activist disagrees with another participant about interlacing race and class to negatively characterize poor blacks:

Nah, nah . . . you become a victim of the same stuff that everybody else has been a victim of . . . you categorize folks inappropriately . . . you're saying the folk where you live currently are acting differently than the folks in [a middle-class white suburb] . . . that's bullshit . . . and the system does that to you and to everybody else. . . . I mean . . . in the same environment, people respond in the same way. . . . it ain't no different between how black people respond in the same environment as a white person. . . . you gotta understand that . . . the whole thing with crime affecting Columbus and people are always referring to the [black side of town] . . . obviously that's bullshit . . . how's the [black side of town] gonna be [the adjacent trendy white urban enclave]?

Martin, Malcolm, and Everyday Talk

These three vignettes offer a snapshot of the composition and sentiments derived from intimate conversations of ordinary citizens in their private homes. They highlight conflict and consensus, unity and division, and hope and pessimism about the racial futures of black America and the broader nation—all the motivations that foster and frustrate citizens' ability to make and express political opinions. From these short reports, there was evidence of the diversity of people and positions that informed this work, but more than that, we were able to paint a portrait (if only a small one) of the dialogically complex and sometimes circuitous route used by ordinary citizens to make sense of the political and social world. Reading them, many might argue that these are universal questions discussed and debated by all Americans: how to find the best and safest neighborhood, how to interpret the information provided by media outlets, or what is the most efficient and expedient course for achieving the American dream? Indeed, on the surface they transcended social categories, with the exception of the racial ink that marks nearly every conversation. During this process, no conversation was free of racial markers. The presence of race talk was unremarkable; the larger goal was to move the conversations toward race and politics through a common structure across groups. Intuitively, starting with something familiar and widening the discussion seemed most logical.

No other African American leaders have enjoyed the recognizability and popularity of Malcolm X and Martin Luther King Jr. in the post–Civil Rights era. They are studied in schools and portrayed in films, and their images are displayed on T-shirts and baseball caps. In the last twenty years scores of movies have portrayed King or Malcolm X, who have also been discussed in hundreds of books, as apparent from a keyword search at my own university library. In 1993, Spike Lee released the feature-length film *Malcolm X*, which grossed $48 million domestically. These men and their images have both emotional and political resonance in the broad American community and particularly in the black community. Davis and Davenport (1997) examined the stability of African American political attitudes and the impact of viewing Spike Lee's film on those attitudes. They found "individuals who saw the film and received reinforcement from a televised documentary became more racially conscious, more concerned about race relations" (550).[2] For these reasons, I decided to begin all focus groups by providing participants with images of Malcolm X and Martin Luther King Jr. and asked them to discuss these leaders' political beliefs. These focus group discussions, outlined in the introduction, served as an opportunity for average citizens to express their political views in their own words.[3] By starting with the familiar, I attempted to demystify the entire research process and to allay potential beliefs that they, for various reasons, had nothing to contribute to the conversation. After the discussion was under way about Martin Luther King and Malcolm X, I could guide the conversation toward other political questions.

Based on the assumption that these men were famous for their political views and activities, I hypothesized that, when probed, focus group participants would automatically offer political comments.[4] Further, discussing the politics of these famous figures in a group setting like this would also lead to a reflexive discussion about participants' own political beliefs and how those beliefs relate to the political principles championed by Martin Luther King and Malcolm X. These men are often portrayed as oppositional figures—one who supported peace, integration, and nonviolence, and the other who supported black self-help and self-defense. Overall, participants had a lot to say about the importance of these men to the black community and to their personal views. What participants did not do was differentiate these political figures along the expected ideological lines. Participants most often expressed jumbled views about what these men stood for and how each leader's principles were different from the other's. In much the same way that citizens muddled through an enormous amount of facts and myths to form political preferences, these participants' opinions merged ideas in unexpected ways and in ways black politics scholars would view as incongruent. The important point here, however, is that they were grappling with the political meaning of these leaders and came to settled personal conclusions. Some saw the men as sharing similar principles and goals, and when disagreement was acknowledged, it was framed as a disagreement over strategy, not goals. Interestingly, initial comments about Martin Luther King and Malcolm X typically referred not to their political views and accomplishments but to their religious affiliations, such as, "King was a preacher" or "Malcolm X was a Muslim." Additionally, participants mentioned ideas, such as that Martin Luther King wanted equality for everyone regardless of race and was a peacemaker, or that Malcolm X wanted rights for black people only and was a "radical." Participants saw the differences between the two men not as ideological but as strategic and stylistic, such as endorsing violence or nonviolence and being confrontational or nonconfrontational.

Surprisingly, very few participants invoked the dichotomy that I hypothesized except to talk about how one or the other man was potentially misunderstood or how each simply represented different constituencies within the black community but essentially had the same goals. For instance, Leslie, a corporate researcher who is also the single mother of another participant, Evelyn, acknowledged differences between the two men but went on to talk about their similarities. She believed Martin and Malcolm were on

> divergent paths with the same goal. Where a person draws his strength whether it's his religion or faith . . . Malcolm X was a part of the black Muslims, but I think his power was a lot of his personality, his life experiences. [Martin and Malcolm] still called the people in the same way, both being strong from different points of view.

Rahim and his wife, Janet, were nearing retirement and the end of child rearing and were among the oldest participants in the focus groups. With a longer view of black history than others, they were quite concerned about the future of the black community and unsure if its current course would lead to progress or destruction. Rahim suggested that Malcolm and Martin had appeal in specific and separate geographic regions, which was dependent on the political context:

> Malcolm was a transition for me. He represented [large northeastern city] more than Martin did, because of the politics of that city. Um, Malcolm hit things on the head, whereas Martin hit some of it, but Martin was

dealing with larger geographics, the nation. Malcolm pretty much had his appeal to people who lived in urban areas, not rural areas.

In only one focus group, a participant outlined the difference in the expected way. Delia, a single professional in her midthirties, asserted:

> I have to disagree about their political thoughts being the same; at least early on in Malcolm X's career they were very different. I think . . . Dr. King's viewpoint was "We will, as a people, get better when everyone learns to integrate and whites and blacks can go to school together and live together and have equality in that way." Malcolm X's idea was exactly the opposite, "We will get better when we as a people learn to do for ourselves, stay to ourselves, and make ourselves stronger. We don't need the white man to make us stronger, we need each other to lift ourselves up." So I think, in that way, their viewpoints were very different.

This would be a much shorter intellectual exercise if every member of all the groups adequately differentiated among Black Nationalism or other ideological positions as did Delia, but they did not. Instead, discussing these two men evoked abstract references to equality, peace, and confrontation, which were more difficult for participants to connect to their own views. This exercise underscored the importance of persistent probing as a useful methodological technique and the need to ask both directed and more subtle questions to deduce political views and values. What follows for the rest of this chapter is what happens when members of the focus groups are encouraged to talk about various political questions related to the black community and its political future. These discussions were based on direct questions about the desirability of interactions with whites, voting for black candidates, and other political issues.

"I Don't Know Where They Hiding It, But My Vote Counts": Voting and Candidate Evaluation

Participants in all the discussion groups expressed clear frustration with the conflict between a desire to live out the American dream fully and a belief that they were somehow hindered by race and socioeconomic status. Several participants talked about voting, for example, as a treasured right of all Americans; however, when asked if it was an effective practice, they were not enthusiastic because of a lack of accountability of candidates of all races. This belief reflected opinion dynamics in the larger population. When questions about political responsiveness were first asked in the National Election Study during the 1950s, more than 60% of respondents disagreed with the statement "I don't think public officials care much what people like me think." That number has steadily decreased, and now more than half of NES respondents agree with the sentiment that public officials do not care what they think (www.electionstudies.org). Participants in these focus groups were squarely aligned with contemporary beliefs about the level of concern held by public officials.

References to the duty to vote because of the sacrifices made by African Americans throughout history often were coupled with a profound belief that voting did not result in real progress for African Americans as a group. Put simply, voting was framed as an obligatory nod to ancestral sacrifices rather than an effective form of political participation. Thus, voting was equal parts right and ritual. Their references also demonstrated the complicated relationship blacks have to the American political system in which they were simultaneously socialized (like all citizens) for patriotic attachments and primed for resistance based on history and experience. Focusing on the importance of voting also represented an ongoing desire for connection to and engagement with the American political system. What surfaced, then, was both individual internal conflict and discordant views about optimal empowerment strategies. Another example of this frustration was provided by participants' suggestions that the government and politicians rarely have black interests in mind when they are making policy decisions and that politicians (regardless of race) are tied to whites because whites underwrite candidates' political aspirations.

While the presence of black candidates did not guarantee that participants would vote for them, it did motivate participants to gather information and participate in the political process.[5] Some participants suggested that they would pay more attention if there was a black candidate in a particular election, and if two candidates running for office seemed to be equally qualified, they would vote for the black candidate. Thus, race played a part in the decision calculus, but not the central part, and not always in the way scholars have predicted. The diminished importance given to race often echoes in the opinions of younger African Americans who were less likely to make reference to direct racist experiences and systemic causes and more likely to embrace popular beliefs of multiculturalism and color-blind societies.

One of the most striking findings in relation to traditional political behavior was the attitude of participants toward involvement in the American electoral process. Previously, I wrote about the frustration that many focus group members expressed surrounding the perceived futility of the vote. Participants also cautioned against unconditional support of candidates (including African American candidates.) This makes the fact that there was almost a universal belief in the power and necessity of the vote counterintuitive. All but one participant felt that the vote was absolutely imperative to the progress of African Americans. In conjunction with this belief in the vote, participants were also effusive when asked to discuss their judgments of black candidates. Dialogue surrounding both the vote and the evaluation of candidates originates from the perspective of individuals who see themselves as active members or citizens of America. This becomes more important as the process of defining and framing Black Nationalism through participants' everyday talk begins in the next chapter.

In every focus group, I asked participants to discuss their thoughts about and opinions of black candidates. I asked whether or not they felt black candidates were more attentive to black constituencies, whether they thought it was important to always vote for black candidates, and whether it was important for black candidates to represent black people. All but seven participants either disagreed or strongly disagreed with the statement that blacks should always vote for black candidates whenever possible. Most participants were opposed to having rigid standards for choosing candidates. Instead, they examined qualities beyond race based on information gathered about all candidates without regard to race or party. Participants fell into the following opinion categories.

Some participants demonstrated a special affinity for African American candidates that was different from their attitudes toward white candidates.[6] For some, the mere presence of an African American in elective office was a positive thing. Crystal, a student in her early twenties who had been raised in an upper-middle-class family in a small, predominantly black midwestern city, admitted:

> It's good to see . . . I love to see black people running for office because there was a time when we couldn't do this. You know . . . so it's just good to see that . . . and like when Bill Clinton won . . . I know he's not black . . . but from what I know he helped a lot of black people out, so you know that all the black people love Bill Clinton . . . if it was a black

person in office or a white person in office, I would vote for the black person, but I would like to know are they going to help me?

Other participants argued that using race as a factor in voting was acceptable only when all other candidate characteristics were comparable. Cameron was the oldest and most politically active member of his discussion group. In his late fifties, he had been a community activist and neighborhood advocate for his inner-city neighborhood for several decades. When discussing black candidates, Cameron asserted:

I would like to think that the best candidate is the one I selected, but obviously I have some bias toward a black person. I'm going to tell the truth. We have similar lifestyles, history. I'd like to think that I pick candidates based on skills and abilities. But all things being equal, I am biased toward the person of color.

Shandra suggested that expecting special favors from candidates of your own race was a part of the American ethnic political tradition. She was raised in midsize northern industrial city and is highly educated, married, and the mother of small children; she and her husband, Henry, own a home in Fairview Pines. Referring to her own experiences, Shandra shared:

Every ethnic group . . . I know in [northern industrial city], where I'm from, when the Italian mayor got elected, my side of town which is predominantly Italian, got our streets plowed. We saw street cleaners. When the Irish guy was in, the south side and the police department was primarily Irish. I'm not saying that's good or bad, but people expect . . . and [my city] is more ethnic than black or white, so you get to see the dynamics of different ethnic groups. You expect someone who looks like you to somehow share some of your same values.

This observation led me to ask the entire group whether or not black candidates have a special obligation to the black community. Delia asserted (and others agreed), "I certainly hope so. If they don't, who is supposed to? I mean, if the black candidates don't hold a special responsibility for black people, then who is?"

Another opinion category stopped short of full support of black candidates and instead paid more attention to elections in which black candidates were vying for political office. These participants revealed that when black candidates were running for office, they were more likely to pay closer attention to politics. Although this did not guarantee that they will vote for the black candidate, the candidate's presence gave them more incentive to get involved in the electoral process. Leslie made the point especially clear:

> I must say that I might read more and investigate more when there is a black candidate to decide whether or not I want to vote for them. Some things that are being run I don't particularly care. Before I check yes on the brother or the sister, I will read more. It's really hard with the *Dispatch* locally. But national issues, I guess I want to be sure, but in the same respect usually I leave it blank in a lot of presidential elections. It's like do I pick the electric chair or the gas chamber. Many a year, I have written my own father's name in, and one of these days he's going to win something. But if it's an election that I care about and there's a black person who is running, I might read up more.[7]

For members of this opinion category, the mere fact that the person was black was not enough to ensure support, but it increased their level of attentiveness. For many, this increased interest has also resulted in more scrutiny of candidates. In their view, not all black candidates were the same. Franklin suggested that when deciding to vote for a black candidate, it all depended on which candidate you were talking about. For him you had to really know more about politics than just race, because you had to "categorize black politicians. You [have] liberals on one side. You [have] blacks who are more conservative." These participants recognized that there are important substantive differences between black candidates. Rahim echoed Franklin's sentiment that black candidates were not all the same:

> That's the interesting part about it. We aren't all rural. We aren't all urban. It's like saying Jesse Jackson and Sharpton. Sharpton don't play well outside of New York. In New York he makes sense. In Altoona, Pennsylvania, he don't make no sense whatsoever. Jesse, he runs to and fro. But who Jesse represents, maybe a DC urbanite. For me, Jesse, I don't need ya. I can do it myself. I can argue and fight for my own.

A third category felt that there was no reason to hold black candidates in any special esteem because while in office they govern no differently from their white counterparts. Many believed that black candidates were not responsive to black constituents because many of them only had black faces but did not promote black interests. For them, phenotype was not a clear indication of support, attachment, or any sense of responsibility on the part of black candidates. According to some participants, candidates were only responsive to money, which blacks either lacked or were unwilling to give. Shandra's husband, Henry, a young professional who was a Fairview Pines resident, offered:

> When we have a black candidate it would be someone that we have financially supported so that he would be engendered to us and not to Schottensteins or someone else he's working for. So a quote-unquote black candidate doesn't matter if he is engendered to white people who don't really care about you. So it doesn't matter who you vote for in today's society because we don't pay for them to get elected. They are not engendered to us because we . . . have no economic basis for keeping ourselves together.[8]

Other participants were less likely to differentiate black candidates from any other politicians because they felt that black candidates had not lived up to expectations that they would effectively advocate for community needs. These participants no longer felt allegiance to black candidates because, according to Rahim, "a lot of time they put a black person in certain positions or categories just to get the vote . . . knowing that he is not running for the right things and he really isn't running for you. So, no, I don't go by color lines." Thus, the rejection of black candidates was often attributed to the candidates' shortcomings. One participant, Neil, was a successful professional in his fifties. Though he offered some opinions during his focus group, he also served as a devil's advocate by challenging the positions taken by other members. Neil suggested that this failure on the part of black candidates has been detrimental to the black community: "I think that we are in a very precarious position in black politics right now. I think that blacks . . . we have had in positions of authority for whatever reasons haven't done a good job in those positions, and that doesn't look well for the future endeavors." Members of the focus groups viewed black candidates in varying ways; there was no denying, however, that voting was an important component of their political behavior.

Several reasons were given in the course of the group discussions for this strong attachment to the vote. First, they suggested that voting was the right of all citizens, and they, as citizens, wanted to exercise that right.

Sharon, a single mother who recently relocated to Fairview Pines from the suburbs, was one of several participants who were a part of a pioneering black family that integrated white neighborhoods when their children were small. She argued:

> This is my father's saying, but I agree with it. If you don't vote, you don't have any right to complain because if you didn't vote to make a change and that person didn't get elected. But at least you tried. I heard my grandmother complain about the condition of life, and close to when she died, we were just talking, and she said she never voted a day in her life. And I'm like . . . oh . . . and she grew up in the South, where she couldn't vote. Then when she got up here, she wouldn't vote, and that never dawned on me that she hadn't voted because we always voted.

For these participants, voting was an important activity that should be ingrained early and one that people should approach from a more analytical standpoint. When asked what the most important political goal is for African Americans, Paula reiterated her own and other group members' beliefs about the value of the vote. An outspoken single mother of an adult son, she resided in Fairview Pines but had been recruited to participate in a focus group as one of Keesha's natural hair care clients. Paula recommended:

> Your school experience should start teaching you at kindergarten about how the election process, how the voting process works in this country if we are going to continue to participate. My other viewpoints . . . as far as politics is that we should extract ourselves from both the Democratic and Republican aspects of voting and we need to become independent and let folks figure out where we are going because we used to be Republican and then we became Democrats, and now both of those parties have bamboozled us and taken us for granted, and we continue because my mama and daddy was a Democrat instead of doing it from a thought-provoking experience as to why I need to vote the way I am. I have become an Independent this year. I am no longer a Democrat, and I will vote whatever my conscience decides. If I have to become a Republican, I will do that too because I am no longer going to decide because I have two brain cells that do rub together that I am going to participate in a party that has historically been the party of my quote unquote people and I think if black people began to do that from a thinking process instead of a historical process, then they can begin to turn some things around politically in this country.

Throughout most discussions, participants justified their support for voting while discussing parts of the process that were corrupt, unfair, or even futile. With all that, they still endorsed voting as an appropriate and necessary activity for blacks. This contrast was demonstrated in the following exchange between three women about voting and the 2000 presidential election—Paula, who offered the preceding opinion; Adrienne, a clerical worker in her midforties living in the inner city; and Janelle, a suburban educator:

ADRIENNE: My vote counts.

JANELLE: We learned that in the last election . . . my vote counts. . . . I don't know where they hiding it, but my vote counts . . . [Laughter from the group]

PAULA: Irregardless.

JANELLE: That's right. . . . Irregardless . . . my vote still counts.

ADRIENNE: But you can't stop, you gotta keep trying, and the only way that you can show that you are still trying is to get out there and check things out and vote.

Second, there was a heightened sense of being obliged to vote because of historical struggles surrounding African American suffrage. When asked whether or not they thought it was important to vote, many participants said yes because so many people had died for that right. Not voting would be a disservice to people who had been sprayed with water hoses, attacked by dogs, and humiliated by voting judges. Janet, Rahim's wife, relocated to Fairview Pines several decades ago and lived with her family through much of the urban blight about which Fairview Pines residents seemed most concerned. As a grade school student, Janet was involved in early school integration efforts. During the course of the discussion, she expressed how living through the Civil Rights Movement era and her own personal experiences with racial integration profoundly shaped her views of race and politics. In a discussion about the necessity of voting, she explained:

We dishonor our heritage when we don't vote. People died for us to have that right and that privilege and to not vote . . . you know . . . it's a slap in the face to our ancestors. We show up and vote, and if the election is such that there are three good people on there that we want to vote for and the rest of the people we could care less, we go to vote for those three good people. Because, you know, to just . . . to do otherwise is to say that those lives that were lost for us for the right to go vote didn't mean anything so we got to go.

There were constant references to the dual meaning of voting by participants across all age-groups, which was seen as symbolically and substantively important. Not all participants had a positive endorsement of voting, with some mentioning the amount of corruption and unfairness built into the process. Only one participant admitted withdrawing from political life, however. Sasha, a college student from a military family that eventually settled in the Midwest, acknowledged that although she did vote at one time, she had decided not to participate in the electoral process and to instead attempt to effectuate change through individual interactions with others. She explained her feelings:

> I just feel that the political climate that we have now in the United States is a joke. So I mean it's like Pepsi versus Coca Cola. It's the same thing. I just don't care for the political climate in the United States, that's why I don't vote. The way politics has gone over the years, and the way people have allowed it to go. I just don't participate in it. . . . Voting for somebody hoping that they will do that for you is ridiculous, and they don't know you 'cause they got other things to worry about. A part of being in politics is a career choice whether you believe it or not, and these people are public servants, but this is a career choice. So they have to keep their job. I mean, there's a lot of things going on in politics that have nothing to do with getting us to the next level.

These reasons illuminated two important themes that emerged in discussions of political participation—a mix of disenchantment and patriotism. Blacks, even those who were extremely dissatisfied with the political process, still conceptualize politics and other issues related to race in terms of their "Americanness." Participants across economic, education, and gender categories put forth American democratic ideals, they asserted rights and privileges as Americans, and they talked about African American contributions to U.S. political development. Discussions of their connection to their American identity, however, were laced with expressions of mistrust, dissatisfaction, and disappointment with the relationship African Americans have with each other and the larger political system.[9] A further research question might be whether African American voting really can be seen as the result of patriotism and good citizenship, as voting is so often framed. Perhaps for blacks, voting connotes something other than good citizenship; another set of factors might contribute to African Americans' decision to vote—namely, respect for ancestors and commitment to the black community. This commitment and references to ancestral obligations should tie into Black Nationalism quite easily. However, this is mitigated by the fact that the behavioral recommendation resulting from racial awareness is continued and active participation in the American political system. Endorsing American political participation would temper wholehearted support for, or at least extreme adherence to, Black Nationalist ideology, which supports withdrawal from the political system.

Distrust and Disenchantment

Because of their abiding presence in this discussion, there should be some mention of the role of distrust and disenchantment in black political opinion. Only 15% of focus group participants felt they could trust the government; the majority felt they could trust the government very little of the time. They cited specific examples, especially from the Jim Crow and civil rights eras, in which many of the older participants came of age. The intensity of the distrust was demonstrated in discussions about voting, reasons they cannot trust black candidates to support black interests, and the persistence of crime and other problems in the black community. The findings related to trust were not surprising. The National Election Study has consistently tracked governmental trust among Americans since 1958, and the data demonstrate that trust has declined significantly. In fact, in 1958, 57% of Americans felt they could trust the government most of the time. By 2004, only 43% reported trusting the government most of the time. Even more dramatic, in the lower category of trusting the government some of the time, the number of respondents increased from 23% in 1958 to 52% in 2004.[10]

Another form of trust emerged as important to participants in these focus groups. This form of trust initially seemed to be a feeling of optimism about race relations and the possibility of integration on the part of younger participants. However, it could be more correctly characterized as a combination of universal mistrust of others regardless of race and confidence in their individual ability to achieve their goals. It involved a focus on the responsibility of the individual to progress or make things happen in her own life. This is best exemplified in an exchange between several of the college students when they were asked to explain the mistrust conveyed by their comments. One student, Breanna, emerged in her group as the most talkative; she was in her early twenties, was academically accomplished, and was raised by a single mother and maternal grandparents in a small city in Ohio. She often used the metaphor of a game to describe politics. Players must learn to play a game in which corruption, injustice, and other problems were built into the rules. When asked if there was a specific racial identity attached to the major players of this political game, she responded there was not. So for these students, targets of mistrust were colorless. Alternatively, this phenomenon suggested an emerging collective action problem resulting from a disconnect between the idealized unified black community, as characterized by linked fate, and the one that has resulted from a shift toward expanded individual opportunity in the face of perceived problems.

Besides distrust, there was also palpable discontent in much of the discussion. There were several areas of dissatisfaction. First, participants were dissatisfied with the level of understanding and regard other Americans had for blacks' predicament. When they were talking about social and economic gaps between blacks and whites, gentrification's impact on urban communities, or blacks' portrayals in the media, there was a general belief that blacks are disposable Americans.[11] Next, there was displeasure with what blacks themselves had made of opportunities available since the civil rights movement. Among younger participants, for whom the sixties were remote, there was a high level of black blame for the problems faced by the black community. Additionally, there were critiques of many of the social and political policies that were direct results of civil rights efforts, such as affirmative action. For older participants, the dissatisfaction reflected a firm belief that the American political system had not really changed as much as many hoped it would, and that many opportunities had been wasted by black leaders and thwarted by whites.

A Burgeoning Divide:
Contours of the Generation Gap in Black Political Attitudes

Differences in the political and racial climate in which participants were socialized revealed important differences in the way older and younger participants talked about race. Younger people were much less likely to rely on direct racist experiences as explanations for their opinions. This is in contrast to older participants, who clearly saw race and racism as important determinants in their lives. In fact, younger participants were more likely to downplay or rebuff their parents' and some of their peers' reliance on racism as an explanation for problems in the black community. When positive white affect was expressed, it typically was done by younger participants. Thus, age differences and socialization emerged as prominent factors in this analysis. Younger participants were less likely to see racism as an impediment to individual or group progress. For instance, Breanna asserted:

> I have an issue with the whole idea of we were oppressed and yada yada and we were. We were . . . past tense. Right now is what we need to be worried about. "We were" was a time period in which I was not even around. My mama wasn't even born. So I mean, you know, I don't know about the "we were," I know what I can do right now. I think it's important to know about the past but not to hold on to it so tightly.

Andrea, another college student, pointed out that although many African Americans may believe there is a wide chasm between the worlds and experiences of blacks and whites, she was doubtful. Andrea, who is of Caribbean ancestry, was the only participant who was not a descendant of Africans enslaved in the United States.[12] She had lived in the United States only briefly before beginning college and stated:

> I listen to the talk of the building of the bridge and the closing of the gap and I want to say I just don't . . . I don't think . . . I don't see the gap sometimes. I don't see the need for a bridge. And yes it's all really nice and wonderful to stand up and use the flowery language and say yes we need to bring the two worlds together, but to me . . . it's all really well and good to get up and say that . . . realistically is it going to happen? I don't know. Why? Because we're all sitting around here waiting for someone to get up and use the flowery language and say let's build a bridge. What I do day-to-day is I go out and I interact with white people.

Breanna and Andrea were not alone. Like her peers, Sasha, based beliefs about appropriate interracial relationships on her personal interactions. Her mother's negative experiences with whites did not affect her "because any beliefs I have about other races is because of my encounters with them not [my mother's] encounters." The only focus group in which a majority of the participants expressed opposition to affirmative action, complete abhorrence to the formation of a black nation, an enthusiastic embrace of multiculturalism, and the need for diversity was the group composed of young college students.[13]

Older participants, when discussing race and racism, were much more likely to draw from their experiences as direct victims of racism. Members of these groups talked about affirmative action and integration (though rarely using that conceptual label) as by-products of the Civil Rights Movement and as difficult experiences for those participants who were the first to integrate workplaces, educational institutions, and neighborhoods. One participant talked about integrating a middle school in a border state in the sixties and how difficult and hostile it had been. Janet reflected on this period:

> It was a challenging experience and one that still haunts me. One that I think haunts everyone in the community of my age. I went to an all-black elementary school, which was wonderful and was a wonderful experience . . . and they really educated us. . . . They [referring to the teachers] did their job . . . when we got to September . . . we ended up . . . they wouldn't send the bus to our neighborhood. They sent it to the white neighborhood next door, and our parents had to transport us over to the white neighborhood to catch the bus. Once they got that straightened out and they picked us up in our neighborhood, they would pick the white kids up then pick us up and go to school. But we ended up with race riots on the bus every day. You know, we were spit on; we were cursed at . . . that's when I learned to curse. Because before that I never heard that. I didn't hear that, but you know they put us through it. Um . . . it was a very hostile environment.

Her husband, Rahim, talked about integrating a small midwestern college and what it was like to deal with both the university and the surrounding community. Both of these participants classified their experiences as negative and immersed in racism. Both also made it clear that they saw no particular reason to racially integrate their lives in any way. Also participating in that group were people whose families had pioneered residential integration when the participants were children. They talked about periods when blacks could not live in certain areas and how some of their families participated in tearing down racist residential boundaries. Donna, a Fairview Pines resident in her midforties, recalled one such attempt by her family, in which they were

> thinking of buying some land . . . and they would not sell to blacks. That really devastated me as a child growing up to know that this was a place that we would go on Sunday afternoons, after church and play . . . people were friendly, but how could this place be a place where blacks weren't permitted to live? So that was . . . um . . . a really . . . um . . . devastating situation. Just to see that people don't like black people and don't want them next door. That was rough. That was difficult.

These efforts seemed to profoundly shape participants' current understandings of how race works in America, including the need to maintain a sense of cautiousness with nonblacks and in some ways temper their desire to live in integrated settings.

Few younger participants made references to direct racist experiences. These references were usually coupled with statements that attribute fault to African Americans for not taking advantage of opportunities, along with any racism they have experienced. For instance, Melissa noted:

> So I understand, like, how she said she doesn't see the race card. I see it definitely. I have experienced racism in very subtle forms and so I'm not . . . it's not that I hate white people. . . . I don't hate white people, but there are certain things I see in the black culture based on what we had to go through. I think we are . . . I'm biased. I like my culture. I like where I come from, but I do see a lot of times too where we play off the idea that everything should be handed to us . . . and true I think that there are some things that we deserve in terms of reparations, but you have to know, kind of, how to get the message across. You have to take what we are doing based on historical things and make yourself better.

Whereas Melissa's comments offered less detail about the nature of the racist experiences she has suffered, another of her peers, Aminah, pointed to a specific experience. However, statements that attribute the problems of blacks to individual negative behavior flank her retelling of the experience:

It's just that I have experienced racism too. For example, when I just came back from Ghana this past Christmas, everybody who was, this was just after the September eleventh thing, so everybody who got pulled to the side for a second screening had a funny-looking name or was black so, um, that was one experience I had of racism just recently. So I understand the racism part too, but I also don't agree with that [belief on the part of black students that] oh I can't move forward because I'm black and oh I got a 2.0 GPA and my mom is going to buy me a car. I was like, nobody was going to buy me a car, and I have 4.0. I was like, hey, where's my car, where's my bicycle?

Both of these references to direct racism were told in a way that is very different than the descriptions of the older participants. The experiences of the younger participants were either vague, as in the case of Melissa, or they were cushioned by statements that point out the shortcomings of individual blacks in a way that discounts the impact of racism, as in the case of both women. Older participants did not do this. It was not that they did not offer black blame sentiments. Instead, they offered accounts of racism to demonstrate their level of identification with the struggles of the Civil Rights Movement, to explain their preference (or lack thereof) to live in all-black surroundings, and to discuss the development of their views about politics and race. They provided their own share of black blame, but not as a way of devaluing the shock of racism.

The members of one focus group were also trying to maintain a community with specific demographic characteristics. These participants lived in a neighborhood that was rapidly gentrifying. Many of their sentiments potentially stemmed from a feeling that if they were in a place where people looked like them, they would also be more readily accepted. Another community resident, Shandra, pointed to her desire to reside in a predominantly black community:

It's really sad. When people are selling houses around here, like that house across the street is for sale, and so many white people . . . well first of all, she tried to keep it on the DL.[14] Like, do you know any black people who would buy this? She did do that, and then a lot of white male gay couples came by and looked . . . so it's really sad. I really want to see young black couples live in my neighborhood. I want my [child] to have somebody to grow up with. I want to have a reason to keep her in the school system, but I don't have one right now, and she will probably be going to private school out of here. . . . Its okay for gay people to live here, but it's also okay for married black couples with children and elderly people to live here.

Last, in recognition of contrasting views on race and racism due to age and socialization, one participant, Neil, pointed to differences between his and his daughter's experiences with race. Neil explained:

I've been through a lot of things as a black person, and I've got a kid who is now in college, and her black experience is probably very nil. She probably doesn't care about the black experience, and yet I try to instill that in her. I think young people today do not see the black community the same way possibly your generation [referring to author] and I know my generation, and I think that's unfortunate. I think we have to keep trying to instill close relationships with them.

Another example of a generation gap among respondents was their beliefs about the motivations and behavior of whites. There was discussion in every group about the character of the relationship between blacks and whites, and most people advocated a cautious approach to any dealings with whites at the very least and strong negative sentiment toward them at most. The only people to express any positive white affect were members of the younger cohort. Andrea, who interrupted a discussion about the relationship between blacks and whites, most vividly relayed this:

I like white people . . . I just want to put it out there that I like white people. Yeah . . . you know white people ain't bad where I come from . . . I talk to white people. I like them. I don't have a problem with them because I think individually I don't have a problem with myself. I don't see myself as a lesser person than anybody else who is white or colored skin. I don't see myself as having less opportunities. I don't see myself as less bright, so when I go out there I portray myself as being not just their equal because I know that I am better [there is laughter from others] and that commands . . . it doesn't matter to me . . . it doesn't matter that my skin might be eighteen times darker than their shade of pigment because I am representing myself as a person with this amount of value . . . of this amount of estimation.

Evelyn, a college student who was raised in a predominantly affluent white community and the youngest focus group participant, reported that she has always been treated well by whites and that she identifies with whites as much as she does with other races.[15] Evelyn suggested:

> I honestly . . . I don't want to say that everything I have I owe to the white community, but I've never not fit in [or was made] to feel like, I couldn't identify more with one group or another. Like I said before, the only time I felt like I didn't belong was with the black people who thought I wasn't black enough. We [referring to black people talking about themselves] speak this way. You seem white. I mean all I see is just a lot of division [among blacks], so if there was a black America, I can't really say how I would fit into it.

Notably, both of these comments encouraging strong positive affect, and relationships with whites were coupled with expression of negative black affect. This was a component of black blame, mentioned earlier, that will be discussed more fully in chapter 4.

Defining "Us" and "Them": The Endurance and Metamorphosis of Linked Fate

In the decades since the initial research findings, linked fate has continued to be a catchall category for understanding why African American group orientations persist in political and social arenas. Linked fate is the feeling of connectedness that individual African Americans have to the fate, image, and progress, of African Americans as a group. African American survey respondents have demonstrated a resounding belief that their personal progress is connected to the progress of other African Americans. This belief was also held by participants in this sample—to varying degrees, African Americans consider the implications of events, ideas, and so forth, for their entire racial group. Throughout the discussions for this research, there were repeated references to black people as a group rather than to the participants themselves as individual African Americans. Younger participants were tied less to their racial group and at times even desired to distance themselves from it; however, they still focused on race. African Americans are aware that externally they are lumped together even if they do not want to lump themselves. Participants felt their political, social, and economic fates rose and fell with the tide of sentiment toward African Americans as a whole. Participants used words signaling a collective outlook, such as "we," "our," or "us."

Recognizing that African Americans still focus on their "groupness" as an overarching lens for much of their discussion of social and political issues, there were also some unexpected nuances in the way that participants created boundaries around their racial community. This was especially evident in the focus groups that were composed primarily of older, more educated, and middle-class participants. This discussion shed light on the fact that sometimes it is very important to simply ask more questions about what participants mean when they say things like, "It's important to me to give back to my community." Often in homogeneous black settings, "community" is assumed to have a universal definition when, in fact, it has vastly different meanings across individuals, time, and space. For instance, when participants were asked how they saw themselves in relation to the black community, without any cuing, most answers were based on geographic boundaries rather than the idea of a larger, national, and fluid definition of the black community. The respondents recognized their membership in multiple communities, but when actually discussing their specific role in their community, they often did so in reference to their geographic community.[16] Terrence, a university administrator and married father of a small child, illuminated this point. Responding to the question of whether he bears some responsibility to his community, Terrence explained:

> I think . . . first I think we do have a role in our community just like the sister was saying, but I think the question is that we have a number of communities to be a part of, like me . . . you know . . . I've grown up all over the place. I've never stayed in one locale for a long period of time due to my father being in the military, but every place I was I was a part of that community. Even now I am a part of my community where I live over in [a mixed-race middle-income neighborhood]. So, yeah, I do believe that we have a role and a responsibility in our community. Just like the example earlier . . . we are the same way in [my neighborhood]. We're vested in our community. We want our property value to stay at a comparable level. We watch our streets. We want our kids to be safe. If there is something going on, we are calling the police, we are talking to our neighbors, we know our neighbors, so there's a really good communal base there. So I think, yeah, we do have . . . our communities are important to us, but I would like to make it a little bit broader . . . I mean . . . we've all got multiple communities. The question that I would like to pose is . . . how we are as blacks working within our communities, plural?

This definition runs contrary to the way scholars have both conceptualized and empirically analyzed linked fate. Questions about black representation, the success of social movements, cohesion in public opinion, and bloc voting in national elections all contend that African Americans see themselves as members of a broad national (and sometimes global) black community. The fact that the most affluent and educated members in this analysis and potentially a good proportion of African Americans were constructing narrower borders around their definition of community will have strong influences in future black political and social dynamics. A decrease in affective orientation toward blacks should also diminish support for Black Nationalism, for which more global racial connection is central.

Class differences also emerged during discussions of community and linked fate. Class became a huge factor in the maintenance of black residential communities and individual ability to succeed. Class served as a latent influence on the larger argument made here about racialized ideologies; dialogue about class was framed as the choice between cross-class incorporation and class isolation within a black framework. For some participants, there were clear boundaries defining "the black community" that moved beyond the geographic boundaries. In these cases, there was a clear and intentional separation between African Americans with higher incomes and social status and poorer African Americans. Shandra, in the opening vignette in this chapter, outlined her goals for the black community using class differences as a delimiter. Her statement is worth repeating:

> I want us to have political power. I want us to have economic power. I'm not saying . . . There's a place for, you know, lower-class blacks, and I want to see a little bit of that. I don't mind people who are poor. I just don't want to see them bring the drugs, the guns, and the alcohol and the violence.

To many African Americans who are more educated and wealthier than their racial peers, poor people bring the same social pathologies and problems that are cited in popular media and by other wealthy citizens. An interesting and lengthy exchange emerged around this particular topic. One of the participants, Neil, a middle-aged architect, played devil's advocate by asking the other participants to really think about what was most important to them—race or class.

NEIL: But the question is . . . let's say across the street, and you live here . . . say somebody . . . let's say you got a white couple who wants to buy that house, you got a gay couple who wants to buy that house, and you got me [who is black] who wants to buy it for Section 8 . . .

SHANDRA: If they were to manage that building . . .

HENRY: No . . . no . . . I'm just going to stop that. I mean we're talking about a race and a class issue . . .

HENRY: Somebody who can afford . . .

LESLIE: Yeah, there are a lot of class issues within our own race.

NEIL: But I'm talking about putting black people over there. Isn't that segregation?

HENRY: No . . . no, it isn't.

DELIA: Economic segregation . . .

HENRY: If you can afford to live there, then you can live there.

SHANDRA: But most of us can't afford . . .

NEIL: That's what they say about black folks . . .

HENRY: Well . . . they have 5% who are upstanding, and that 5% gets off it eventually.

AUTHOR: So isn't . . . when you define your black community, economic status plays an integral role in that, and so then it becomes not just a black community but a black, and I hesitate to say it . . . black middle class.

NEIL: Black caste system . . .

AUTHOR: Or a black upper class but not just a black community, or do you see yourself as a part of a black community more globally rather than based on . . .

HENRY: It can be a black community. People can even rent over there. What I'm saying is . . . somebody who moves in and has no responsibility whatsoever, that's trouble. We all know it's trouble. We all know that. A black person can buy that and put black people in there, and they can rent from him. That's beautiful, but if a black person buys it and puts black people in there which he knows is going to tear down the community, that person is no longer black to me. I'm sorry. He's not black. He's classified as something else.

For these participants, both class and race emerge as seemingly equal factors in their decisions.

According to some participants, African Americans of different social and economic classes should try to live together and interact because their fates are interdependent; consequently, some level of interaction is important for community maintenance and progress. They pointed to the ability of blacks who are better off to help uplift others and serve as role models. When asked directly if they thought it was a good thing for poorer and wealthier African Americans to live in close proximity, Janet volunteered:

I think it's a good thing actually . . . um, diversity is a key word today . . . and if they neighborhoods were more mixed, more diverse in terms of income, there would be less negative impact on our neighborhoods. Because people think . . . well, really you could be in a $300,000 ghetto as easy as a $50,000 ghetto. [Others agree] If those are the only people you associate with. When you have a mixture of people . . . different economic groups, different backgrounds . . . they improve each other's lives when they get to know each other. You know . . . and just because you might only own $10,000 today . . . tomorrow it might be a $100,000 . . . and by perhaps interacting with people who have that kind of income, it might change your aspirations for what may be.

To Janet and others who concur, such a relationship was not just a drain on middle-class resources; it is a symbiotic relationship in which each group contributes and benefits. Sadie, another Fairview Pines resident, went so far as making sure her daughter interacted with poorer African Americans. She had grown up in a totally white environment and had admittedly lived an extremely sheltered life. So when her daughter was coming of age, Sadie wanted to provide her with a different experience. She said:

And the experience that I had growing up, I said that I would never let that happen to my child. So I actually introduced her to the inner city, ghetto, or whatever. And I would take her over there to Atkinson, to the Neighborhood House. Uh, so that they helped me raise her. You know, I would take her there. Of course, once again, my family was against it. All my sisters thought I was going crazy. But I thought it was really important to make her well rounded, to understand everything is not just what you have, but what they have. And I remember one day pulling up, and there were all these kids around her. And I was like, "Oh my God, what are they doing to my baby?" And they were saying, "Talk for us." You know, because she talked proper English. And she didn't talk any slang. It was a foreign language to them. So she learned from them, and they learned from her. So it was an exposure-type thing. And then I learned, you are doing the right thing, because that exposure is important, because

I didn't have it. And it hurt me in being brought up, in my marriage, everything, because I was so sheltered. I didn't know people were really mean. I didn't know people were dishonest. I didn't know people lied. I thought everyone was good. You know because I wasn't exposed . . . they sheltered me from everything, and it's really not for the best. You have to be exposed, be diverse, and be exposed to everything. And there's a reason for it. That's for your survival.

Conclusion

Knowing and interacting with blacks across economic classes (within clearly delineated limits) is desirable to all participants. It is also true that, with mixed feelings, these participants see themselves as inextricably linked by shared racial group membership. This is significant for any discussion of linked fate because it tells interested scholars that the link constantly referenced and implemented as an explanatory variable may be an unwanted tether for some and a welcomed connection for others. Either way, it deserves more scholarly inquiry. If the connection is unwanted, then individuals seeking to distance themselves from their own race and endorsing the elimination of race as a defining social category would be more likely to reject a race-centered ideology like Black Nationalism. The primary goal of this chapter has been to give readers a sense of how the focus groups were conducted and to provide a sample of the discursive structure of the group discussions. The next chapter will elaborate on how participants' political views inform their support for or rejection of Black Nationalist principles. It begins by outlining a typology of Black Nationalist support and rejection.

3

Rights and Resistance

Mapping the Terrain of Black Nationalist Adherence

Thus far, *Dreaming Blackness* has elucidated the guiding principles and scholarly theories regarding Black Nationalism and characterized the structure and tone of the group discussions. Here, I return to my original argument that African Americans' ideological positions related to the appropriate relationship between the black community and the larger American society shape their overall political views. For blacks, their race and racial group membership play central roles in many areas of life. Essentially, the unspoken question that African Americans find themselves asking is, Should they as individuals and as a collective try to incorporate themselves into the larger (and mostly white) American social and political structure, or should they opt for withdrawal and seek to extricate themselves from that structure? Returning to that question, this chapter will lay out the political and social psychological characteristics that emerge as important when individuals choose to embrace or reject Black Nationalism or plot a course that falls somewhere in between.

The focus group participants, with few exceptions, did not refer to ideological labels during these conversations. So, the excerpts offered are based on several prompts. First, all groups began by discussing images of Martin Luther King and Malcolm X. As mentioned earlier, it was hoped that Martin Luther King's and Malcolm X's political beliefs would spark discussions about individual ideological positions. After this discussion ran its course, participants were asked how important it was to have contact with whites, as well as other political questions previously addressed. These questions were related to candidate evaluations, black organizations, political trust, and voting. Occasionally participants made unanticipated but useful interjections, and I would prompt them to elaborate and encourage others to weigh in. This chapter reflects answers to those prompts. Did participants ever say things like, "I am a Black National-ist, and this is what I think"? No. Nevertheless, within the dialogue there were ideological structures and cogent arguments. Without question, par-ticipants took sides. The systematic differences in participants' opinion are taken up in this chapter.

The fundamental project undertaken in *Dreaming Blackness* is to sys-tematically understand individual Black Nationalist adherence among Af-rican Americans in the post–Civil Rights era. To that end, table 3.1 lists attitude and issue positions that function as ideological characteristics. This information is presented in tabular format to facilitate cross-category comparison. It is vital to note here that these categories should not be viewed as mutually exclusive. Participants in the focus group and the Na-tional Black Election Study samples rarely expressed opinions that fit into single ideological categories. As with other political questions, one group of respondents expressed moderated opinions that both embrace and re-buff Black Nationalist principles. Thus, the categories delineated here are archetypes, with adherents subscribing to most characteristics rather than absolutely all of them.

At the outset, I call attention to the first attitude orientation outlined in table 3.1—linked fate. From earlier discussions and a long line of schol-arly work, it is evident that linked fate serves as an important starting point in this and all African American political analyses. African Ameri-cans feel attached to each other in significant ways, and that remains true across this ideological typology. In many ways, the presence of linked fate among African Americans has become a constant in the analysis of Af-rican American politics. Stipulating this fact allows this project to move beyond linked fate and to speak more directly to the nature of that asso-ciation and its impact on blacks' worldview. To accomplish this, I discuss in detail the categories listed in table 3.1.

Black Nationalists

Relying on historical racial conflict and hostility, as well as a desire to reconnect to African cultural origins, Black Nationalists have called for various levels of withdrawal from the American political system. Black Zionism represents the most extreme form of Black Nationalism, and its proponents have rarely been able to muster the support necessary to amass and sustain an emigration movement. More popular, instead, have been more reserved forms of Black Nationalism that endeavor to protect

TABLE 3.1
Typology of Black Nationalism: Attitudes and Issue Positions

Ideology by Attitude Position	Black Nationalists	Moderate Black Nationalists	Black Nationalist Rejecters
Belief in linked fate	Strong connection	Strong connection	Strong connection
African American vs. other identities	African American dominant identity and cognitive liberation process	Primary African American identity/ secondary identities considered	Multiple identities recognized or no identity emphasized
Social outlook	Collective	Individual and collective outlook	Individual
Group problem perceptions and origins	System blame/low black blame and institutional cause	Moderate black blame and ambiguous cause	Black blame and individual failure
White affect	Negative	Mixed positive and negative (cautious)	Positive
References to racist experiences	Direct racist experiences	Indirect racism/ mitigated direct racism	No references
Racial identities attached to government actors and institutions	White	Both black and white	Colorless
Whites and institutional motivations	Intentional and malicious race-specific problems	Combined race-specific and universal problems	Universal government problems and not race-specific

and maintain African American culture, institutions, and traditions separate and apart from others. The latter type of Black Nationalism is demonstrated most among participants here.

For Black Nationalists, their African American identity is central to how they define themselves. Identity transformation is a crucial mobilizing element of Black Nationalism, accomplished largely by strengthening connection to individuals, cultural traditions, and struggles throughout the African Diaspora. Keesha, a civil servant and natural hair salon owner who has worked, resided, and raised her children entirely in the center city, summarized these essential beliefs in her discussion about why she agrees with Malcolm X:

Well you know if we read the books that Malcolm told us to . . . we always talk about what we can't do. What we are not able to do; we have not analyzed why we are there mentally and how do we break that mental slavery . . . um . . . the fact that when you go over to Africa, not in the colonized areas because you know they are just as confused as the black folks over here but in the rural areas . . . people eat out of the same plates, people see each other as one. If you're hurting, I'm hurting. If you don't have, I don't have. If you have, I have. So I feel good when you get because that means I got, and I feel bad when you don't have because that means I don't have. So I'm saying that being kidnapped and then being raped of our identity, and like Paula said you ain't going to get it back in thirty years, but to be able to identify that I don't trust people and why don't I trust people and work on that because the only way you're going to get through it is—it's almost like having a phobia, you have to expose yourself to it—and say, okay, I'm going trust Jerri and Paula and Adrienne, and somebody's going to let me down, but it's okay. That's where we're human. But the point is—are we looking out for the group? We've been so Europeanized that it's me and I. And we forgot about you and us.

Keesha's sentiments encompass many characteristics of Black National-ism. For instance, she demonstrates a social outlook that emphasizes the importance of taking care of the collective. Community empowerment and progress are central to the beliefs of Black Nationalists, who look in-ward for resources to address the needs of the community. The ability of blacks to rely on community resources and the belief in black interde-pendence is realized through frequent interactions and transactions with black businesses, community centers, and other organizations. Reflecting on this need to preserve community, Paula referred to a time when this type of community-based living was the norm:

PAULA: There was a time in school when we were on our own and our teach-
    ers were black . . . then when we weren't subjected to [negative treatment
    and stereotypes by white teachers] even though we were still being taught
    the dominant culture because for you to survive that's the culture you had
    to live. You had to have two personalities . . .
JANELLE: It's called by W. E. B. DuBois duality.
PAULA: Duality . . . you had to have it.

Paula and Keesha also point to another component of Black National-ism—the recognition that there are important differences between the way blacks and whites think and interact with each other and within their own cultural groups. Part of this seems to be the belief that African Americans have to undergo a cognitive liberation process in which they eschew white American norms and values. Social movement scholars Frances Fox Piven and Richard A. Cloward (1979) and Doug McAdam (1982), define cognitive liberation as a multistage process in which individuals relinquish their faith in the "legitimacy" of the current system, understand their current situation is changeable, initiate demands, and believe they are capable of changing the system through their own strategic actions. For Black Nationalists, cognitive liberation is similar in the sense that ideological adherents recognize the illegitimacy of the American political system; however, instead of making demands and asserting rights in that system, they choose to withdraw and effect change by creating a new system. Recall Keesha's earlier assertion that black Americans need to relinquish those beliefs and behaviors that are "Europeanized"—read white. The desire to alter ingrained views that are biased toward the dominant is a unique feature of Black Nationalist ideology. Other ideological groups discuss the best tactics for maneuvering within the current system that for various reasons fails to live up to its stated goals.

The focus on their African American identity and history, when added to the obligation to work for group empowerment, leads Black Nationalists to engage in the cognitive liberation process. Having gone through the process, Black Nationalists participants begin to define problems within the African American community quite differently from other participants. They see many of the problems in the black community as evidence of inequality and bias within the American political system. The government and its actors use institutional rules and norms to prevent black progress. Further, other institutions that shape American life, like schools, businesses, media outlets, and banks, form a constellation of rules and norms that render black success more difficult on multiple fronts. The attribution of blame and its political implications will be discussed more thoroughly in the next chapter, but it should be noted that how individual participants attributed blame was often connected with the way in which they viewed whites' motives.

As expected, Black Nationalists exhibit less trust in government and are more supportive of withdrawal from the American political and social "game." In the focus group discussions, participants were also more likely to employ testimonials of direct racist experiences to reinforce their arguments. For instance, Leslie offered:

I feel like I've already lived in an all-black America. When I was in elementary school, very few white people came into my life except a few teachers. The businesses we went to, the doctor, almost everybody. The year we moved into our neighborhood, there was a whole bunch of empty houses around us all of a sudden. All of the white people moved out, and it was an all-black neighborhood, all-black elementary school, like 95%. We went to Long Street for businesses, the beauty shop, the doctor, or whatever. You just didn't come in contact with white people. I thought I had a good life. I don't feel like I missed anything by not having white people in my life.

Leslie's statement revealed dual points in relation to Black Nationalism. First, in agreement with earlier discussions, Leslie told the story within a cognitively liberated framework. She understood the impact of white racism on residential or business opportunities for blacks, which did not diminish her evaluation of black spaces. Second, the anecdote provided an example of how participants who adhere to Black Nationalism identify and implicate racism as a problematic and enduring American feature. Leslie did not point to her experience as especially negative, but other participants reported explicitly negative interactions with whites. Keesha gave her account:

That's what I really want to push out on my children, and I probably was pretty blatant because I came up during the sixties and seventies. It wasn't no joking and playing around, and I told them, see, I came up through Catholic schools, and I went to elementary school with all white children, so I know what it is like . . . so I'm speaking from experience, and if you think for a moment that just because your kids are around white people that's going to make them better . . . ha, ha, ha, ha . . . one thing it will make you is very cautious and strong.

In another group, Gina, a youth leader and community activist at one of several black Catholic churches near Fairview Pines and North End Community Center, talked about her experiences with whites and why she was more comfortable in racially homogeneous contexts:

I prefer to be with all blacks. For instance, when I go out I want to go to a black club, I don't want to go to a white club. I just prefer to socialize with black people more than white people. I try not to be—I try to make sure that my daughter knows that God loves everybody equally. It is just that I don't want her put through that. When I was growing up, we were a very small portion of the people going to Catholic school in the south end. We went to school with some terribly, terribly racist people . . . Well, I am just saying that because of some of the experiences that I have had with white people, that's all. I am a lot more comfortable around black people than I am around white people—socializing and everything. I have people in my family that are the opposite.

Nationalists both experience racism and use that experience as evidence of white malevolence and the need for blacks to coalesce. Keesha believed that recognizing color differences is normal and appropriate behavior. She had a problem, however, with race consciousness that moves into the area of discrimination; she "feels like genetically whites are told that you're better. I mean in this country anyway." This belief that the system is permanently tilted in favor of whites has led Black Nationalists to actively withdraw, on either a limited or a more comprehensive basis, from a system they perceive already excludes them from full participation. More than simply withdrawing, Black Nationalists take up a larger task of shifting the racial paradigm by reframing the meaning of blackness and galvanizing an independent power base.

Black Nationalist Rejecters

Much of American political history encompasses the conflict resulting from the demand for minority incorporation and an unwillingness to incorporate smaller groups into the larger American community. The incorporation process for African Americans has been challenging and drawn out, but still there are many African Americans who are committed to the goal of full incorporation. It is a big leap, however, to say that this commitment is premeditated rather than a subconscious process. During the course of the focus groups, participants rarely said that it is important to make a conscious effort to integrate. Instead, such sentiments are revealed in more roundabout and subtle ways. Participants described experiences with racial integration efforts and the lasting impact they had on their lives, or they relayed the feeling of being the only African American in certain settings and what the appropriate reaction to that experience should be. They provided a contrasting portrait between those participants who embrace Black Nationalism and those who do not.

Participants who rejected Black Nationalism were more likely to acknowledge and incorporate multiple identities into their decision-making process. These participants were clear that they did not want to be thought of as just one thing—a black person. Despite this preference, rarely did they offer other prevailing identities as alternatives. Being college educated, having multicultural awareness, or having direct ties to another country were identities that impacted their beliefs about the level of association African Americans should have with whites. For example, Andrea, a student reared primarily in the Caribbean, was the most effusive of all participants about integrating with whites. Her motivation for this support for integration had a lot to do with her admitted inability to identify with much of the African American experience, including a history of negative interaction with whites. Andrea stated:

> I have been listening, and I didn't grow up here. I don't know anything about Martin Luther King or Malcolm X. I don't know . . . I saw the movies. Basically that's what its come down to . . . from what I have witnessed because I don't play the race game . . . I don't pay attention to it. It doesn't figure into how I think. People always ask me if it feels weird being the only black person in a certain setting. I don't notice. I actually think it's a little sad that people do notice it and they have to point out, "Oh my God. You're the only black person here."

Andrea was not alone in her belief that race was not the most vital filter through which she viewed the world. Her statements connected to other participants' beliefs about multiple identities and the importance of intraracial and interracial diversity. Sasha, who grew up in a military family, suggested that for her parents it was very important for her and her siblings "to be ourselves, be citizens of the world." Non-Nationalist participants consciously avoided being boxed in by prevailing stereotypes that narrow their field of opportunity. Breanna, chiding her mother for her narrow definition of blackness, offered:

> [My mother thinks], like, we need to stand up for ourselves and you should not let other people enter your black circle. . . . she's kind of becoming an extremist as she gets older . . . she appears to be like, okay,

well, not only can they not be white, they can't be anything else either. They have to be black. And we're talking about black and straight.

Breanna and her ideological peers were attempting to transcend other people's perception of "authentic" black characteristics and behaviors. Strong desires to shatter popular images of blackness, however, did not result in expressions of other identities that more accurately captured their perception of themselves.

With no other prevailing identities, these participants often championed the benefits of individual recognition without regard to race. Some simply wanted to associate with people who espoused shared values, which were not bound by racial categorization. Sasha made the point:

> I want to live in a culture or around people who are on the same level as me because my biggest gripe about being here in Ohio is that in Ohio everybody thinks in terms of black and white, and there is a whole world out there of people . . . and never mind that there are many shades of black. There are also people from different parts of the world who might on sight look black but not consider themselves black . . . or like even in whites there might be people who look down on being called white . . . they are, like, I'm not white, I am Croatian or Ukrainian or whatever, or I'm South American. For me I want to be around people who are like-minded. I don't care what race. I don't want to be around people who are all the same. I don't want to be in a society that is all of one anything, to be honest.

Others emphasized good character, harmonious values, and the establishment of sound relationships as more important than race in deciding which interactions were appropriate. For instance, Adrienne saw it as progress that her grandchildren do not focus on race as much she and previous generations did. In an exchange between Adrienne and Paula, Adrienne highlighted her beliefs about this point:

> ADRIENNE: My grandchildren, they don't have a color thing going on. They don't care. That's my friend. They don't see it. They haven't been through what we've been through. They haven't been through what my parents have been through, so that's just their friend. That's their little friend they go to school with, and can she come over. And, girl, you ought to see the look on my face when I see that they friend ain't one of us. [Laughter]

As Mama used to say when I was a kid, if they can't use our comb, don't bring them home.

AUTHOR: So do you see that change as progress?

ADRIENNE: I think it's progress. Because when my children were coming up, they had only had a little exposure to white people. They thought only their face and hands was white. They called them the people with the white face. My grandchildren, they don't even think of them in terms of color. That's Megan. That's Amber. That's my friend. Can she come over?

PAULA: Well color is taught anyway. That's a learned behavior.

ADRIENNE: So I notice that they don't care like we were brought up to care or like our parents were brought up to care.

The beliefs of participants were also informed by their common social outlook, which emphasized the individual. These participants recognized that society categorizes and evaluates them (to a greater or lesser degree) on racial group membership, yet they rejected or ignored these assessments and chose to focus on the individual. In her discussion of the NAACP, Breanna exemplified this belief in the importance of moving beyond race toward critically examining individual worth:

And like sometimes [people say things like] I don't want to be in that organization [referring to some fictional organization] because it's an all-white organization . . . but it's important to know that, like, the NAACP was set up by a group of definitely intellectuals and thinkers but was mainly, like, pushed through by an older white gentleman who saw that there should definitely be an advancement of a group of people that was not as knowledgeable about things that was going on. The NAACP has definitely been the one [organization of this kind] that has lasted the longest just because . . . it helps to . . . it helps people to see that, like . . . it's important that we work together, that we work as a collective. It is being a part of those organizations that not just help black people but help people in general to be . . . that help with advancement . . . I hate to say that . . . that helps with the advancement of any good people. It doesn't have to be about a group, just individuals overall.

Breanna's support for organizations that help "any good people" encapsulated many of the sentiments held by supporters in this category. They viewed themselves and wanted others to view them from a nonracial perspective in which good moral character, individual effort, and sound judgment are the relevant standards.

The focus on the individual and her ability to impact personal circumstances resulted in unambiguous definitions of the causes of enduring problems in the black community. These definitions usually surrounded the theme of black blame and individual failure. Briefly, there was a significant tendency for members of this group to see blacks' choices as the primary reason for community problems and lack of success. The tendency of those in this opinion category to focus on individual failure diminished the amount of blame attributed to other sources, including inherent biases in the American political system or white racism. They saw whites as less hostile to the black community than did Black Nationalists. Indeed, only members of this opinion category voluntarily expressed a desire to seek out cross-racial friendships and interaction. Rarely did they reference the existence of racism without simultaneously discounting it as one of many obstacles that all people face. Or they saw racial prejudices as a trap that you have to be smart or strategic enough to avoid.

Participants who soundly rejected racial categorization as an evaluative category were the only ones to offer any form of positive affect toward whites. Andrea and Evelyn, who were mentioned in chapter 2, were two college students who participated in separate groups and freely talked of efforts to deal with whites on a daily basis, the high comfort level they felt around whites, and the need for a "symbiotic" relationship with whites. Although not everyone in the sample expressed negative attitudes toward whites, all but Andrea and Evelyn fell short of offering unwavering positive evaluations of whites. However, most did not find interactions with whites problematic or undesirable; these participants were also less likely to reference direct experiences of racism and racial hostility. Andrea's and Evelyn's comments in the last chapter were the starkest example of this, but others exemplified this way of thinking as well. In this case, the positive affect was not detected in the verbal presence of positive white evaluations; instead, it was visible in the absence of references to racism and hostility from or toward whites.

In the course of every discussion, participants were frequently asked to expound when using general or vague labels such as "they," "them," or "some people." When participants in one focus group began a discussion of the media, an interesting dynamic emerged. I suggested there was "a high level of mistrust." I added that "mistrust was possibly the wrong word, but [members of this focus group] see some kind of low-level deceptiveness on the part of whites." Again, Breanna emerged as spokesperson, while others indicated agreement through nonverbal cues. In a rather long but important exchange, I encouraged Breanna to provide more detail in explaining her views:

BREANNA: It's not necessarily a deception or like a convincing of like, oh, okay, I can use your life up to like help me cause you're white and you're going to make a whole lot of money because you're white. I mean, I don't think that that's what happens. I think it gets more into being a misunderstanding. And I think it gets into trying to become more . . . not necessarily become more of the ignorant person like Sasha was saying but more of the intelligent and using the system to your advantage. Does that necessarily mean the white man? No, that's talking about the government. I mean we are talking about using what you have available to you to your advantage. Now, that sometimes entails manipulation.

AUTHOR: On your part or on the part of white people?

BREANNA: On your part. Not on the part of white people. All people are manipulating the system at any point in time, just period. But, I mean, it just takes a need to understand and have the education in order to better understand how this whole bureaucracy or institution works. And I don't think that that has anything specifically to do with just white people. I couldn't say that it's Justin or it's Allen or any other just white person that I can think of.

ANDREA: Just being white.

BREANNA: It's not any of that. It's the institutions. It's the system in which we are that they just so happen to be the majority of. So, I don't think that's necessarily a black-on-white attack. I think of it more of trying . . . of not trusting the system . . . of not trusting or trying to better understand the system at large or as we know it . . . i.e., the United States.

AUTHOR: So, when you talk about the institution or the system or the government you are not referring to white people?

BREANNA: No. I'm saying the institution itself. I don't know if it has anything to do with the mistrusting of white people like, you know, they are running around with clouds, and they are like trying to "trick" us. [She makes a gesture indicating quotation marks]

AUTHOR: Oh . . . what do you mean by running around with clouds? I'm lost.

BREANNA: It's not like they are trying to trick us. It's just that you are basically conditioned to try to get a better understanding of or perception of what is going on. And being aware of what is going on around you. Not necessarily tricking anybody or not trusting them.

This exchange also informed another category from table 3.1—motivations and intentions attached to the white behavior. For these participants, rather than perceiving whites as having bad intentions for blacks, whites were mostly just "ignorant" or unaware of other cultures. Unlike for Black Nationalists, there were no assessments of white prejudices as knowingly hostile, no recognition of institutional structures purposely designed to prevent black empowerment, and no race-based assessments. Whites simply needed to reach out to other communities to overcome that ignorance. Then, with a certain level of education, society would improve. Sasha demonstrated this point:

SASHA: I think the most important thing about us is that white people need to come to us. I've got a white friend, and the thing that staggers me is their ignorance of other people in general. Never mind black folks, but just in general. It saddens me just how ignorant they are of other people's cultures. They know all about rich white people and poor white people, but they can't translate that to other cultures. They just . . . they are blind. I have a friend that's white, and I have known him since like seventh grade. He probably knows me the best, and he is white, but I have had to educate him on some things. He just doesn't have a clue, and that feeds into the media. [White] people are ignorant. They might even be stupid. You have ignorant people watching stuff on TV, and unfortunately they just become more ignorant. Ignorance begets itself. I think we can educate each other as much as we want, but white people need to come to us.

AUTHOR: Us as in black people?

SASHA: Any minority groups . . . so white people, and the word needs to get out . . . you need to come to us. You know, I am tired of those few white people who come to me and I tell them what the deal is. The few that have that nerve to ask, and I don't care what kind of questions. You know, I have had questions about my hair, skin color. It's ignorance. Just ignorance. Even as if a child were to ask you a question. You can't get angry because they don't know. They have no concept of it. You know, I feel sorry for them. Honestly, I have deep sadness for them. [Laughter] Because they are so ignorant, and they're gonna be because they don't have to worry about us. Why should they? You know . . . they are on top of the game. Why should they have to worry about us?

Breanna did not necessarily agree that whites need to come to other races to make amends; however, she did agree that whites should be educated about the needs of other groups. She added:

And I think it's not even just saying that white people need to come to any group of people to have a better understanding, but I think even just the ability of that group of people to say let me show you what happened. You need to come over here with me, and you need to see what's going on at my house. And have a better understanding and a more realistic perspective than what they see on TV. I mean . . . that's not necessarily realistic.

This attitude was echoed by Delia, who on several occasions referred to the need for blacks to educate whites as a method of countering stereotypes whites have about the black community.

Among those participants who rejected Black Nationalism, institutions lack racial specificity in the sense that actors' behavior and policy implementation were not race specific; rather, they were race neutral. Because Non-Nationalists focus on the efforts of the individual and the importance of individual effort in changing circumstances and do not attach racial labels to forces governing those institutions, they are also less likely to believe that there is race-specific targeting of blacks and less likely to support race-targeted programs. This was best demonstrated in the least Nationalist focus group—the one composed of young college students. Breanna's earlier comments showed the same regard for the political system expressed by many of the others in her group. In essence, these young people seemed to view political and social interaction as a game that is competitive, flexible, and winnable; they position whites and blacks as equal and undifferentiated players in that game. Their beliefs resembled those of Melissa, a participant in her early twenties who was raised in an upper-middle-class family in a predominantly white suburban enclave.

AUTHOR: There seems to be a high level of mistrust even among those of you who think that cooperation with whites is important. It seems to be a high level of mistrust of whites, or is it that I am just reading that wrong?

MELISSA: As far as we use white people, but we don't trust them.

AUTHOR: That's what it seems like most of you are saying to me . . .

MELISSA: Yeah, I think so . . . I can agree with that . . . I mean, I have white friends cause that's . . .

AMINAH: [Very quietly] I don't trust anybody.

AUTHOR: [Repeating for the group to hear] She doesn't trust anybody.

MELISSA: Well, yeah that's true too.

Because these young participants often evoked this game image, it is also interesting to report the amount of bravado that went into their belief that they would fare well in it. This attitude also seemed to inform their beliefs about affirmative action and its appropriateness as a strategy to equalize the game for black Americans. For various reasons, most of these participants expressed a strong negative reaction to the idea of affirmative action. Although they saw some benefits to affirmative action efforts, there was still a high level of discomfort, so much so that the benefits were questioned because of the negative costs. First, they were very cognizant of and uncomfortable with the amount of hostility blacks received in employment and educational settings because of the perception that their positions were ill-gotten. Melissa offered:

I just don't like the hostility that affirmative action brings, because just the other day, [a friend of mine] and I were talking about applying for different scholarships and applying to [Ohio State University] just because there is such a great need for minorities in graduate programs, and [another white student] . . . she's a sweet girl . . . she says, oh, I wish I had that card to play. And I am so sick and tired of hearing that. And I know it's written out there that they are helping us, but I just get so tired of hearing that.

Melissa acknowledged the benefits of affirmative action; however, she also sympathized somewhat with the feelings of whites. She noted:

There's just so many people always saying that [you have it easy because of affirmative action]. It just . . . it unnerves me . . . it makes me so sick. People just assume that you don't have to work hard and you're going to get into any school you want because you're black. No. You can be black and be as dumb as anybody else and not go anywhere with all the little social programs they have in place. You can still not prosper.

Second, the mere possibility that these students had gotten their position through affirmative action channels implied that they were unqualified. Andrea voiced her concern that blackness should not be the sole reason for acquiring anything; in fact, she did not want a position given to her because of her race. She elaborated:

> My problem is, when I go for a job, I don't want the job because I am a black woman. I want the job because my qualification was better than the white man. That's why I want the job. You know. It was so funny that my Caucasian boyfriend made the comment the other day that, um, because we had both gone out for [the same job] and we had both gotten the job and he was telling me how he felt the need to be so much more competitive with me in the interview room because I was the black woman. I already had three points up on him. I'm like, that has to be the dumbest thing that has ever come out of your mouth. . . . And I know what affirmative action is supposed to do. I know it. I can see the benefits of it, and I can see that it is supposed to do this. But I . . . to me . . . I cannot get over the whole handout issue is what it comes down to, to me. It's like, I don't want you to make a law that says you have to have 2% black people in your company so that you can hire me. No, I want you to [hire me] because I have so much degrees and I can make this contribution to your company . . . because then what it comes down to is that you are going to treat me . . . you are not going to patronize me in my position because of how I got it. And to me that is not fair. That's when racism comes in, if you ask me. That's when it's most prevalent to me. That's why I don't want to deal with it.

Her group mates further echoed Andrea's sense that blacks are viewed as incompetent because of affirmative action. This negative reception by white colleagues exasperated these participants because they were uncomfortable with the fact that blacks were seen as the "face of affirmative action" and received the bulk of the backlash even though white women are the greatest beneficiaries. This is illustrated by the following discussion between various group members:

SASHA: White women get the most from that.
BREANNA: I was just about to say that . . . that's what I wanted to say. Thank you. You have such a good point, you and you [referring to Andrea and Melissa]. Who is the primary beneficiary of affirmative action?

SASHA: White women.

BREANNA: And who is the face of affirmative action? Somebody black. It's the same thing with the welfare issue . . . that's the face of affirmative action. The face of affirmative action is some black woman who got the job because she is black. Some black man who got the job because he is black. Not because of anything else. And, yes, that does tear down basically any movement forward that you may have because it's like, oh, that's the only reason why you got it. Um, excuse me, no that's not why I got it. It's because I did a better interview than you did because you don't know how to speak. And you know that's what it has to do with, and it has nothing to do with anything else, and I think that that's a problem. I don't think of it as necessarily a handout. It's supposed to be a hand, but to some people that is what it is. And I mean it can be kind of nasty.

This reaction reinforced the interconnection of individual effort and personal outcomes for participants who rejected Black Nationalism. American history is filled with tales of rugged individualism and the power of one's effort to make life better for you and those around you. African Americans who reject Black Nationalism as the appropriate strategy for group advancement affirm that tradition. They are aware of their race and are willing to acknowledge that all Americans are grouped and often judged based on racial categories. The difference, however, lies in their refusal to engage in such broad-brushed categorizations themselves. They recognize that historically whites have behaved in ways that were hostile to blacks, but for them it represents the past. Now blacks often are the predominant obstacles to their own progress. For them, whiteness (and even blackness) is secondary to normative evaluations of how they choose to order their social and political worlds. These characteristics then become the basis for distinguishing Black Nationalist adherents, moderate Black Nationalists, and Non-Nationalists.

Moderate Black Nationalists

The categories offered here represent a continuum of Black Nationalist support from complete adherence to complete rejection. Participants who occupy the opposing poles possess clearly delineated positions on issues related to race, perceptions of problems within the black community, and the best strategies to address those problems. For opponents of Black Nationalism, interactions with whites and other ethnic groups are appropriate and even necessary for the progress of blacks. In contrast, for proponents of Black Nationalism, interactions with whites are not necessary for black progress. Ideally participants conceptualize and cogently express their views about race, politics, and a multitude of other issues about which scholars are concerned. Participants in these focus groups struggled with these questions, and like many other individuals, they fell short of taking extreme stances on most political issues. For that reason, a third or middle-range ideological category is outlined that contains the largest subset of participants, whose beliefs both incorporate and reject Black Nationalism.

Like Black Nationalists, they primarily identify with their African American experiences when making political decisions. However, similar to Non-Nationalists, other identities emerge as secondary lenses in addition to race. A good example of this was one focus group's discussion surrounding the influx of gay white couples into an established black middle-class neighborhood. This group was mainly composed of Fairview Pines residents, who were feeling uncomfortable with the changes in the community. These are the same residents discussed in the vignette at the beginning of this chapter; the discussion is reiterated here to highlight another important aspect. Participants readily admitted that they preferred African Americans to live and raise families in their own community. Thus race and association with people in their own racial category were important to these participants. However, another identity emerged as important in this scenario, and that was class. Participants were unwilling to accept all blacks as neighbors; they also wanted their neighbors to have similar economic backgrounds.

Participants in the mixed category focused on both individual and group concerns. They used black blame to explain community problems such as unemployment but also acknowledged the impact of historic and current discrimination on persistent unemployment. They oscillated between a strong endorsement of self-help and racial group cloistering and a lamentation for why this is not always possible or preferred. This was the only group that demonstrated reluctance when employing black blame, and group members were openly averse to saying that they are sometimes distant from and in judgment of their own community. The resulting quandary rendered them cautious of both blacks and whites and, subsequently, supportive of black self-segregation and cross-racial integration. They saw the benefits and detriments of both.

People who fell into this ideological middle ground were distinctly aware of the existence of racism; however, they were more likely to refer to indirect forms of racism or direct racism that is mitigated by black blame. Sharon, for instance, recounted an instance of indirect racism that she heard about from a friend:

> One of my coworkers just told me that her brother just got a house . . . and up until the last minute he didn't think he was going to get a house. Now someone who helped him with the paperwork put a blatant lie on the paperwork. He put down that the person who is purchasing was a white man. And he said, he thought he wasn't going to get the house because he had a spotty credit record, but the fact that that little box was checked, white male, his spotty credit record didn't matter.

Others pointed to racism that is both mitigated, which serves to diminish the degree of impact, and indirect. Talking about his daughter's experience with whites, Rahim pointed to her disregard for color in general and offered that whites still do not really understand blacks. His point was mitigated, however, by the assertion that blacks do not really even understand themselves:

> RAHIM: Kids today are in a different place, different time, and different set of circumstances. So what they might do and how they would react . . . my daughter reacts different than I do. For *her* [referring to his daughter], white folks are just white folks.
>
> AUTHOR: Do you see that as progress or . . .
>
> RAHIM: Neither . . . neither . . . I'm glad that she has come to terms with our culture and is beginning to realize people as people. But there are still a lot of things they don't accept us on. Like historically they don't understand our . . . where we truly came from . . . they're beginning to get a clue, but they still haven't embraced it all. Even us, we still haven't embraced it all.

This group walks a tightrope between ideological communities. Whites have hurt them and members of their racial community, but they do not see all blacks as allies either. They stop short of attaching a racial designation to government actors and institutions. Instead, they view the country as being governed by moneyed interests who lack concern for all people. Rahim and others in his group illustrated this point:

RAHIM: So sometimes your vote is not your vote . . . they got their plans. They got their plans already.

AUTHOR: And when you say they, who are you referring to?

RAHIM: Oh . . . the powers that be. They say all you have to do is run in this election, and then after it's over you can go and do what you want to do, and we'll shuffle positions, and you can run for state senate or whatever . . . but in the meantime you need to get this through.

AUTHOR: Do you think that there is a particular racial makeup of the people who are in power?

RAHIM: No.

DONNA: Whoever has the most gold . . .

FRANKLIN: . . . makes the rules.

Opinions for this middle group were muddied by conflicting views about whites and blacks. For instance, they were perfectly happy to work with whites but wanted only limited interactions with them in social arenas. They tried to incorporate the ideas and the rhetoric of leaders and personal experiences into a worldview that allowed them to navigate both the black and white communities. Janet summarized:

When I think about [Martin Luther King and Malcolm X], I think about the fact that they were both agitators. And just like in a washing machine, you need agitators to get the clothes clean? We needed them both. At the turn of the century it was Booker T. Washington and DuBois. In the middle of the twentieth century, it was Malcolm and Martin. We're in 2002 now. . . . I'm waiting.

Individuals in these focus groups often were conflicted, both explicitly and implicitly, by their own oppositional views. Though I label this a middle category, I am not suggesting that its members do not take positions. Instead, they exhibited ideological thinking that lacked constraint but supplied the map for how they maneuver through the political world. They often struggled with the awareness that their racial group membership carries with it both push and pull effects. They embraced and expressed racial pride but also engaged in black blame. After establishing definitions of each ideological category and providing examples from ordinary citizens' dialogues, one is left wondering how these attitudes are transmitted across generational cohorts. Is it true that, as Keesha and Paula suggested, you have to be diligent about teaching children about race and racism? Or is it a maturation process in which age and social context become crucial factors in how individuals view race and at what points they might embrace or reject Black Nationalism?

Conclusion

Keesha's views, in this chapter, were a clear and concise representation of her Black Nationalist views. Other focus group participants were also able to express consistent views that can then be systematically connected to the ideology of interest here. Like most Americans, the vast majority of participants held views that are complicated, malleable, and sometimes contradictory. The goal of this chapter has been to compare and contrast the manner in which Black Nationalist principles are employed or rebuffed by ordinary citizens in the language of those citizens. Most participants fell into the moderate category not because their views are necessarily ambiguous or indecipherable but because they actually had divided loyalties that have led them to support some tenets of Black Nationalism and not others. This makes it more difficult, but not impossible, to tease out the systematic ways in which individuals choose positions that are congruent with their own beliefs.

Additionally, focus groups are highly variable in the tone they take, topics discussed, and backgrounds of participants involved. One thematic frame that was particularly significant in these discussions was blame attribution. Participants in all groups were very aware of the disparities between blacks and other groups across multiple social and economic indicators, and they developed explanations for why these disparities continued to persist despite civil rights gains. Two explanations received the bulk of the credit—African Americans' failure and system failure. The next chapter takes up the meaning and impact of blame for African Americans.

4

The New Old School Blame Game

*Blame Attribution and Ideology
among African Americans*

From the previous two chapters we have seen how ordinary citizens consider political questions and draw political conclusions. How can the increasing achievement gap between blacks and whites be explained? Why has the American dream remained beyond the grasp of most African Americans despite civil rights gains? Often with whites as the main comparison group, though there were others (new immigrants, Latinos, Asian Americans), these were the types of questions participants were using to evaluate black progress. As they assessed the topography of the political landscape and were able to see (from their perspective) challenges and opportunities available to them and to groups in which they hold membership, they inevitably offered diagnoses for persistent community shortfalls. Along with an evaluation of problems, participants often looked for and found targets of blame. The primary culprits identified were either blacks themselves (black blame) or some kind of systemic or institutional factors (system blame).

First, there was a compilation of reasons that fault blacks and their individual shortcomings for persistent lags. These took the form of criticism for the lack of racial unity, poor behavioral choices that lead to poor life circumstances, and other personal and political pathologies. This constant criticism, or black blame, then became the primary explanation for the failure of the black community to keep pace with whites as well as other racial minorities. This was juxtaposed with system blame, where there were systemic targets toward which fault could be attributed such as breakdowns in the political system or even the obstacles constructed by racist or malevolent whites. For example, Smith (1995) suggests two themes that dominate Western research on poverty (especially on impoverished blacks): "a structural one that emphasizes enduring features of the economic and social systems (including racism) . . . and a culturalist one that emphasizes the values, beliefs, attitudes and lifestyles (intergenerationally transmitted) of the poor themselves" (107). The division that was most prevalent was between system blame and black blame. At times, however, the "system" had a clear racial label, and other times it was less racially defined.

Despite using the same explanations for community problems, Black Nationalists and their opponents utilized them quite differently and drew different conclusions. For Black Nationalists, black blame was an acknowledgment of the continued impact of past injustice on current outcomes. Blacks Nationalists viewed many of the bad choices that society labels as pathological as a direct result of a history of enslavement and degradation. They acknowledged the choices as harmful, but those choices did not undermine their desire to immerse themselves in racial group interactions or their belief in blacks' ability to overcome that legacy with the right information and exposure. In turn, they also firmly convicted the American government and its white agents as the fomenters of black problems and as inherently and terminally hostile. Those who rejected Black Nationalism saw black blame as an end. They were aware of past injustices, but the past does not completely explain the present. For them, blacks bear the brunt of the responsibility for the community's current condition. They also acknowledged past and some current racial hostilities on the part of the government, but this explanation did not trump individual responsibility. In terms of contemporary politics, governmental actors are a muddle of racial groups rather than racially specific.

Is It "The Man" or "The Man in the Mirror"? Employing System Blame and Black Blame

Neither group-based attributes nor external hostilities are particularly new targets for blame, and they are not necessarily emerging because of shifts in the post–Civil Rights political climate. In many ways, system blame is easier to understand and define than black blame. Because of the history of racial hostility and violence blacks have experienced in the United States, often under the watchful eye and sanction of ordinary citizens and all levels of government, it is not surprising that blacks would blame the American government and its white agents for many community problems. But system blame is more than a reaction to historical racism. It is a recognition of the myriad ways in which government and social institutions are established and maintained through racist practices, historically and contemporarily. System blame, then, is more akin to Ture and Hamilton's (1992) definition of institutionalized racism. Unlike other forms of racism, institutionalized racism is "less overt, far more subtle, and less identifiable in terms of specific individuals committing the acts" (4). In other words, it "is understood as policies and practices that, controlling for social class, subordinate blacks or maintain or 'freeze' them in a subordinate position" (Smith 1995, 53). It is embedded in the rules and norms that control access to and influence over those institutions where decisions are made. Ture and Hamilton (1992) highlight this in an illuminating passage in their chapter entitled "White Power." Institutionalized racism manifests itself when in Birmingham

> five hundred black babies die each year because of the lack of proper food, shelter and medical facilities, and thousands more are destroyed and maimed physically, emotionally, and intellectually because of conditions of poverty and discrimination . . . But it is institutional racism that keeps black people locked in dilapidated slum tenements, subject to the daily prey of exploitative slumlords, merchants, loan sharks and discriminatory real estate agents. (5)

They emphasize that "institutional racism relies on the active and pervasive operation of anti-black attitudes and practices" (5). Institutional racism does not exist without individual racism; institutions are overseen, maintained, and ultimately dismantled by the people who run them. Thus, diminished levels of individual racism are most laudable when those individuals take stock of how their racism has concomitantly shaped social policy and practices created through the lens of their racist worldview.

In his study of the changing (and persistent) nature of racism in the post–Civil Rights era, Robert Smith (1995) characterizes both individual-level and institutional racism as having a "now you see it, now you don't quality," which "demonstrates that race is still from time to time and place to place taken into consideration in a manner that denies blacks equal access to societal values and resources" (141). Using five policy areas—education, housing, employment, health care, and consumer services—he demonstrates how government regulatory policies have borne responsibility for black subordination. Focusing on examples of white privilege as a method of exposing the ways in which government agencies and actors have used public policy initiatives to simultaneously advantage whites and disadvantage blacks, Williams (2003) argues, "The welfare state was grafted onto preexisting conditions of race relations." Thus, "segmentation in American social policy . . . grew out of established boundaries that privileged whites and penalized blacks" (13). She is clearly and aptly demonstrating how racism has been institutionalized in America by focusing on what whites have historically gained through the development of social welfare policies. By turning the gaze to whites rather than blacks as beneficiaries, Williams is able to identify institutionalized forms of racism by highlighting black exclusion from social programs (New Deal programs) and invoking blacks' presence to render some programs illegitimate (President Clinton's welfare reform).[1]

In *Dreaming Blackness,* participants were not offering historical accounts of the development of the American welfare system or expressly saying that "white privilege" serves to disadvantage blacks in the political process, but they clearly were expressing parallel sentiments by pointing to historical and contemporary examples of racism and discrimination. They were talking about the ways the system is designed to advantage whites and deny blacks similar opportunities, and their comments formed a worldview in which large-scale problems in the black community signal problems with the broader American political system. But even the staunchest invocation of system blame was softly tempered with another kind of blame—black blame. In many of the discussions it seemed that black blame and system blame were different sides of the same coin, permanently joined and competing for dominance as the legitimate explanations of black problems. In fact, Hanes Walton (1985) suggests in *Invisible Politics* that even black politics research is guilty of "ignoring systemic external influences, identifying black pathologies and black deviation from the 'norm' as the crux of the problem" (9). This is important to keep in mind as a definition of black blame is offered and participants make plain their understanding of black problems.

The perception by blacks that despite racism and other obstacles, they can shift their social and economic status by revamping values and behavioral mores is not new. Neither is the belief that if they do not make changes, they are somehow complicit in their own regress. This line of thought has a long historical reach. African Americans who engage in black blame believe racism is not a free pass to abdicate personal responsibility. This belief resonates with social group cleavages that have existed since Africans were enslaved in the New World. In the Southern plantation system there were hierarchies among enslaved Africans based on job assignments, skill level, skin complexion, and the degree of autonomy and freedom of movement (Quarles 1987; Blassingame 1979). These hierarchies, though beneficial to and reinforced by whites, were often diligently policed by blacks as well. Since emancipation, blacks have been engaged in various racial group uplift efforts. In the discussion of early Black Nationalists in chapter 1, we saw prominent leaders discussing their view that persistent subjugation fostered a belief among some blacks that they were inferior.

In his study of black leadership in the twentieth century, Gaines (1996) emphasizes that racial uplift runs contrary to the way some scholars and leaders have traditionally viewed the goal of racial uplift as solely middle-class black desire for whiteness and antipathy for their own racial group. Instead, according to Gaines, for black elites "uplift, among its other con-notations, also represented the struggle for a positive black identity in a deeply racist society" (7), but that "vision of self-help" prioritized "bour-geois values of self-control and Victorian sexual morality as a crucial part of the race's education and progress" (34–35). For these reasons, he suggests that this "class-bound argument for black humanity was deeply contradictory" because elite efforts to manage the public image of blacks were often couched in "claims of racial and gender hierarchy" (xiv). Ad-ditionally, he offers "two general connotations of uplift": group efforts to-ward advancement stemming from emancipation, and as a class signifier for black elites to distinguish themselves from their lower-status racial counterparts. In her historical account of the Black Women's Club Move-ment, Giddings (1984) distinguishes black women's efforts from those of their white counterparts because black women were required to battle racism, classism, and sexism simultaneously.[2] She points to famous club woman and educator Mary Church Terrell's declaration, "Self preserva-tion demands that [black women] go among the lowly, illiterate and even the vicious, to which they are bound by ties of race and sex . . . to reclaim them" (97). In this way, Terrell both affirms and disavows the relationship that exists between her and her peers and less fortunate blacks.

Uplift narratives and reinforced class distinctions are often viewed as the milieu of African Americans whose primary goal is full integration into American society, but Black Nationalists, especially in the pre-emancipa-tion period, were also making distinctions between themselves and their enslaved brethren. It is important to reiterate here the ways in which they accomplished this. First, they were making the very same class distinctions outlined here. Early Black Nationalists shared unique privileges for blacks of their time—they enjoyed free status, were literate and formally educated, and enjoyed some wealth. This afforded them the ability to engage in early Black Nationalist projects and distinguished them from enslaved blacks. Like Terrell, they saw the differences and acknowledged a connection. Second, Black Nationalists from all periods have endorsed conscientious attention to and compliance with conservative moral values despite renouncing European philosophies of black inferiority. This is evident from David Walker's mention of Haiti's need to abandon Catholicism and take on Protestant values to the Nation of Islam's strict behavioral and dress codes. Beyond religion, organizations such as the Universal Negro Improvement Association and the Black Panther Party viewed self-presentation as a way of modeling the external impact of internalized beliefs about black pride for other blacks (Rhodes 2007; Stein 1986; Abron 1998; Jones and Jefferies 1998). Additionally, for Black Nationalists much of what blacks had come to believe about their racial group and its ability to self-govern had to be rethought. Blacks had to shed white-centered perspectives of what the black community could achieve and embrace new narratives of blackness. Because expectations of white attitudes and behavior toward blacks were so low, Black Nationalists saw reforming black thinking and behavior as key to black liberation. Those blacks refusing to shed negative perceptions and behaviors were ultimately deemed just as damaging to black progress as whites.

The question of who is responsible for the African American community's failure to thrive has become particularly relevant in recent years after the hoopla and debate provoked by Bill Cosby's comments at the NAACP's commemoration, on May 17, 2004, of the fiftieth anniversary of the *Brown v. Board of Education* decision.[3] At this event, Cosby excoriated poor blacks for their destructive choices and behavior. Cosby admonished,

> Ladies and gentlemen, the lower economic people are not holding up their end in this deal. . . . These people are not parenting. They are buying things for kids—$500 sneakers for what? And won't spend $200 for "Hooked on Phonics" to improve their children's reading and speech. (Tucker 2004, A15)

In this speech, which lasted about twenty minutes, Cosby critiqued family structures, use of slang, name choices, and inappropriate public behavior of poor men and women and their children (King 2004). Noted black journalist Cynthia Tucker (2004) labels Cosby's comments and the public debate that resulted a "watershed event—a sign that black America is now comfortable enough with its accomplishments to discuss its shortcomings." The comments resulted in a media blitz in the black and mainstream presses but also became fodder for watercooler conversation. Tucker's editorial offers a quotation by then NAACP president Kweisi Mfume in which Mfume suggests that Cosby's remarks opened the door for "a tough love conversation" in the black community. This seems to be a clear case of blaming blacks for their lack of empowerment that is also couched in class arguments. Indeed, it mirrors the discussion that has taken place throughout African American history.

The tenor of African American views about the appropriateness of Cosby's assessment of poor blacks is hard to determine. While it seems that many in the media lauded Cosby's comments and his right to speak, he also came under fire from people who vehemently disagreed with his position. Immediately after Cosby concluded his remarks, in fact, Theodore Shaw, director-counsel and president of the NAACP Legal and Education Defense Fund, "rushed to the podium to serve up a rejoinder, noting that the larger [read 'white'] American society still bears some responsibility for the failure of so many black Americans to join the economic and cultural mainstream" (Tucker 2004, A15). Michael Eric Dyson (2005) later released *"Is Bill Cosby Right?" Or Has the Black Middle Class Lost Its Mind?*, which *New York Times* writer Deborah Solomon (2005) called a "rhetorical screed against Bill Cosby." Dyson claims that Bill Cosby and what Dyson labels as the "Afristocracy" (e.g., middle-class and wealthy blacks) have turned against the "Ghettocracy" (e.g., poor blacks). Dyson suggests, "For Cosby, self-initiative, not systemic solutions, is the way to black salvation" (182). But when Cosby and other members of the Afristocracy view the black poor in this way, Dyson believes they are mistaken to believe that "by assuming such responsibility the problems of the poor will disappear" (182). Further, when these problems of the poor fail to disappear through efforts to take personal responsibility, it would only serve to "bring greater social stigma to the poor" and further isolate them from the black elite. Interestingly, Dyson champions Cosby's right to speak to important issues in the black community and affirms any claims he makes for all people to take more personal responsibility; however, he takes issue with Cosby's failure to recognize the systemic ways in which the black poor are kept stagnant.

The invocation of black blame should not be seen solely as a function of class stratification. In the focus group data analyzed here as well as in other studies, blacks across the economic spectrum expressed sentiments that reflected black blame. In a study of attitudes toward social mobility among low-income black men on Chicago's Near West Side, sociologist Alford Young (2004) found that many of the men, especially the most isolated, lacked the ability to express how "the external social world might matter for their lives," and because of that they "emphasized personal initiative" (189) as the key to mobility. In this case, personal initiative is viewed as compliance with mainstream behavioral norms and acquisition of the social capital required to succeed in mainstream or white America. Most of the men agreed that following the prescribed method would yield social mobility and respect, and when they and others did not comply, then they would fail to thrive. Young attributes this focus on individual effort to minimal contact with people outside of their neighborhoods, which limits both cross-class and cross-racial contact. This suggests that the lack of experiential knowledge leads to a focus on personal responsibility, in much the same way that some African Americans in this project focused on personal failures in their quest to explain enduring inequality.

Also working in inner-city Chicago, Melissa Harris-Lacewell (2004) recounts a political conversation witnessed through participant observation at a black barbershop on the South Side. She found that the customers and barbers all shared a communal vision of black empowerment, but the government also received a significant amount of blame for black problems. This combination of communal vision and government accountability was also augmented with a certain level of black blame. For instance, she recounts a discussion about money, black churches, and banks by one of the barbers, Hajj, and two customers, Bill and Wes. After one of the men suggests that black churches in Chicago deposit a million dollars into white banks every week, the group not only discusses how taking black dollars out of the black community is problematic but also emphasizes that black banks are "unprofessional and untrustworthy" and "that the federal government is more interested than black banks in contributing to the growth of the neighborhood" (193). This exchange is important for ideological reasons, as Harris-Lacewell highlights, but it also resonates with the question of who is to blame for lack of economic empowerment. Clearly these men believe that blacks should ultimately be able to recycle black dollars within their own community and that relying on white banks is not optimal. Interestingly, whites' discriminatory behavior or other systemic reasons for black failure are paired with the attribution of blame to black institutions and their failure to conduct business properly and professionally.

In what may be the only empirical study of the political impact of blacks blaming themselves for their failure to succeed in the American political and social system, Parent (1985) uses belief in the American ethos as a backdrop for understanding black blame. The American liberal tradition entails a belief in the ability of the individual to succeed based on hard work and initiative (Hartz 1983 [1955]). According to Parent, "Blacks have been the most glaring exception to the uniquely American experience" of equal opportunity, yet studies have consistently demonstrated black support of the American creed. He hypothesizes that adherence to individualistic beliefs should yield individualistic explanations for why blacks fail to succeed despite systemic barriers. He confirms that "blacks are more likely than whites to refuse to attribute responsibility to the individual in the black case" (16). Thus, blacks in his study engaged in less black blame than whites. Additionally, he found that, among blacks, union membership diminished the level of black blame, and Protestantism increased attribution of blame to the individual, which would result in more black blame owing to blacks' greater religiosity and membership in Protestant denominations relative to other Americans.

Rebukes of poor Americans for lacking the personal responsibility and determination needed to succeed are cross-racial phenomena. In the now classic study *What's Fair?*, Jennifer Hochschild (1981) examines "the fact that the American poor apparently do not support the downward redistribution of wealth" (1). When comparing her findings to the results derived from a study of working-class men in Robert Lane's *Political Ideology* (1962), she finds that "perceptions and explanations of poverty apparently have changed since the 1950's" (280). Most Americans she interviewed did not see poverty as a result of personal pathologies; rather, they were likely to attribute the status of the poor to "bad luck or even structural biases" (280.) Hochschild follows this assessment by noting that some participants in her sample made clear divisions between the deserving and undeserving poor. Some poor Americans, due to unfortunate circumstances or systemic failures, deserved help, but others did not. Interestingly, the participants saw the undeserving poor as a much larger category. Thus, Hochschild's participants, through their own contradictions, were making similar blame attributions as participants in my sample. This is true even though Hochschild felt her subjects had much more sophisticated reasons for poverty's existence than did Lane's sample from the 1950s.

This begs the question, Why isn't black blame called individual blame? Does labeling it black blame unnecessarily marginalize the black poor and render African American mass opinion as somehow aberrant when compared with other racial groups? I label this concept black blame for several reasons. First, because of the complicated interaction between race and poverty in American society, there is a history of characterizing black poverty and low achievement as uniquely pathological or genetic (Herrnstein and Murray 1994).[4] Second, even more recent structural arguments have served to isolate black poverty, especially in urban areas, as permanently entrenched and a settled fact, so much so that scholars have developed the designation of urban underclass largely to classify the black poor who have been systematically shut out of the American economic and political system (Wilson 1997, 1978; Jencks and Peterson 1991). The last and primary reason I label this concept black blame is because focus group participants locate and operationalize it with racial specificity. It is black people, their people, who are not taking responsibility for their actions or not taking full advantage of the opportunities afforded them in the post–Civil Rights era. While it is important to understand that blacks exist not in a sociopolitical vacuum but in a larger multidimensional political system, the fact that whites engage in black blame and that poor people regardless of race are often castigated for lacking personal responsibility is interesting but not the focus here. Instead, I am interested in the ways African Americans strategically employ blame to make sense of their social world.

The purpose of this analysis is not to suggest that African Americans (or any subgroup within the black community) invoke black blame due to self-loathing or racial group loathing. Nor does it suggest that referencing system blame connotes anti-American or unpatriotic sentiments. Indeed, one could argue that individuals' deep affection for members of their own racial group causes them to make critiques of their community when it seems they are not living up to their fullest potential. Earlier I mentioned Mfume's reference to "tough love." After all, many, including Dyson to a degree, found Cosby as the source of the comments more problematic than the actual content of what he said. It seemed that Cosby's wealth and history as an apolitical, race-neutral comic made him the wrong person to speak, but his comments seemed to be received as timely, accurate, or at least in need of voicing by someone in the black community. Alternatively, it could be strong national zeal that makes individuals want to ensure that America remains true to its stated principles. Rarely does anyone question Martin Luther King's patriotism because he fervently critiqued the American government and its racist practices. For either perspective, a combination of both strong affection and frustration could be the best characterization, depending on the sample used. For this project, we are interested in blame attribution as a question of framing and problem definition rather than a measure of self-esteem, racial group esteem, or national esteem. Nelson, Oxley, and Clawson (1997) define framing as "the process by which a communication source constructs and defines a social or political issue for its audience" (221). They suggest that framing "represents another subtle, yet important, manner in which political communication shapes popular thinking about politics" (223). In their view, "frames serve as bridges between elite discourse about a problem or issue and popular comprehension about that issue," and for this reason frames "can be meaningful and important determinants of public opinion" (224).

In an experimental study using a predominantly white sample, Iyengar (1991) found that, unlike other issues, race and welfare frames were quite malleable depending on the kind of frame used by news outlets. He found that television news uses two major frames—episodic and thematic. Episodic frames "take the form of a case study or event-oriented report and depict public issues in terms of concrete instances (for example . . . bombing of an airplane, or an attempted murder)" (14). Alternatively, thematic frames "place public issues in some more general or abstract context that takes the form of a . . . report directed at general outcomes or conditions. Examples include reports on changes in government welfare expenditures" (14). Inyengar's project, fittingly titled *Is Anyone Responsible?*, looked at several issue areas, one of which was racial equality. He found that "episodic framing of black poverty elicited a significantly higher frequency of individualistic attribution" (122). In addition, he found that because the media largely provide news coverage using episodic frames, "television news leads viewers to issue-specific attributions of responsibility and these attributions tend to shield society and government from responsibility" (137).

Although these data do not allow us to speak directly to media attention, we have been able to examine how the black elite have framed black political problems. Additionally, through the focus group discussion we can identify whether black blame or system blame is employed, and we can also examine the logic behind the usage of these kinds of justifications. We know that African American elites have historically utilized system blame and black blame to shape protest arguments, within and external to the black community and as in-group recruitment and mobilization appeals. The rest of this chapter uses focus group participants' everyday talk to provide evidence of system blame and black blame in African American political opinion and to draw conclusions about how blame is reflected in the participants' ideological outlook.

Messed-Up Priorities: Ordinary Citizens' Expressions of Black Blame

Black blame is the attribution of fault to African Americans for persistent problems or failure to keep pace socially and economically with whites and other minorities. This attribution often comes in the form of references to vague problems such as the inability to facilitate cooperative efforts or to poor behavioral choices such as failure to work, unplanned pregnancies, or illegal activities. Black blame was present across each focus group and even across age cohorts, economic and educational cohorts, and ideological categories. Participants commented on how blacks have allowed certain things to happen to their own community or how socially unacceptable behaviors explain community problems. Overall, there was no focus group in which black blame was not employed as an explanation, and very rarely was black blame countered as inappropriate, stereotypical, or unjustified. For instance, among some of the college students who talked about why black students were not thriving in universities, the most common answer proffered was best expressed by Andrea, who said:

> My problem with a lot of the race questions, just because I haven't experienced it, is that my experiences with black people have been not that they aren't holding the torch but they are holding on too tightly and for the wrong reasons. I have heard so many excuses for not living up to potential, not being able to do things because I am black. That to me should not be an excuse for anything because I'm black. Maybe there is racism that I just don't notice, that I am ignorant to, but I myself personally I don't believe in the, you know, the white man's trying to keep me down and it's the white man's fault that I didn't get this job. No it's because your hair is not combed, your shoes are dirty and you're not wearing a tie. That's why you didn't get the job. That's my take on it.

Andrea and others who engaged in this kind of black blame point to individual problems or behaviors. Evelyn, another young college student who participated in a different group, expressed frustration that misplaced values and popular cultural images are problematic for the black community:

But I think one of the problems is . . . you know . . . you have kids who can work at McDonald's and can afford an Escalade and that's all they care about. You see it in the videos. You hear it in songs. They wear this and they wear that. . . . The black community in terms of motivation and in terms of duty . . . I mean . . . it's hard for people to see white people wanting to help black people.

While it may be difficult to believe that salaries at McDonald's could yield the status symbols she mentioned, Evelyn's comments denoted the severity, in her view, of black problems, as well as the reason for whites' refusal to help. Delia, a college-educated professional, chided herself for believing and verbalizing this view but made a similar comment about the problems of black America when she said:

But boy I have to negate myself on top of that. There are times when even within your own culture group there are social economic differences. There are some black folks I cannot relate to. There are just some things that I just don't understand, like how you can not have a job and continue to have children. How you . . . in that way I consider myself to be pretty conservative. I just don't understand . . . you know . . . what our own people are doing, so I really, really vacillate between many different opinions, politically.

Even when participants felt like what they were saying was not quite right or appropriate, they still attributed problems to poor personal behavior. They suggested that if African Americans would correct particularly aberrant behaviors that are inappropriate in the larger society, or if they would focus on other goals, then their life outcomes would be dramatically improved. This point was cogently demonstrated in a dialogue between several members of one focus group:

SHARON: If they could stop striving to look as good. You know, I have a seven-year-old goddaughter who goes to Afrocentric School[5] and doesn't want to wear the uniforms anymore because they don't look good. And I said, "Baby, at your age, you should not be worrying about how good you look, you should be getting your mind together so that when you get to a grade where the clothes matter, you can focus. You know it's not what's outside; it's what's up here [pointing to her head]."
RAHIM: Our priorities are messed up.
[OTHER participants agree]

RAHIM: They are more concerned with whether they get school clothes and not the question, can they read? You know, I got the first day of school. I got to be looking good.

DONNA: Or can they see? You know . . .

JANET: And the whole push is to get the clothes for school, but no one says anything about buying a book. Do they?

Beyond personal shortcomings, black blame also took the form of general statements about the manner in which African Americans have squandered opportunities and betrayed the efforts of older generations. These views were in sync with arguments referenced by Cosby at the beginning of this chapter. Sasha pointed out:

We have to carry the torch, not white people. We have to keep that torch burning . . . and by keeping that torch going as individuals, we have to do more to keep those things alive as individuals. I can't look at Breanna, Aminah, or even you and expect you to keep it going so I can keep doing what I want to do. I have to do what I need to do to keep alive what those people did forty, fifty years ago. So I guess that's my big thing. They did a lot of work, and they worked really hard, and they tried to get it out there, but nobody kept it going . . . it's gotten better. Granted, my father's generation wouldn't have had all the opportunities that I have had, but at the same time we are not taking advantage of them, as they would have if they were getting them. If they were getting the opportunities, they would have been on them like white on rice . . . you know, but people aren't taking advantage of opportunities that our forefathers have worked so hard to set up.

Another way in which this kind of blaming took place was when blacks are blamed for aspects of the black community that were perceived as ruined or destroyed. Problems tended to be attributed less to individual behavior and more to broad group pathology. For instance, Cora described a group of women who were trying to help African American teen mothers make better lives for themselves and their children, but the women have found it very difficult to raise funds and resources among members of the black community. Cora pointed to this as an example of how blacks fail to act when there is a problem:

Even if you're not willing to do it, let me help someone who is. Where I am not willing to go out and try to stop young girls from getting pregnant but you are, how do we help them in doing that? Well, we're not. [Referring to African Americans] I think that's part of the problem because we don't support each other in doing things that we can't do or we don't want to do.

Gina echoed Cora's sentiment when she countered another group member's argument that it was unfair that white people get things they do not deserve just because they feel like they are owed more than other racial groups. Gina, however, defended this behavior as appropriate and further stated, "If we [referring to blacks] were cockier as a people, we wouldn't be in the shape that we're in." When the topic turned to the state of predominantly African American urban communities, black blame became a principal reason for why many communities were so blighted. Hank, a professional in his thirties, suggested:

> [This community is] theirs [referring to blacks], but they have devalued it. They have no stake in it. So they bring nothing to the table. Like, if I were to come and say I want to do something, I could bring the value of a house. I can bring something to the table. If I mortgaged the house that could bring me $200,000, I could leverage that and I could do something. You can't leverage a Benz because it devalues. It's just a great expense. It doesn't have any value to it all. That's the difference between, I think, black and white. Whites, kind of, pander to us those things and we accept it. And they laugh at us. I'm a sell you this car for $50,000. I made it for $15, and it's not gone be worth $5 when you get done with it. And we accept that.

These types of sentiments were numerous, and even those participants who indicated strong positive support for African American culture and the desire to be around blacks predominantly engaged in this behavior.

Messed-Up System: Blaming "the System" among the Black Mass Public

An alternative to black blame that was often invoked in these discussions was system blame, or attribution of fault to the governmental and social institutions, norms, or agents that prevent black achievement and exacerbate problems in the black community. Arguments in this vein often cited the design of the system as a cause of black problems. For participants who utilized this type of blame, the American social and political system has built-in obstacles that prevent black progress. Thus, African Americans must be cautious. When employing system blame, focus group participants often pointed to events and periods in history such as slavery or Jim Crow as times that have delayed African American progress. For instance, in one group a participant stated that she was able to deal with whites because she knew that they were no better than her. I asked whether she thought low self-esteem is the reason that blacks do not deal with whites more, and she agreed that it is. Aminah then provided an explanation using a more conciliatory form of system blame:

> Black people have been . . . um . . . they've been degraded for the longest time. They've been put down. They've been tortured, and slavery hasn't happened to anybody else. And, seriously, if a white person had gone through slavery, they probably would not have survived it, so I'm just saying that black people have gone through so many things in their lifetimes. And I think their self-esteem is kind of hard to come by when your parents have gone through some things and maybe they don't know how to teach you how to have that self-esteem.

A less conciliatory but still moderate form of system blame pointed to history as well, but it emphasized how changes in the system have been detrimental to blacks. The argument generally entailed some disappointment over the loss of community businesses and institutions once racial integration opened access to more mainstream enterprises. Pointing out one of the losses that resulted from school desegregation, Rahim said:

> Another thing that happened is the education system fell apart in America. Integration forced black teachers into losing their jobs. Okay, white teachers didn't lose their jobs. It was the black educators that lost their jobs. And they just got spread across, and all the principals and all the administrators in those black schools, they were the ones that suffered. So now we had a system that totally changed, because they used to train you on how to think, how to read, and how to reason. That system is no longer in place.

Focus group participants also employed a stronger form of system blame that more directly targeted American culture and government as forces that work against black Americans. Keesha pointed out on more than one occasion that systemic forces are put in place to hold black Americans back. For example, she stated:

I think that first of all we have to recognize that the system has been designed to put us where we are, which means that we have to create our own system. That does not mean that we exclude anyone, it just means that we support ourselves, and in doing so we are able to support other people. The system I live under right now is designed to keep white people in power, and I can design a system where I can empower myself as a group, as a people, and then I'm of more benefit to this country and to the world globally.

Cameron, mentioned in the North End Community Center vignette in chapter 2, was one of the few participants to counter the black blame process. He became visibly annoyed and pointed out:

Nah, nah . . . you become a victim of the same stuff that everybody else has been a victim of . . . you categorize folks inappropriately . . . you're saying the folk where you live currently are acting differently than the folks in [a white middle-class suburb] . . . that's bullshit . . . and the system does that to you and to everybody else. . . . I don't know if you're old enough to remember growing up hearing a news person on TV, and he would tell people that were vacationing . . . coming to Columbus during the holidays, don't go to the east side, but what he was saying was is that it's niggers out there, but I'm saying that was the media, and they do that all the time and you gotta understand that . . . and all he was basically saying was reinforcing . . . now he was supposed to be totally neutral and he was buying into that same mind-set. . . . don't go over there where them niggers are. . . . this was done on TV . . . and it's done consistently, you just don't pay any attention to it . . . but they do that to us all the time . . . and we buy into it . . . we get to believing that stuff.

When they invoked system blame, participants were signaling problems in the American political system rather than internal problems in the black community. Although system blame was used to a lesser extent than black blame, it was still used frequently—so much so that one was puzzled by other statements that were made in which participants wholeheartedly endorsed mainstream political activities and policies in that same system. One example that reverberated throughout these discussions was the area of electoral politics and political opinions surrounding voting and African American candidates. Why did participants acknowledge an inherent bias in the system and yet continue to endorse participation in that system? Probably the most ardent Black Nationalist in the sample, Keesha, was a prime example. She quoted Malcolm X, suggested that his principles were the solution to black liberation, subscribed to the major tenets of Afrocentrism, and had carved out an almost exclusively black existence, yet she was adamant that black people need to exercise their right to vote.

Another example was age differences, with younger members of this sample relying more heavily on black blame than system blame as an explanation for black problems. Breanna and other members of her discussion group saw blacks as having failed to properly understand and utilize the norms and structures currently in place. This system (though probably or at least sometimes racist) is still navigable and remains a potential arena for black success. Racism was viewed as either constant or extremely diminished; thus, other social variables could and should be manipulated to achieve the American dream. Those variables were almost always, in their opinion, determined by individual behavior and decisions. Rather than external factors being the predominant determinant of achievement, rigid adherence of individuals to social norms such as doing well in school, obeying the law, abstaining from drug use, and practicing responsible family planning foretold one's ability to thrive. When individuals chose not to engage in achievement-producing behaviors, they were also choosing their social and economic lot in life, which was most assuredly negative.

Truths and Consequences: Blame Attribution and Ideology

Obviously, how the problems in the black community were framed had a powerful impact on who got blamed for those problems. From the focus group data, we saw a relationship between blame attribution choice and ideological adherence. At the outset of this chapter, I stated that all groups employed some form of black blame in their explanation of community problems. No subset of the sample ignored the potential impact of individual motivation and behavior on individual success. However, the amount of weight given to individual action varied greatly. The same could be said about the weight given to the impact of systemic forces on black social outcomes. The mediation of blame between these two options also led to differential assessments of the motivation of whites among ideological groups.

Like Ture and Hamilton, Black Nationalist participants placed primary blame for persistent inequality and racial hostility squarely on the shoulders of whites and the institutions (social and governmental) that they control. For them, African Americans have been casualties in the American nation-building process. They expressed negative evaluations of black Americans, but this was because some blacks have bought into the negative perceptions held by other groups—especially whites. Adopting these negative images leads to poor choices that result in bad outcomes. Participants' predominant target became, however, American institutions and actors whose racial designation they saw as white. Keesha, Adrienne, and Janelle engaged in a lengthy dialogue about the lessons learned from Martin Luther King and the Civil Rights Movement that illustrated not only the way that Black Nationalists defined blacks' inability to overcome racism but also the motivations attributed to whites.

KEESHA: I think that Martin Luther King Jr. . . . he clearly demonstrated that you can have that theory and idea to be peaceful but through the experience he showed that even though it put us in the right direction, it still didn't solve the problem of racism. So I think that we learned from that experience. . . . I'm grateful for that experience because without that experience with Martin Luther King we would go through that cycle again. So I think if we analyze and study we will clearly understand where we would take parts of it out, and we can see where that was a benefit and the other parts, either we can learn not to do it that way again or refine it some other way.

ADRIENNE: We are not the only ones who learned, though. They learned too. They learned how to hide it better . . . how to go about it a different way . . .

AUTHOR: When you say they, who are you referring to?

ADRIENNE and KEESHA [simultaneously]: White people.

ADRIENNE: I think [white people] learned how to get us from the right direction. And saying no, that is not how it was meant to be. You got it all wrong and trying to make us [referring to whites] feel bad. And you're like, well maybe they didn't mean that . . . well, yes.

JANELLE [in background]: Yes. They did

ADRIENNE: They mean us harm. And I think they mean us harm because they think in their own heart that if someone was to do this to me and mine, I would get them. So they are afraid of us. So that is why they are trying to hurt us, and they think our mentality is to try and hurt them. That's why they can't leave us alone. They're scared.

JERRI: They're terrified.

[OTHERS nod in agreement]

Black Nationalists saw whites as intentionally malevolent. The American political system and its social structure are, in Keesha's words, "designed to put us where we are." So, in recognition of inherent flaws, Black Nationalists searched for alternative value systems or normative structures. Keesha offered:

> I just feel like the Nguzo Saba, which is the seven principles of Kwanzaa . . . I just feel like if we even operated by something that simple, it would bring us up as a people, and then we wouldn't have to be angry at other people for designing a system that keeps them strong and healthy.

With that assessment of the American political system and its white actors, it was very difficult for individual blacks to want or attempt to integrate fully, any cross-racial interactions were limited to low-contact occurrences such as voting, and it was all tempered by a high level of suspicion.

Moderate supporters of Black Nationalism wanted to see blacks prosper and work more cooperatively to effect community change, but they did not want an excess of poor people in their neighborhood, bringing down property values and contributing to increased crime. They wanted political candidates who are responsive to the needs of the black community, which is poorer than white communities, but they did not want to elect a candidate who was going to significantly increase their taxes—this was because they usually diagnosed social problems as the result of both individual black failure and problems that are imposed on blacks from outside their groups. For instance, they employed black blame when trying to understand why some blacks refuse to work, and they simultaneously acknowledged that the system is often unfair and that whites are not in touch with blacks. Terrence admitted that some dissonance occurred when he tried to sort out the politics of race and other issues. He expressed how this worked for him:

> I think it depends on the day and the situation. Sometimes you do want to be with people like you, so you don't have to have all these different masks and other facades, because . . . you know . . . when you're at work white people don't understand you and understand how you are when you want to express yourself in a particular way. And sometimes you just want to be able to do that without being questioned, without being chastised or going through this thought process as to how they are going to view you.

Although, in his assessment of his relationship with whites and other blacks, Terrence indicated that "sometimes" he prefers to associate just with blacks, at other times he finds it acceptable to be around whites. Moderate Black Nationalists fluctuated between wanting blacks to do for themselves and wanting to believe in the ability of all human beings to cooperate. Delia asserted:

> Sometimes both of them [being in all-black or racially mixed settings] are more appealing. There are times when I truly believe that black folks need to take care of themselves and stop worrying about integrating and being with other people. And there are other times when I really believe that at the bottom of it all we are all human beings.

Terrence and Delia, while partially supporting both integration and separation, illustrated the kinds of opinions held by participants in this moderate category. There was ambiguity built into their assessment of why they preferred to retreat into the black community at times. Further, Terrence, Delia, and others were cautious of the motives and behaviors of whites.

Non-Nationalists tended to see blacks as the authors of their own misfortune. As in Cosby's assessments, blacks were cast as both perpetrators and victims in the explanation for why African Americans fall short of other racial groups in numerous social and economic categories. As discussed previously, many of the participants across the ideological spectrum employed black blame. The differences outlined here were in the manner in which black blame was employed. For this group, black blame was the central reason for black problems, and because their focus is on the individual, then individual failure provided the explanation for why blacks cannot and do not overcome these problems. In a discussion of how blacks are often portrayed negatively as the mythical welfare queen and other images, one group's members acknowledged that this is a stereotypical portrayal but then continued to employ black blame as a reason for why blacks cannot get beyond these stereotypes. They suggested that individuals have to be "smart enough" to counter those stereotypes; otherwise, it becomes a "self-fulfilling prophecy" that blacks live out or emulate the behaviors outlined in these stereotypical images. Other adherents pointed to refusals to work, to conform to mainstream standards of dress, to maintain a "normal" family structure that entails having a reasonable number of children, and other behaviors to explain why blacks are not taken seriously, are turned down for jobs, and experience numerous other negative reactions by nonblacks. Even blacks who are not living "deviant" lives and achieve success are blamed for how they choose to use or not use their successes. Evelyn explained:

> When you ask what that relationship [between blacks and whites] should look like, I think it's more of a symbiotic relationship. We have to be able to feed off of each other equally. I know we're not at that point yet, but I think a lot of that's because black people don't care and it's not affecting them every day, and if they manage to surpass living in the ghetto, to have money and nice clothes . . . it's like, well, I got out and no one helped me. Then they don't think they need to help others who didn't have opportunities.

In essence, they were all saying that black people continuously find themselves at the negative end of statistical results because of individual personal failure on the part of blacks. Interestingly, they also did not see the government as having racial specificity. When I asked whether or not the government or any other agents of authority have a specific racial designation, they answered with a very strong no. When probed further, they suggested that these actors could be of any race. In fact, they were resistant to giving most referents a definitive racial designation just as they shunned others who attempted to categorize them.

Conclusion

It is difficult to see a problem and not search for an explanation for its occurrence. Surely, racism and racist practices in the United States have been problems for multiple centuries. There have been political efforts to diminish the impact of racial hostility, but the extent to which it has diminished is open to debate and difficult to assess. Members of these discussion groups sought not only to explain problems but to attribute blame. In their assessment, there were two main culprits: either blacks themselves or the American social and economic system. These forms of blame were not mutually exclusive, though often one was given priority over the other. Those who emphasized black blame were likely to discount the impact of systemic forces on community problems, and vice versa. Interestingly, a high degree of focus on black blame could result in a tendency to believe that systemic factors are either nonexistent or irrelevant to black progress. African Americans held themselves accountable regardless of how they define problems. Even if the system was designed to prevent black progress, African Americans did not let themselves off the hook when they did not succeed; however, when African Americans failed to adhere to societal norms or make poor lifestyle choices, systemic problems were viewed as absent or less relevant.

So far I have used these focus group descriptions to give an idea of how Black Nationalist beliefs are expressed among ordinary citizens in the post–civil rights era. Each chapter moves farther from the writing of elites and closer to how citizens utilize everyday talk to articulate a worldview. This chapter has also exposed the way in which ideology informs political opinion and decision making, especially when it comes to assigning blame. Thus, the groups proved to be an especially useful setting for observing the anatomy of political discussion among intimates in homogeneous and fairly relaxed settings. The goal of this project is to use multiple approaches to examining evidence of ideological thinking among ordinary African Americans in the post–Civil Rights era. Thus far I have presented semistructured discussions to provide a sense of black political opinion. At this point I turn from qualitative data to the development of a statistical framework to analyze and draw conclusions from a larger sample. The rest of this project bridges the results from this small sample with the findings about Black Nationalist ideology and political opinion from a larger sample. Using the 1996 National Black Election Study, the rest of this project makes further explanatory and predictive statements about the role of Black Nationalism in black political decision making.

5

The Measure and Meaning
of Black Nationalism

Conversations about race and politics are often shaped by the context in which they take place. The important events of the day and the background of the individuals involved all strongly influence the subjects addressed and the tone of the discussion. To be sure, Keesha's vehement support for Black Nationalism may have invoked different responses and explanations had it not been expressed among a group of African American women sitting around her dining room table or if white or Latina women were present. Despite possible differences the changed context would make, closer examination of Keesha's group and others allows us to view a microcosm of African American political opinion. Indeed, it offers a skeletal model that we can now test using a national sample.

This chapter begins the process of adding more substance to the model developed in previous chapters through an analysis of the National Black Election Study. Black Nationalist and other ideological positions have been widely discussed by African American elites, but until recently their presence in the mass public was measured by organizational members and activities or speculation. In contrast, I focus primarily on developing a measure of subscription to a specific ideological category by the black public and making predictions about differences across multiple characteristics of those individuals who subscribe to or reject basic Black Nationalist principles. Where the previous chapters explored these issues in focus groups; this chapter examines national survey data that explore the attitudes of a cross section of black Americans.

Measuring Race-Specific Ideology: The Black Nationalist Index

There is no preexisting direct measure of adherence to Black Nationalism or other race-specific ideologies in African American surveys. Respondents in national surveys are not given the opportunity to self-identify as a member of a particular ideological category as in traditional liberalism/conservatism measures. Given the findings in previous chapters and by other scholars, it is doubtful that asking respondents to self-identify with a particular category would yield substantive insight. Therefore, I use a multi-item index, which combines several related questions from the 1996 NBES and creates a "composite measure of complex phenomena"—in this case the variance in the degree of adherence to Black Nationalist beliefs (Johnson and Joslyn 1991; McIver and Carmines 1981).

Four items from the 1996 NBES are combined to capture respondents' support for Black Nationalism. Those four items asked respondents whether they thought blacks should (1) attend Afrocentric schools, (2) always vote for black candidates, when available, (3) shop in black-owned stores, and (4) have nothing to do with whites.[1] All four of these items speak to the question of whether blacks should become more community-centered and internally focused. These questions address respondents' beliefs in cultural arenas through support for Afrocentrism, in political arenas through support for black candidates, in economic arenas through patronage of black businesses, and in affect toward whites by their willingness to associate with them.[2]

Before examining the impact of this index, it is important to discuss, in some detail, the development of the measure using statistical indicators of reliability. First, all items are significantly and positively correlated with one another, which is prima facie evidence that they have some similarities.[3] Chronbach's alpha assesses scale reliability; the alpha coefficient for these items is .628. This suggests that the items individually measure parts of the same phenomenon to a considerable degree (Spector 1992). When combined, they reliably measure a single phenomenon—in this case African Americans' beliefs about racial group empowerment and community relationships with the broader American community—Black Nationalism. One last statistical test of this measure involved subjecting the four variables that make up the Black Nationalist Index to a factor analysis.[4] The results indicate that one underlying factor explains half (48.9%) of the variance among the components of this scale (Kim and Mueller 1978a; Carmines and Zeller 1979). This factor, I argue, is the degree of respondents' adherence to Black Nationalist principles. The percentage of explained variance by this first factor is more than twice the amount of any other component.

After satisfactorily determining that these items are indeed related and should be used in forming one additive measure, the index is created by adding all four items together into a five-point scale.[5] A score of 1 represents Black Nationalist responses to all the items in the index and an adherence to strong Black Nationalist sentiment. Alternately, a score of 5 represents complete rejection of Black Nationalist principles. The distribution of respondents along this scale is reported in figure 5.1. About 12% of respondents fall within either the Strong Nationalist or the Nationalist category; conversely, the majority (59.2%) endorse categories that measure either Strong Nationalist Rejection or Nationalist Rejection, which constitutes the largest cluster of respondents. The second-largest category of respondents is categorized as Neutral.[6]

The most important feature of this sample is the dearth of Nationalists. There are several explanations for the large number of Nationalist Rejecters. First, the items used in this index, although the only available NBES items that address Black Nationalism directly, prove to be a hard test for Strong Nationalist support, especially support for separatism. Dawson (2001) finds that very few African Americans actually endorse the formation of a separate black nation; however, more are supportive of moderate withdrawal efforts. Agreement with some questions such as

FIGURE 5.1
Frequency Distribution of Black Nationalism

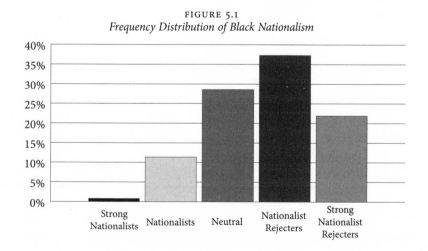

not having anything to do with whites is difficult and may be viewed as a utopian rather than realistic goal. Support for black-owned stores could be another example of a utopian goal. In the 1996 NBES, respondents were only slightly more likely to strongly agree (28.2%) with this question as to strongly disagree (16.7%). Some respondents might believe that it is important for African Americans to patronize black-owned and black-operated businesses, but they may also recognize the difficulty in finding businesses to meet certain needs.[7]

Second, it is important to mention that although there were fewer Black Nationalist respondents in the 1996 NBES, a longitudinal analysis of this measure might yield significant changes in this distribution. The works of Taylor (1989) and Henderson (2000), discussed in the introduction, successfully demonstrate the temporal nature of ideological prominence and mass ideological adherence. Consequently, there is no reason to believe that simply because Black Nationalism proved not to be the dominant ideology among African Americans in 1996 that it will remain or that it always has been the subordinate ideology. Whereas the youngest NBES respondents were more supportive of Black Nationalism, analysis of focus group data seemingly demonstrates an ideological shift toward less support of Black Nationalism in the youngest cohort. It should be noted that the youngest focus group participants are anywhere from five to fifteen years younger than the youngest respondents in the NBES sample. Though they were the youngest of their data cohort, there is a substantial difference between the political climates in which these two groups were socialized.

The Black Nationalist Index: What Can It Tell Us?

When new measures are created, it is important to make sure that they accurately capture the phenomena of interest. To explore this question, the Black Nationalist Index (BNI) was correlated with several variables, which should have clearly identifiable Black Nationalist positions (table 5.1). It is expected that Black Nationalists should be supportive of Louis Farrakhan (as indicated by raw feeling thermometer scores that range from zero to 100) because of his role as the preeminent Black Nationalist and separatist leader in the last few decades. Additionally, because Black Nationalism emphasizes reclamation of black pride through increased awareness of black history and African cultural traditions, Black Nationalists should think more about being black. Alternatively, affective orientation toward

TABLE 5.1
Correlations Used to Assess Predictive Validity

Feeling Thermometers	Black Nationalist Index
Louis Farrakhan	-.206** (.000)
White Feeling Thermometer	.173** (.000)
Think about Being Black	-.105** (.004)
NAACP	-.07* (.053)

** Indicates significance at the .01 levels.
* Indicates significance at the .05 levels.

whites was analyzed. Due to support for a more egalitarian, less race-specific ideology, respondents who reject Black Nationalism should display warmer white affect. Also the National Association for the Advancement of Colored People was born out of racial integration efforts. Therefore, Black Nationalists should have weaker affective orientations toward whites and the NAACP.

The correlation between the BNI and the Farrakhan feeling thermometer shows that as respondents move away from Black Nationalist support, their support of Farrakhan decreases. Although the explained variance is small, the relationship is highly significant. Because of their emphasis on a Pan-Africanist identity, it is expected that as individuals become more Nationalistic, they are significantly more likely to think about being black. Respondents reporting higher scores on this item hardly ever think about being black, and ones with lower more nationalist scores frequently think about being black. Like the Farrakhan feeling thermometer, this coefficient is small but significant. As support for Black Nationalism increases, so does the frequency with which respondents think about being black. This finding is logical, since two of the primary tenets of Black Nationalism is self-determination and increased black pride.

A surprising finding was that as respondents become more Nationalistic, they are also more likely to have higher scores on the NAACP feeling thermometer.[8] This relationship falls just short of significance, which may be related to the changing role of the NAACP. From the NAACP's inception, its primary goal was to promote integration through cross-racial unity and cooperation. Since the end of the civil rights movement and the elimination of de jure segregation, the NAACP has transformed itself into a general advocacy group for the entire African American community.[9] Additionally, the NAACP and historically black colleges and universities were the only organizations mentioned when focus group participants were asked to discuss organizations that were helpful to the black community. Hence, many individuals with a community-centered focus are likely to support any group working to improve the lives of black Americans. This is especially true given the paucity of national black organizations with as much prestige and influence as the NAACP.

Having established the BNI as an appropriate measure of African American ideological views, this chapter seeks to relate this scale to various measures of political behavior and participation as well as sociodemographic variables. The primary objective is to provide a portrait of the people who subscribe to this ideological position and, once they are identified, to address what this means for their attachment to a race-specific political ideology. To this end, the rest of this chapter is divided into four sections. The first section examines socioeconomic characteristics and other variables that provide a contextual picture of members of each ideological subgroup. The second section examines the relationship of this ideological category to traditional measures of liberal conservative ideology. It will also relate Black Nationalism to other political variables such as linked fate and religiosity, which are measures historically associated with African American political behavior. Finally, the chapter ends with an analysis of an ordinary least squares (OLS) model that examines the determinants of Black Nationalism. Because of the explanatory power demonstrated by the perceived race of the interviewer measure, it is examined more closely by analyzing two models of Black Nationalism determinants that separate the sample based on perceived race of the interviewer.

What Does a Black Nationalist Look Like in Post–Civil Rights America?

Categories such as race, age, and gender can sometimes allow us to predict a group's propensity to hold specific preferences based on historical trends. For instance, it is fairly safe to assume that most African Americans vote Democrat because of their overwhelming Democratic electoral support for more than a generation. Here the goal is to make similar claims about the characteristics impacting respondents' preferences for Black Nationalism. Are older African Americans more likely to reject withdrawal efforts because they have had longer ties to their American citizenship? Do the less educated support withdrawal from the system in which many are already marginalized? Does religiosity play an important role in black political ideology formation in the same way that it informs political behavior? For answers, I analyzed several sociodemographic variables in relation to the BNI.

First, as the focus group results suggest, age is an important factor for determining ideological preference. For this analysis I divided respondents into six age cohorts: 18–24, 25–34, 35–44, 45–54, 55–64, and 65 and older. Respondents were overwhelmingly young, with nearly 70% less than forty-five years old.[10] Age is significantly related to ideology. Table 5.2 demonstrates that within each age cohort, nearly a third of respondents fall into the Neutral ideological category. Beyond this, there appears to be a curvilinear relationship between age and Black Nationalism. Black Nationalist support is strongest in the two youngest age categories of 18–24 and 25–34 and the oldest age category of respondents over the age of 64. Alternatively, Nationalist Rejecters are clustered in the 35–44 and 45–54 age cohorts. Interestingly, the youngest participants in the focus groups were in their early to late teens when the 1996 NBES was conducted and were not very supportive of Black Nationalist beliefs and efforts. Why this younger group was different from the youngest members of the NBES sample, who are just a few years older, is unclear. Possibly, subscription to Black Nationalism requires a rejection of the current American political system, which is a major undertaking for people who have been socialized as American citizens. This is especially the case when individuals are socialized during a time of prosperity like the youngest focus group participants, who came of age primarily during the Clinton administration and a time of record economic growth. Alternatively, some might see Black Nationalism as an extremely radical step. Thus, younger participants in the NBES sample might be more inclined toward making this step because they came of age during the Reagan-Bush era, which was characterized by economic and social (especially racial) conservatism. Additionally, the oldest group of African Americans might be more inclined to support Black Nationalistic goals because of disenchantment with the historical relationship of blacks as a group and their personal history with the American political system. Similar to the focus groups, the oldest participants are much more Nationalistic than their younger counterparts.

A major Black Nationalist tenet is the reclamation of a glorious and male-centered African past, which is predicated on restoring African males as rightful heads of the black community. It follows that Black Nationalism would be more attractive to African American men, who would be greatly advantaged by and desirous of these leadership positions. Women in the most recent wave of Black Nationalism in the 1970s spoke about their distaste for those males who thought that the appropriate role for women in the Black Power movement was as mothers, cooks, and

TABLE 5.2

Cross-tabulation of Age and the Black Nationalist Index

	Black Nationalist Index				
Age	Strong Nationalist	Nationalist	Neutral	Nationalist Rejecter	Strong Nationalist Rejecter
18–24		12.1	25.9	37.1	25.0
25–34		15.9	25.8	37.4	20.9
35–44		9.4	28.2	43.6	18.8
45–54	.8	7.8	29.7	37.5	24.2
55–64	2.5	11.4	31.6	30.4	24.1
Above 64	3.8	15.1	34.0	24.5	

Chi-square test is significant at $p < .001$ levels.

TABLE 5.3

Cross-tabulation of Gender and the Black Nationalist Index

	Black Nationalist Index				
Sex of Respondent	Strong Nationalist	Nationalist	Neutral	Nationalist Rejecter	Strong Nationalist Rejecter
Male	.7	7.6	31.9	36.1	23.6
Female	.8	13.6	26.7	38.1	20.9

Chi-square test is significant at $p < .10$ level.

typists (Bambara 1970; Brown 1992; Davis 1974). Despite these expectations, however, the findings from table 5.3 suggest that gender differences in ideological adherence are only marginally significant.

Collectively, men are more likely than women to fall into the Neutral and Nationalist Rejecter categories. Alternatively, women are more likely to be Black Nationalists. This counterintuitive finding evokes more questions about why respondents subscribe to a particular ideological category. There are several potential explanations for this finding. First, the fact that women are more Nationalistic could signal their agreement with the need for a male-focused uplift agenda given the negative social statistics associated with black men.[11] This seemed to be demonstrated in black women's support of the Million Man March (Gay and Tate 1998; Smooth and Tucker 1999). Second, women are less likely to fall into the Neutral category and more likely to take clear stances, which are presumably a by-product of other findings that African American women are more politically knowledgeable and engaged than African American men

(Burns, Schlozman, and Verba 2001). Indeed, African American women have been courted as a distinct voting coalition because of the small black male presence on registration rolls and the resulting high percentage of black women in southern states' Democratic parties in the 2008 election (Sinclair-Chapman and Price 2008). This may also account, incidentally, for the dearth of males in all the samples used in this analysis, as less politicized people are less likely to respond to a request to be involved in a survey or any other political activity.

Education is significantly related to position on the BNI. The results reported in table 5.4 demonstrate that although Nationalist and Neutral respondents seem to be fairly evenly distributed across education levels, a different trend emerges for respondents who reject Black Nationalism. Increased education leads to an initial decrease in Black Nationalist support, but at some point this relationship plateaus, and respondents with higher education levels are just as likely to adhere to or reject Black Nationalism. Several reasons can be offered for why Black Nationalism is less appealing to the moderately educated groups. Members of these groups might see integrating into mainstream America as more available to them than do respondents who are less educated or more educated. For instance, respondents who are high school dropouts know that few opportunities to integrate are available to them. This is especially true given the research agendas by Wilson (1999, 1997, 1978) and others who suggest that there is an economic chasm between the suburban, educated, and largely white middle class and residents of the center cities who often are less educated, unskilled, and unable to access higher-paying suburban jobs—and often are black. Additionally, the most educated NBES respondents may be more sensitized to the rewards and benefits that should come with increased education and somehow feel unfairly denied opportunities, which make them more likely to agree with items in the NBES that measure Black Nationalist beliefs (for example, see Feagin and Sykes 1994).

How does Black Nationalism relate to conventional ideological differences in American politics? To test this, I examined the relationship between the BNI and liberalism and conservatism. This is important because self-placement on the liberal-conservative scale has been regarded as a fairly good predictor of political behavior, especially voting behavior. Within each ideological category, the respondents overwhelmingly see themselves as moderates (table 5.5). Beyond this, we see that both the Nationalist and the Neutral respondents are more likely to place themselves in the liberal categories. Nationalists are almost twice as likely to be liberal than conservative. Additionally, Nationalist Rejecters demonstrate a greater tendency toward conservatism. Although chi-square tests are not significant, Kendall's tau-b and gamma are significant at the .001 levels, both indicating an ordinal relationship between these two measures. Adherents to conservative ideology are more supportive of the status quo, in the sense that they are more likely to buy into the major tenets of a particular country and are less tolerant of change. Thus, it follows that respondents who reject Black Nationalism and who simply want to be a part of the existing system are more likely to subscribe to some form of political conservatism and its close ally, racial conservatism. On the other hand, Black Nationalists, who reject all or part of the existing political system, are also more likely to be more liberal and supportive of change. It is important to reiterate, however, that the overwhelming subscription of NBES respondents was to a moderate position.

This finding is somewhat counterintuitive given the conservative leanings embedded in Black Nationalist ideology, such as a strong emphasis on the maintenance of traditional family structures, black male leadership, and strict rules of personal behavior and ethics. Additionally, during many Black Nationalist periods, there has also been a strong embrace of capitalism and entrepreneurialism as a method of black advancement. Chapter 2 notes that early Black Nationalists rejected white supremacist notions of black inferiority while holding fast to Judeo-Christian values and norms. Even cultural Black Nationalists, who reject Western (or white) cultural norms and practices, champion rigid (and often patriarchal) value systems. This has led some scholars to note the strong similarities between the political preferences of Black Nationalists and Black Conservatives (Orey and Price n.d.; Dillard 2001; Simpson 1998). Dawson (2001) notes that Black Conservatives "are just as likely to frame their analyses as being critical to the advancement of the African-American cause as are Black Nationalists" (23). Orey and Price (n.d.) have found empirical confirmation that Black Conservatives and Black Nationalists have some overlapping political preferences; however, the ideological similarities of these groups is undermined by differences in racial outlook. Black Conservatives are more likely than Black Nationalists to express feelings of racial resentment toward and engage in negative stereotyping of other blacks.[12]

More than two decades ago, a research agenda led by Pat Gurin and other scholars at the University of Michigan established overwhelming evidence of a key component of African American political calculus—that

TABLE 5.4

Cross-tabulation of Education Level and the Black Nationalist Index

	Black Nationalist Index				
Education Level	Strong Nationalist	Nationalist	Neutral	Nationalist Rejecter	Strong Nationalist Rejecter
Less than High School	4.2	12.5	32.3	21.8	29.2
High School Graduate		8.6	25.4	37.3	28.7
Some College; No Degree	.3	11.7	29.7	39.7	18.6
Bachelors Degree		12.7	29.1	42.7	14.5
Graduate or Professional School		13.2	28.9	40.8	17.1

Chi-square test is significant at $p < .05$ level.

TABLE 5.5

Cross-tabulation of Black Nationalist Index and Liberal Conservative Ideology (%)

	Black Nationalist Index				
Liberal Conservative Ideology	Strong Nationalist	Nationalist	Neutral	Nationalist Rejecter	Strong Nationalist Rejecter
Strong Liberal		15.9	33.6	32.7	17.7
Weak Liberal	2.1	13.5	33.3	35.4	15.6
Moderate	.3	11.3	28.0	38.4	22.0
Weak Conservative		8.8	25.0	42.5	23.8
Strong Conservative	1.1	9.6	20.2	38.3	30.9

Chi-square test not significant. Kendall's tau-b and gamma significant at $p < .001$ level.

of group consciousness or linked fate (Gurin, Hatchett, and Jackson 1989; Gurin, Miller, and Gurin 1980; Shingles 1981). Thus, any new measure of African American political preferences or behavior must include an analysis of the relationship between that measure and measures of linked or common fate. The result of this analysis demonstrates a tendency for Black Nationalists to be more group-centered. The findings in table 5.6 show that Black Nationalists are significantly more likely to say that much of their future is tied to other blacks. This is expected, since a feeling of linked fate is crucial to Nationalist ideology in that these individuals are more likely to connect their identity to the African American community

TABLE 5.6
Cross-tabulation of Black Nationalist Index and Linked Fate

Linked Fate	Black Nationalist Index				
	Strong Nationalist	Nationalist	Neutral	Nationalist Rejecter	Strong Nationalist Rejecter
Yes, a Lot	1.5	13.3	29.6	36.7	18.9
Yes, Some		11.7	29.1	38.5	20.8
Yes, Not Very Much	2.7	9.5	37.8	29.7	20.3
No		7.9	19.8	40.5	31.7

Chi-square test is significant at $p < .05$ level. Kendall's tau-b and gamma are significant at $p < .05$ level.

as a part of the African Diaspora rather than connect themselves to people of other races. Notably, although their actual numbers are small, no Strong Nationalists believed they lacked a common fate with other blacks.

Substantial research in both political science and sociology has documented the significance of religious institutions to the political development of the black community (Frazier 1964; Harris 1999; Lincoln and Mamiya 1990; Lincoln 1974). The Civil Rights Movement, for instance, was carried out by marshaling the resources of African American churches in terms of manpower, institutional structure, community networks, and financial resources (McAdam 1982; Morris 1984). As in other ideological constructs, there are both secular and religious factions. Within Black Nationalism, religion and religious imagery have been fairly constant. Because of religiosity's influence on behavior, it is also important to assess whether or not it plays an important role in determining ideological positioning. In this analysis the relationship between the BNI and religiosity is not statistically significant.[13] Results in table 5.7 suggest that there are no significant differences between Black Nationalists and Nationalist Rejecters in relation to attendance at religious institutions.

More sophisticated analysis could potentially tease out a relationship between ideological position and religious beliefs. Additionally, church attendance may not be as important as the type of church individuals attend. Scholars have noted that some churches are more explicitly political than others (Harris 1999; Calhoun-Brown 1996). For instance, some churches are very involved in registering their members to vote, encouraging them to turn out on election day, and holding meetings for candidates to present their platforms. Others, however, rarely mention anything political and even suggest that politics and religious life are incompatible. This suggests

TABLE 5.7

Cross-tabulation of Black Nationalist Index and Church Attendance

	Black Nationalist Index				
Church Attendance	Strong Nationalist	Nationalist	Neutral	Nationalist Rejecter	Strong Nationalist Rejecter
Twice or More a Week		5.0	20.0	50.0	25.0
Every Week	.8	9.6	31.0	35.6	23.0
Almost Every Week	.7	13.5	30.4	34.5	20.9
Once or Twice Monthly	1.1	13.0	25.4	36.2	24.3
A Few Times a Year		12.7	27.3	42.7	17.3
Never	2.2	6.7	28.9	37.8	24.4

Chi-square test is not significant.

that a measure that captures whether or not individuals attend a political church might be more appropriate when attempting to analyze the effects of religion on subscription to an Integrationist or Nationalist ideology. To test this, a multiple-item measure of a political church was created that asked respondents if their place of worship was involved in politics, whether respondents heard about the presidential campaign at church, and whether their place of worship encouraged respondents to vote. The relationship between the BNI and political church attendance, like frequency of church attendance, however, proves not to be significant.

Predictors of Black Nationalism

Although contingency tables allow us to examine the relationship between variables, they provide little in the way of predictive ability. Therefore, an OLS model is used to identify which factors significantly influence individual adherence to Black Nationalist views (table 5.8). Previous analysis explored the impact of standard socioeconomic status (SES) predictors, such as education, income, gender, and age, and they are included in this model as well. In this analysis, gender is coded as a dichotomous variable in which females are assigned a score of 1. Young people are less likely to engage in political activity, and because they are politically inexperienced, their attitudes and ideological orientations are less stable (Jennings and Markus 1984; Flanigan and Zingale 1998). Actual reported ages are used, and as an individual's age increases, so too should his or her score on the BNI. Scholars have shown that educational attainment and income, which are interrelated, make individuals more politically informed and engaged and more tolerant of others' opinions (Verba, Schlozman, and Brady 1995). A higher score for income and education indicates increased wealth and educational attainment. All these factors should also foster coherent political beliefs and definitive position taking. Subscription to Black Nationalism requires a willingness to reject prevailing narratives of "authentic" black political behaviors, as well as political narratives among the dominant racial group. Thus, young blacks, who have less entrenched political loyalties, and the less educated and less wealthy, who have fewer investments in America's social and economic future, will be more likely to embrace Black Nationalist principles.

Long-established political variables like liberal or conservative ideology and region are included because of their enduring ability to influence political behavior. Liberal or conservative ideology is measured on a seven-point scale from strong liberals on the low end to strong conservatives on the high end. The variable for region delineates respondents living in the South from those who reside in the rest of the country. For various reasons, many of which are directly related to race and the treatment of blacks, southern culture and politics differ from culture and politics in other regions of the country. Thus, this analysis includes a dummy measure of region, in which respondents residing in the South are assigned a score of 1. Additionally, linked fate is particularly important because African Americans overwhelmingly demonstrate a belief that their fates are connected to the fate of other members of the black community. This survey measures linked fate by asking respondents about their level of agreement with the statement "What happens to black people has a lot to do with me." High scores on this item suggest that the respondent strongly disagrees with this statement and believes that his or her individual fate is not tied to that of other blacks.

Certain variables provide scholars with information about the environment or neighborhood context in which respondents live. To that end, several of these environmental variables have been added to the data using census block data. The kind of neighborhood one lives in can impact ideological positions in several ways. First, supporting racial integration may be related to other decisions such as whether to live in a racially mixed or segregated neighborhood. Second, the racial and economic makeup of the neighborhood will have a potentially significant impact on the life experiences of individual respondents, such as influencing the amount of

TABLE 5.8

Regression Model of the Predictors of Position on Black Nationalist Index

Variables	β	SE	Significance
Education	.013	.034	.710
Income	-.023	.021	.278
Age (18–43 Dummy = 1)	-.004	.098	.970
Gender (Female = 1)	-.088	.098	.369
Region	-.099	.099	.381
Liberal/Conservative Ideology	**.060**	**.024**	**.012***
Linked Fate	**.095**	**.045**	**.007***
% Poverty	-.006	.006	.821
% Black	.002	.001	.126
Religiosity	**.088**	**.042**	**.035***
Feeling Thermometer: Blacks	-.001	.003	.666
Feeling Thermometer: Whites	**.010**	**.002**	**.000****
Perceived Race of the Interviewer	**.470**	**.101**	**.000****
Economic Position of Blacks vs. Whites	**-.078**	**.039**	**.044***
Will Blacks Ever Achieve Full Equality	.001	.052	.983
Constant	**2.839**	**.393**	**.000**
Adjusted R²	.172		
N	340		

Significant variables are in bold type.
** Indicates significance at $p < .01$ level.
* Indicates significance at $p < .05$ level.

contact respondents might have with nonblacks. Huckfeldt (1984) found "that the political influence of context is realized through social interaction processes" in that it impacts both "intimate" and "casual, less personal, and nearly inexplicable encounters" (416). Additionally, Cohen and Dawson (1993) have found that "living in a neighborhood with high levels of economic devastation leads to greater isolation from social institutions that are most involved in black politics such as the black church and organizations dedicated to social affairs" (291). Despite high levels of isolation, many respondents in the Detroit Area Study still reported high levels of political efficacy. All these factors suggest that the model should include not just fixed demographic measures like race and gender but also measures that account for the social context. Using the census tract and block codes of respondents in the National Black Election Study, variables were included that measured both the percentage of residents living in poverty and the percent black population within the outlined geographic boundary. These variables report actual percentages; consequently, as scores increase, so does the number of black or impoverished residents.

Some variables included in this analysis are specific to the African American community in that they have been found to have a significant impact on African American political behavior. These variables include religiosity, attitudes about the economic positioning of blacks versus whites, and the ability of blacks to achieve full equality, as well as feeling thermometers measuring affect toward blacks and whites. Citrin et al. (1975) found a strong connection between alienation and negative evaluations of government institutions; consequently, respondents who see the system as permanently closed and who perceive high levels of economic disadvantage in relation to whites are prone to both increased criticism of the government and greater political alienation. Religiosity is measured by assessing the level of importance placed on religion. A high score is assigned to those respondents for whom religion is not important in their daily lives. Respondents were asked whether they thought blacks were worse off, better off, or about the same economically as whites. If respondents believed that blacks are economically disadvantaged in relation to whites, they will look for reasons why this might be the case and move toward either black blame or system blame. Thus, it becomes important to know if this relationship is significant or not. A high score on this item represents a belief that blacks are much worse off than whites; a low score represents a belief that blacks are much better off than whites. As a proxy for black blame and system blame, I include feeling thermometers that measure black and white affect. The intuition underlying the inclusion of these items is that respondents who engage in high black blame will offer lower scores on the black feeling thermometer. In turn, those respondents who attribute blame to the system vis-à-vis its white agents will provide lower thermometer scores (i.e., negative white affect). The raw scores used for both feeling thermometers were included in this analysis; lower scores indicate negative affect, and higher scores indicate positive affect. Another item used in this analysis asked if respondents thought blacks would ever achieve full equality. Individuals who believed in the possibility of black equality received the lowest scores on this item. High scores on this item mean that respondents believe that blacks will not achieve full equality with whites. Last, perceived race of the interviewer effects were accounted for by including a dichotomous variable in which nonblack interviewers are scored as 1.[14]

Although SES appears to be important when analyzing contingency tables, a very different picture emerges in more rigorous analysis. Although the coefficients move in the same direction, SES variables fall well short of significance in the regression analysis. Several traditional indicators of political behavior prove to be statistically significant in predicting where individual scores will fall on the BNI. Both liberal or conservative ideology and the variable measuring belief in linked fate are significant indicators of where respondents fall on the BNI. As respondents become more conservative, they are also less likely to identify with Black Nationalist ideology, which confirms the evidence provided in the contingency tables. As stated earlier, the nature of conservatism has to do with the preservation of the status quo and orthodox interpretation of constitutional questions, including those regarding racial equality. Liberals, in contrast, are more open to ideas or strategies that challenge enduring American traditions that have been exclusionary and unjust. Thus, liberals may also be open to the transformative or revolutionary appeal of Black Nationalist rhetoric.

A recent study has shown that although Black Nationalists and Black Conservatives share some beliefs about self-help, they ultimately "are much more likely to engage in negative stereotyping and express sentiments of racial resentment than Black Nationalists" (Orey and Price n.d., 20). Additionally, linked fate is significantly and positively related to scores on the BNI. This suggests that those who disagree with the statement "What happens to blacks has a lot to do with me" are much more likely to disagree with Black Nationalism. Thus, for Nationalist Rejecters, intraracial connections are less significant than for Nationalists, for whom group identity is integral to their worldview. The finding that linked fate significantly predicts African American political ideology of any kind is not surprising given the well-established research demonstrating its importance and the discussion of linked fate in previous chapters.

A feeling thermometer measuring affect toward whites on a scale of 0 to 100 was included in this analysis. A score of 0 represents absolute negative or unfavorable white affect, and a score of 100 represents absolute positive or favorable white affect. Although the actual coefficient is small, positive white affect predicts Black Nationalist rejection, a finding that is congruent with an understanding of this ideology. As discussed in previous chapters, Black Nationalist ideology recognizes and to some extent exposes both historical and ongoing contentiousness between African Americans and whites that reflects an enduring history of oppression of blacks by whites. Thus, it follows that Nationalists should be more likely to express antiwhite sentiments or negative affect toward whites. Alternatively, beliefs held by supporters of some forms of racial integration emanate from a humanist perspective in which racial prejudices and the resulting behavior serve as a by-product of inequality. Just as blacks do not want to be collectively judged, they are reluctant to hold negative views or judge whites collectively. This is demonstrated here and in the earlier focus group analysis.

The vast majority of African American respondents in the 1996 NBES believed that religion is important in their lives. Nationalists place less importance on religion than do Nationalist Rejecters. The importance of religion partly stems from the role the church has played in providing manpower, structure, and leadership in popular movements such as the civil rights movement. Also, this may be less true for African Americans whose faith traditions are not Judeo-Christian-based. For instance, African American Muslims have traditionally been more Nationalistic than other African Americans because of the role the Nation of Islam has played in both Black Nationalist and separatist movements (Gomez 2005; Essien-Udom 1962). Unfortunately, the 1996 survey does not provide information to allow the role of various faith traditions in determining ideological views to be teased out.

In response to an item measuring respondents' beliefs regarding whether African Americans fare better, worse, or about the same economically as whites, very few African Americans were willing to say that blacks were better off than whites (less than 10%). However, a little more than half were willing to say that blacks were worse off than whites. As respondents become more Nationalistic, they also become significantly more likely to believe that blacks are worse off economically than whites. Though not surprising, the direction of the causal arrow may be more complicated than it appears. Do blacks see the economic advantages of whites and become more Nationalistic? Or do blacks become Nationalistic and thus focus more on inequality? The answer to that question is unclear and difficult to tease out through statistical analysis. Given the evidence found in the focus groups, the answer is likely a combination. Certainly, there are some Nationalists whose beliefs are the result of perceived inequality between blacks and whites. There may also be others for whom an intraracial focus is more appealing and would support

Nationalist beliefs even in the absence of inequality. Not only is this difficult to deduce in the data; it is made more difficult by the enduring and constant presence of stark racial inequality.

The race of the interviewer can play an important role in shaping the responses offered by survey participants. In this case, the perceived presence of a white interviewer made respondents significantly less likely to express Black Nationalist sentiments. The race of interviewer effect is one of the strongest indicators of rejection of Black Nationalism. The strength of the indicator is surprising; however, it is not surprising that talking to nonblack interviewers will change responses. This corroborates results in a pair of articles by Anderson, Silver, and Abramson (1988a, 1988b) in which they assess feelings of warmth and closeness by black respondents for whites and blacks. Anderson et al. defined closeness in terms of a strong feeling of similarity with the target group and warmth as simply an affective evaluation of the target group. They found that blacks were more likely to express feelings of warmth and closeness toward whites when questioned by white interviewers than were blacks who were questioned by black interviewers. This is in contrast to black respondents' feeling of closeness to other blacks; regardless of the race of the interviewer, blacks felt a strong sense of closeness and warmth toward individuals with whom they share common racial designations. As discussed earlier, Non-Nationalist African Americans were more likely to express positive affect toward whites in the focus group sample; the same holds true for this sample as well.

Examining Race of the Interviewer Effects More Closely

Because perceived race of the interviewer effects are so strong, it is important to examine their impact on any potential differences in willingness to express certain beliefs. This relationship was examined in several ways. First, although the coefficient is low, there is a significant and positive correlation between perceived race of the interviewer and scores on the BNI. The coefficient of .181 is significant at the .001 level. Additionally, a contingency table of this relationship indicates that there is a significant relationship between differences in respondents' perception of the race of the interviewer and their scores on the BNI. Table 5.9 indicates that respondents who thought they were talking to a black interviewer were almost twice as likely to fall into the Black Nationalist category as those who thought they were talking to a white interviewer. Alternatively, respondents who perceived their interviewer to be white were almost twice as likely to disagree with Black Nationalist sentiments. Thus, the inclusion of the race of the interviewer in this analysis would serve to diminish the presence of Black Nationalist views in the sample by decreasing the number of respondents who are willing to identify strongly with items that support Black Nationalist views. The impact of the race of the interviewer effects is particularly important in light of the fact that nearly 60% of the respondents thought the race of their interviewer was white.

If blacks' responses about Black Nationalism differ when they believe that whites are interviewing them, then the factors that contribute to ideological positioning may differ as well. To analyze this, separate OLS models were run, with the sample divided on the basis of perceived race of the interviewer. The variables used are identical to the OLS model in table 5.8. The perceived race of the interviewer is used as a filter variable. The first difference that emerges is that there are fewer significant variables in the filtered models. This may be due, in part, to the decrease in the number of respondents. A larger N yields more stable results; however, the findings here are not trivial. The results are reported in table 5.10.

When respondents believe they are speaking to a black interviewer, fewer variables impact their ideological positioning. In this case, when respondents believe that blacks are disadvantaged economically in comparison to whites, they are significantly more likely to support Black Nationalist views. This finding mirrors those in the larger sample in that blacks who recognize disparities between their own community and the white community also endorse Black Nationalism. As respondents report more positive white affective orientations, they also become less Nationalistic. For many blacks, like those Black Nationalists in the focus group, the American political system and white people are inextricably linked. Therefore, as respondents become more withdrawn from and critical of the American political system, they also demonstrate more negative evaluations of whites generally. This is also important given findings by Anderson et al. (1988a, 1988b) that blacks do temper their racial attitudes when being interviewed by someone they perceive as white. These two variables are the only significant predictors of adherence to Black Nationalist ideology when respondents believe they are speaking to a black interviewer.

When respondents perceive that a white interviewer is reading the question, the picture is quite different, and are more significant predictors of support for Black Nationalism. First, as one's household income

TABLE 5.9
Cross-tabulation of Black Nationalist Index and Perceived Race of the Interviewer

	Interviewer Perceived as African American	Interviewer Perceived as White
Strong Nationalist	.8	1.1
Nationalist	15.4	8.0
Neutral	34.6	25.3
Nationalist Rejecter	34.2	38.3
Strong Nationalist Rejecter	15.0	27.4

Chi-square tests are significant at $p < .001$ level.

TABLE 5.10
Comparisons of Determinants of Ideology by Perceived Race of the Interviewer

	Black Interviewers		White Interviewer	
	β (SE)	Significance	β (SE)	Significance
(Constant)	**3.121** (.712)**	**.000**	**3.587** (.522)**	**.000**
Education Level	.002 (.053)	.647	.001 (.046)	.997
Family Income	.001 (.034)	.663	**-.054* (.028)**	**.057**
Actual Age	.001 (.007)	.851	.0004 (.005)	.936
Gender (Female =1)	-.132 (.163)	.420	-.091 (.128)	.476
Region (South =1)	-.156 (.161)	.334	-.066 (.128)	.608
Linked Fate	.001 (.077)	.889	**.166* (.058)**	**.005**
Ideology	.006 (.040)	.125	**.056b (.032)**	**.082**
% Poverty	.003 (.010)	.792	-.013 (.008)	.125
% Black	.001 (.002)	.592	.002 (.002)	.310
Achieve Full Equality	.057 (.087)	.509	-.079 (069)	.256
Relative Economic Positioning	**-.109b (.065)**	**.095**	-.074 (.050)	.142
Black Thermometer	-.005 (.005)	.305	.0009 (.003)	.794
White Thermometer	**.009* (.004)**	**.016**	**.010* (.004)**	**.004**
Adjusted R²	.112		.141	
N	155		181	

Significant variable are in bold print.
**Indicates significance at $p < .01$ level.
*Indicates significance at $p < .05$ level.
b Indicates significance at $p < .10$ level.

rises, individual respondents become more Nationalistic—meaning that wealthier African Americans are more likely to endorse efforts to separate blacks from the larger American political system. This finding ties into arguments by Feagan and Sikes (1994) and others who find that members of the black middle class are extremely disillusioned about their social, economic, and political lot in America. As the most successful members of their community, higher-income and more highly educated blacks also stand to benefit the most from any racial integration efforts. As a result, they are also the most alienated and incensed by perceptions of unfair treatment of African Americans. The opposite may be the case for poorer blacks who live more racially and economically segregated lives and for whom the prospect of living out the American dream may be more abstract and seemingly unachievable, like Alford Young's group of black men in Chicago. Another possibility is that social desirability might be more important to poorer blacks, who are more reluctant to provide more Nationalistic and controversial views about racial questions when speaking to white strangers.

Respondents who disagree with the statement "What happens to blacks has a lot to do with me" are also less likely to sanction the Black Nationalist viewpoint. Adherence to Black Nationalism requires an increased emphasis on race over other salient characteristics. There is a significant and positive relationship between liberal or conservative ideology and BNI score. Even blacks potentially assume or recognize the "liberal bias" among blacks, so those African Americans who are more conservative might be more willing to identify as conservative when speaking to whites and also to associate those views with rejection of Black Nationalism.

Similar to all models examined thus far, white affect is a powerful predictor of the degree of support for Black Nationalism. Respondents with more positive or warm evaluations of whites consistently present weaker endorsements of Black Nationalism. It is safe to say that for various reasons antiwhite sentiment may play a strong role in black respondents' desire to withdraw from the American political system. Respondents and theorists alike suggest that this may not be related to antiwhite sentiments as much as it is a desire for blacks to be a self-determining and self-governing community—efforts repeatedly hindered by whites. Either way, the data show that positive evaluations of whites depress support for Black Nationalism. This finding is equally important given the findings in the focus group discussions that when blacks criticize the government, they often attach the racial label of white to governmental institutions.

Additionally, many participants connected their broad views about race and specific views about Black Nationalism to incidences of negative racial interactions and continued black-white hostility. In a recent study, Sniderman and Piazza (2002) argue that although blacks share common values with whites and other Americans, blacks have "turned inward, having lost confidence in the promise of America" and draw on "their unique experience and traditions to develop their own ideas and aspirations" (180).

Conclusion

The goal of this chapter has been to establish a measure that would capture respondents' positions across the Black Nationalist Index. Using items from the 1996 NBES, a measure was created to assess subscription to Black Nationalism, using questions that asked whether or not respondents supported Afrocentric schools, shopped in black-owned stores, thought blacks should vote for black candidates, and endorsed contact with whites. After running a series of tests, there is strong encouragement that this measure captures the ideology of interest here. As expected, Black Nationalists are more focused on race and supportive of Louis Farrakhan; alternatively, respondents who are Nationalist Rejecters are warmer toward whites. Additionally, contingency tables demonstrate that SES factors such as education, age, and (more moderately) gender impact BNI positioning. It appears that Black Nationalist appeals are more attractive to women, the moderately educated, and both the very young and very old. Last, factors often associated with political behavior such as liberalism, conservatism, and linked fate are significantly related to position on the BNI. Conservative respondents are less Nationalistic, as are respondents who feel less connected to other blacks. These early results strongly suggest that this index plays an important role in the political calculus of respondents in the 1996 NBES and that more sophisticated analysis is warranted.

Traditional socioeconomic status variables do not achieve statistical significance under multivariate scrutiny; however, negative feelings toward whites consistently yield more support for Nationalist ideological views. Also, when respondents believe their interviewer is white, different factors emerge as significant predictors of ideological adherence than when they believe their interviewer is black. First, there are fewer significant predictors with perceived black interviewers. In this case, the perception that blacks are economically disadvantaged in comparison to whites and negative white affect are significant predictors of support for Black

Nationalism. Alternatively, more factors influence ideological position with perceived white interviewers. Respondents in higher income brackets, who are less connected to other blacks, more conservative, and more positive toward whites, are less likely to embrace Black Nationalism.

The findings here demonstrate the difficulty in unpacking the complexities associated with individual ideological adherence. The power of the race of the interviewer is extremely important because it demonstrates that the ability to capture ideological beliefs is vulnerable to nonpolitical factors, such as efforts by respondents to provide socially desirable responses. Quite possibly, black respondents could feel a need to temper positive white affect when talking to other blacks for fear of being perceived as a racial group defector. Consequently, affect toward whites is important. Nationalists report more negative white affective evaluations in general. This relationship is consistent regardless of the perceived race of the interviewer; how respondents feel toward whites matters in their political judgments. But simple affective evaluation does not explain it all. Negative evaluations of whites are tied to respondents' views about the economic and sociopolitical disadvantages of blacks in relation to whites. Respondents must go beyond the threshold of simply disliking whites; they must also believe that blacks, collectively, are disadvantaged in comparison to whites. Blacks see the inherent inequality of a system in which whites receive more than their fair share of the positive ends of American democracy, and this leads to increased negative evaluations of whites and more Nationalistic views.

6

Black Nationalism and
Its Consequences

Mobilization around Black Nationalism has almost always paralleled organization building and an attempt at developing an intraracial infrastructure. Whether it was through the organized African expeditions supported by black separatists in the 1850s and 1860s, Garvey's Universal Negro Improvement Association (UNIA) in the 1920s, or the Republic of New Africa in 1970s, Black Nationalists have mobilized ordinary citizens around ideals that are heavily coupled with focused action. Additionally, because of its focus on demonstrating and practicing self-reliance, self-help, and self-determination, Black Nationalism is equal parts ideology and action plan. Therefore, African American subscription to Black Nationalism should be borne out in Black Nationalists' political behavior, as well.

Now that we have gained a better sense of the correlates of Black Nationalist support, I turn to a final quantitative goal of this project. I hypothesize that this measure is significantly related to political behavior and that it supports the argument that it is a more accurate predictor of political behavior than conventional measures associated with African American political behavior. This is achieved by creating OLS models of political behavior and attitudes and by switching the Black Nationalist Index from the dependent to the independent side of the equation. Here I take up the task of examining the relationship between Black Nationalism and important political variables, including measures of political alienation, partisanship, participation, and policy.

Alienation and Ideology: Analysis of Trust and Efficacy

A democracy cannot sustain itself without popular support; consequently, political scholars and practitioners are interested in both understanding and ultimately preventing the growth of political alienation. Miller (1974) argued that the level of political alienation can be measured along two dimensions—political trust and political efficacy. High levels of political alienation, it was believed, led to increased political tension and reliance on unconventional forms of political expression (Aberbach and Walker 1970b). This was a popular explanation proffered for such widespread support for previously unorthodox political protest in the sixties and seventies. In opposition to conventional wisdom, Pollock (1983) argues that "an increase in cynical perceptions . . . does not necessarily imply an increased potential for extremist behavior. It may, however, imply a change in patterns of conventional participant activity" (406–407). Instead he finds that "politically competent cynical individuals favor high initiative modes of influence—campaigning and contacting as well as protest behavior."

Political trust is a function of several factors, including level of trust in others, social background, political expectations, and feelings of deprivation (Aberbach and Walker 1970b, 1199). Individuals who have a propensity toward trusting other people will also be more likely to trust the government. Political expectations are important in engendering political trust if individuals believe there is a chance that some of their expectations will be met. Closely related to expectations are feelings of deprivation. Individuals who believe that rights and benefits are being unjustly withheld from them are less likely to believe that the government will do what is right. Additionally, social factors can work to make individuals more or less trusting of government. Those individuals who receive more rewards from the political system—the wealthier, better educated, and so forth— are more likely to trust its actors and institutions to do what is right. General levels of trust in the United States have decreased significantly since the 1950s. This sustained period of cynicism toward governmental actors and institutions has been attributed to several factors, including the poor economic environment, dearth of leadership, and political scandal (Citrin and Green 1986; Lipset and Schneider 1987; Miller 1974).

There was a resurgence of political trust in the 1980s that was directly related to increased confidence in the leadership of the Reagan administration and growth in economic prosperity. Citrin and Green (1986) offer, "The current upsurge of political confidence is palpable, but it may be fragile as well. The continued growth of trust in government seemingly requires that good times endure" (450). Agreeing that an "extended period of good news would be required to reverse the confidence gap," Lipset and Schneider (1987) argue that there "seems to be no end to the series of events that create and sustain the confidence gap" (21). Pointing to events such as the Vietnam War, the insurgency of the sixties and seventies, and the Watergate and Iran-Contra scandals, they suggest that Americans are being provided with more (rather than less) evidence to persuade them of the untrustworthy nature of the government and its agents. Given the persistent scandals that characterized the Clinton and Bush years, there seems to be no change in this trend. With political mistrust so deeply entrenched in the American psyche, Hetherington (1998) has found that "rather than simply a reflection of dissatisfaction with political leaders, declining trust is a powerful cause of this dissatisfaction" (791). The end result of entrenched mistrust is "a political environment in which it is more difficult for leaders to succeed" (802).

For African Americans, low levels of trust are more common than in the general population for various reasons related to historical and contemporary disagreements between blacks and the government (Abramson 1983). Examining political efficacy and trust among black students in the seventies, Abramson (1972) found that black children "tend to have lower feelings of political effectiveness" and "lower feelings of trust toward political leaders" (1273) than their white counterparts. Examining the attitudes of African American adults during this same period, Aberbach and Walker (1970b) found that distrust among lower-educated blacks was related to the perceptions of discrimination, but distrust among blacks with more education was based more abstractly on perceptions of group-wide discrimination. These models were based on scenarios in which blacks were denied political power. Using quasi-experimental methods, Howell and Fagan (1988, 343) tested whether or not African Americans' mistrust was simply based on their perception of a political reality in which "leaders treat blacks less favorably than whites." In an attempt to assess whether or not blacks trusted the government more when there were black leaders in power who presumably would be fairer to blacks, Howell and Fagan examined trust levels among African Americans in New Orleans, a city that consistently elected African American mayors for decades prior to their study. They found that blacks exhibited more trust in government in black-led New Orleans. Additionally, Bobo and Gilliam (1990, 388) found that increased political empowerment (measured by the presence of a black mayor) "contributes to a more trusting and efficacious orientation to politics," and it "greatly increases black attentiveness to politics." Both works found that when blacks believed that the system is fairer or at least less biased, they exhibit more political trust. Given that sustained black leadership has escaped much of the country except at the local level, a change in political reality is a more abstract goal rather than an imminent possibility.

As linked fate increasingly emerged as an important explanatory variable, a certain level of distrust by African Americans was included in the way linked fate was defined. Dawson (1994) suggests that linked fate represents awareness that blacks are seen as a collective entity, and that entity has often borne the brunt of racist policies and behavior, either actively perpetuated or at best tolerated by the American government.[1] This means that blacks with an increased sense of linked fate also increasingly recognized the failure of the government to adequately and fairly address black oppression. In turn, they also were less likely to trust the government to do the right thing. However, the effects of linked fate are potentially mitigated in persistently poor black communities because "social isolation and economic distress . . . may be leading to a lack of confidence in black group effectiveness and continued class divisions" (Cohen and Dawson 1993, 288). Diminished trust of black officials and institutions may, in fact, increase government trust.

What about the relationship between distrust and Black Nationalism? In early studies of racialized ideologies, Aberbach and Walker (1970b) found that individuals who were more supportive of a racial ideology were more likely to distrust the government.[2] Although the definition used in this analysis is more refined than mere support of black militancy, it is expected that the results here will mirror their finding of less government trust by Black Nationalists. In the following analysis, trust is measured by asking respondents how often they trust the government to do the right thing. Fewer than 5% of respondents fell into the highest or lowest category, meaning they believed that they could trust the government either just about always or else never. Just over 21% felt that they could trust the government most of the time. The largest group of respondents (71.2%) reported that they could trust the government just some of the time. Respondents were assigned a score of 4 if they reported trusting the government just about always and 1 if they never trusted the government.

Similar to the models used at the end of the previous chapter, this model includes standard SES variables such as education, income, gender, and age. As income and education variables increase, so do actual income and education. Gender is coded as a dichotomous variable in which females are assigned a score of 1 and males are scored as 0. Age is also a dichotomous variable, with those respondents between the ages of 18 and 34 coded as 1 and everyone else coded as 0. A region variable is included in which individuals residing in the South are assigned a score of 1 and everyone else is given a score of 0. One measure reports raw percentages of both the poverty rate and the number of African Americans living in individual respondents' census tracts. The perceived race of the interviewer is included, and respondents who believed that they were being interviewed by a white interviewer are scored as 1.

The model includes variables related to African American attitudes about race and the status of blacks. For example, raw feeling thermometer scores for both blacks and whites are included, and high scores denote positive affect. Measures for religiosity and political church attendance are important behavioral and psychological resources for black Americans and their political evaluations and decisions. A high score on the religiosity measure means that religion is not important to respondents' lives. A high score on political church attendance means that respondents attend a church that is very political. Finally, respondents are asked whether they think that blacks will ever achieve full equality and if they are better or worse off economically than whites. High scores on these items represent a belief blacks will never achieve full equality and that they are worse off economically than whites.

These results indicate that very few factors determine individual levels of trust for African Americans. Both traditional ideology and the race-specific ideology of interest here fail to achieve statistical significance. However, respondents who perceived their interviewer to be white exhibited increased political trust. The degree of openness in the political opportunity structure turns out to be quite important. Those respondents who believe that blacks will never achieve full equality were also more likely to say that they never trust the government. The finding of the significance of perceived race of the interviewer is no surprise. What is demonstrated here and elsewhere is that an individual's belief that he or she is talking to someone of a different race has a profound impact on responses. Additionally, if blacks believe there is no chance their racial group will ever achieve full equality and thus receive no benefits from government activities, they will be less likely to trust the government to do what is right.

A second component of political alienation is a lack of political efficacy. Individuals who feel politically efficacious believe the government and politicians are concerned about their political preferences and that they can potentially influence how the government is run. Political efficacy plays an important role in individual decisions to participate in the political process. Scholars suggest that those African Americans who have

TABLE 6.1
OLS Model of the Political Trust

Variables	β	SE	Significance
Education	-.036	.024	.140
Income	.009	.015	.523
Age (18–34 Dummy= 1)	-.029	.072	.686
Gender (Female=1)	-.0007	.071	.993
Region (South =1)	.110	.073	.136
Black Nationalist Index	-.017	.039	.671
Liberal/ Conservative Ideology	.0003	.018	.987
Linked Fate	-.012	.033	.700
% Poverty	-.0001	.004	.973
% Black	.0009	.001	.407
Feeling Thermometer: Blacks	.0004	.002	.852
Feeling Thermometer: Whites	.0005	.002	.775
Perceived Race of the Interviewer	**.128**	**.076**	**.092[b]**
Economic Position of Blacks vs. Whites	-.023	.028	.406
Will Blacks Ever Achieve Full Equality	**-.104**	**.038**	**.007****
Religiosity	-.059	.043	.170
Political Church Attendance	-.008	.032	.791
Constant	2.646	.312	.000
Adjusted R²	**.025**		
N	**295**		

Significant variables are in bold type.
** Indicates significance at $p < .01$ level.
[b] Indicates significance at $p < .10$ level.

a strong sense of linked fate also tend to demonstrate a high level of political efficacy and mistrust (Shingles 1981). Additionally, blacks whose social and political expectations have been met should be more likely to feel that they can influence the system—thus better-educated and wealthier blacks should feel more efficacious. Again, Cohen and Dawson (1993) are instructive here. They have demonstrated that African Americans who live in persistently poor areas perceive that certain political activities are more efficacious even though they are less likely to engage in such behavior. Last, there should be a significant relationship between Black Nationalism and level of political efficacy. Because Nationalists see the American political system as a source of persecution and hostility, they should be less likely to believe public officials care what they think and that they as individuals have a say in what the government does.

Two items are used to assess the relationship between political efficacy and Black Nationalism. First, respondents are asked whether or not public officials were responsive. A high score on this item is assigned to those who believe public officials care what respondents think, and a low score is given to those respondents who believe politicians do not care about their concerns. Nearly equal percentages of respondents moderately agree (29.9%) and moderately disagree (29.5%) with the statement "Public officials don't care what people like me think." These two categories represent the largest group of respondents. Second, respondents are asked whether or not they have a say about what the government does. This has to do with individual respondents' beliefs about their own ability to influence the system. Approximately 30% of respondents disagree strongly with the statement "People like me don't have a say about what the government does." The largest group of respondents strongly believe that they have the power to influence government actions; the next largest subset falls into the somewhat disagree category. Hence, more than half of the sample believes that they have some degree of influence over the government. Alternatively, very few respondents fall into the neutral category, and 40% feel that they have little power to influence the government. A high score on this item is assigned to respondents who believe they have an influence on what the government does, and a low score represents the opposite. The explanatory variables in these models are specified in the same way as the previous model and are discussed in the paragraph preceding that table. The results of this analysis are reported together in table 6.2 to facilitate comparison of the types of efficacy on government activity.

Two variables related to beliefs about the relationship of blacks to American society proved to be significant. First, the variable we are most interested in—the Black Nationalist Index—is statistically significant. There is a positive relationship between BNI score and beliefs about government responsiveness. In this sample, Black Nationalist respondents are less likely to believe government officials care about what people like them think. Second, African Americans who believe that black people will eventually achieve full equality are more likely to believe public officials also care what they think. This is an intuitive finding in that blacks who believe equality is inevitable should believe elected officials will work toward this goal, thus working toward their benefit.

TABLE 6.2
OLS Model of Political Efficacy

Variables	Political Responsiveness		Personal Influence	
	β (SE)	Significance	β (SE)	Significance
Education	.013 (.725)	.816	.088 (.062)	.152
Income	**.061 (.036)**	**.085b**	.017 (.039)	.664
Age (18–34 Dummy = 1)	.140 (.166)	.400	.162 (.180)	.369
Gender (Female = 1)	.036 (.166)	.825	.088 (.181)	.627
Region (South = 1)	.008 (.171)	.961	**.364 (.185)**	**.050***
Black Nationalist Index	**.206 (.091)**	**.025***	**.198 (.099)**	**.047***
Liberal/Conservative Ideology	.004 (.042)	.916	.068 (.045)	.129
Linked Fate	.041 (.076)	.593	.030 (.083)	.715
% Poverty	-.012 (.010)	.200	.002 (.011)	.885
% Black	-.002 (.003)	.339	.002 (.003)	.417
Feeling Thermometer: Blacks	.002 (.004)	.625	.005 (.005)	.284
Feeling Thermometer: Whites	-.001 (.004)	.719	.00008 (.005)	.987
Perceived Race of the Interviewer	**.346 (.176)**	**.051***	.008 (.181)	.561
Economic Position of Blacks vs. Whites	-.011 (.064)	.866	-.062 (.069)	.377
Will Blacks Ever Achieve Full Equality	**-.229 (.088)**	**.010***	**-.235 (.095)**	**.015***
Religiosity	**-.161 (.096)**	**.094b**	.130 (.105)	.218
Political Church Attendance	.024 (.075)	(.750)	.089 (.082)	.277
Constant	**2.431 (.725)**	**.001**	1.361 (.789)	.086
Adjusted R²	.058		.049	
N	293		296	

Significant results are in bold type.
** Indicates significance at $p < .01$ level.
* Indicates significance at the $p < .05$ level.
b Indicates significance at $p < .10$ level.

There are also several variables that significantly impact individual perceptions of political responsiveness. The first significant finding is that as respondents' family income increases, so does respondents' sense of efficacy. Wealthier individuals are more likely to believe that public officials are responsive to their political preferences. This relates to Aberbach and Walker's (1970b) assertion that when political expectations, in this case a prosperous economic return, are met, individuals are more likely to trust the government to act according to their interests. The presence of a white

interviewer, as in other analyses, is a significant predictor of individual response. Those respondents who believe that a white person was interviewing them were more likely to report that public officials care what people
like them think. Religiosity also serves as an important political variable
for African Americans. Respondents for whom religion is important also
strongly agree that public officials care what they think. Religiosity may be
significant because of the role it plays in the development of social capital
for African Americans. Verba et al. (1993, 491) have found that African
Americans receive more participatory benefits from church because they
are more likely to attend church, affiliate with Protestant churches that
give them the chance to practice civic skills, and receive more exposure to
political stimuli in church. Increased participatory skills and political engagement should also lead to a belief that those skills are taken seriously
by officials and policy makers.

The second aspect of political efficacy assesses whether or not respondents believe they (and people like them) have a say in what the government does. This particular measure captures individual beliefs about the
ability to impact government actions. There are fewer significant variables
related to respondents' scores on this item. First, like political responsiveness, positioning on the BNI is significantly related to political efficacy.
Black Nationalists feel they have less say about government activity, and
rejection of Black Nationalism as well as feelings about the potential for
equality significant increase respondents' belief that they can influence
the government. Belief in eventual equality requires a certain level of
optimism, which is also related to belief in the ability to effect political
change. The historical rhetoric and these data suggest that Black Nationalists do not hold optimism for the government's willingness (and, thus,
ability) to create a more equal society.

Like the results for political responsiveness, respondents who believe
blacks will achieve full equality also believe they can influence government actions. Last, region is significantly related to feelings of personal
influence. Southern blacks are more likely to believe that they can impact government activities, which might be related to the fact that blacks
are often more concentrated in the South. Southern blacks may feel a
greater sense of efficacy because membership in a concentrated group
should lead to more political leverage, resulting in both more personal
and group efficacy.[3] This is also bolstered by a stronger sense of empowerment due to greater political representation in terms of black elected
officials and other civic leaders (Bobo and Gilliam 1990). Overall, we are

able to determine the importance of Black Nationalism in determining political efficacy. Black Nationalists in the NBES are like Black Nationalist women in chapter 2 who, when talking about whether their votes count, jokingly mention that they are not sure where the government is hiding their votes. In this case, they are participating in the political process, but their belief in their ability to influence government and make politicians responsive is undermined by both historical accounts and long-standing lack of government trust.

Ideology and Support for Government Effort

Black self-help is a cornerstone of Black Nationalism. An unhealthy dependence on whites, in general, and the American government, in particular, resulted in negative self-images among blacks. Therefore, Black Nationalists strongly encourage blacks to work as an independent collective to shore up black communities. The relationship between ideology and support for self-help is tested by examining attitudes about the level of effort the government should exert to help blacks versus blacks helping themselves. A high score on this measure indicates that respondents believe blacks should help themselves; a low score represents the belief the government should make an effort to help blacks. The results are reported in table 6.3.

Because black self-help is a key component in Black Nationalist ideology, Black Nationalists should be less likely to believe the government should do more to help blacks. Additionally, this should be the case because Black Nationalists also believe the government will not make any sincere efforts to help blacks. In many ways, beliefs about the government's role in helping any group are clearly tied to individual adherence to liberal-conservative ideology. Conservatives are more likely to support individual self-help rather than government intervention. Given previous findings in this chapter, it also seems that those respondents who believe blacks will never achieve full equality should also be less supportive of government help for blacks. The results are reported in table 6.3.

As predicted, conservative blacks are more supportive of the position that blacks should help themselves rather than the government doing more to help blacks. This position aligns squarely with conservative support for low levels of government intervention into the daily lives of citizens coupled with strong support for rewards garnered from individual effort. Another significant finding is the role of linked fate in predicting

TABLE 6.3
OLS Model of Opinion on Government Effort Scale

Variables	β	Standard Error	Significance
Education	.040	.091	.660
Income	.036	.058	.536
Age (18–34 Dummy = 1)	-.409	.271	.133
Gender (Female = 1)	-.439	.271	.108
Region (South = 1)	.282	.283	.320
Black Nationalist Index	.014	.160	.928
Liberal/Conservative Ideology	**.154**	**.068**	**.026***
Linked Fate	**.334**	**.129**	**.010***
% Poverty	-.004	.017	.804
% Black	.002	.004	.696
Feeling Thermometer: Blacks	**-.013**	**.008**	**.090[b]**
Feeling Thermometer: Whites	-.002	.007	.807
Perceived Race of the Interviewer	-.204	.290	.482
Economic Position of Blacks vs. Whites	-.040	.107	.711
Will Blacks Ever Achieve Full Equality	.021	.146	.887
Religiosity	-.108	.180	.547
Political Church Attendance	.0007	.126	.996
Constant	**3.487**	**1.234**	**.005**
Adjusted R²	**.044**		
N	**254**		

Significant variables are in bold type.
** Indicates significance at $p < .01$ level.
* Indicates significance at $p < .05$ level.
[b] indicates significance at $p < .10$ level.

level of support for government help versus black self-help. People who feel less connected to other blacks also believe that blacks should help themselves. Blacks who demonstrate less group-based thinking should be less supportive of group-based policies by the government. Finally, negative affective evaluations of other blacks make blacks more likely to endorse the position that blacks should help themselves. This finding connects to previous findings related to employing black blame as a reason for negative outcomes in the black community. In many ways, these findings represent a confluence of interrelated positions. Self-identified

Black Conservatives are marginalized in the black community in many ways. They are often seen as racially inauthentic and as possessing strong negative sentiments toward their own group (Dillard 2001). The BNI does not achieve statistical significance. Interestingly, support for community-based self-help efforts is a point of convergence for Black Conservatives and Black Nationalists. Conservatives see self-help as a road map to ending racial hostility, whereas Black Nationalists see it as the path to black independence. Like Black Conservatives, blacks with less group consciousness endorse self-help in the Washingtonian sense. Blacks should develop their social and economic mettle through hard work and individual effort as a pathway to full citizen rights.

Unfortunately, the BNI fails to achieve statistical significance in relation to black self-help. It seems that other factors are more important in predicting support for government intervention in improving the lives of black Americans. Conservatism is a primary determinant of whether or not respondents support government efforts to help blacks over blacks helping themselves. One factor that is a significant determinant of support for black self-help is negative affect toward blacks. Arguing that negative affective evaluations serve as a proxy for black blame, those respondents who engaged in more black blame were less supportive of group-based initiatives to change the status of blacks.

Ideology and Political Parties

High efficacy and issue support should lead to more civic engagement and political involvement. Political parties have been a traditional venue for civic engagement; however, Americans today are less attached to political parties than ever. With the rise of candidates who are able to field competitive campaigns outside the party structure and increased cynicism toward the government and its actors, contemporary scholars are examining the relevance of modern political parties. Wattenberg (1996) has suggested that the decline of political parties represents a movement toward neutrality. Americans have moved toward partisan independence because of dissatisfaction with party institutions. Also arguing that partisanship has declined, Craig (1985) asserts that "high levels of partisan independence" are the result of "changing attitudes about the institutions of political parties" (75). Craig suggests that voters will not return their loyalties to traditional party structures unless party leaders "engender confidence." Alternatively, African Americans have demonstrated strong loyalty to the

Democratic Party since the 1960s, but Katherine Tate (1996) found that the strength of this attachment (although still higher than that of the general population) was lower than it had been in the 1984 and 1988 panels of the National Black Election Study. Nevertheless, any dissatisfaction with Democrats has not yielded less party dominance in terms of black voting. This section examines two party-related questions. First, it asks whether partisanship strength is impacted by ideological orientations. Are Nationalists, who opt for weaker attachments to American institutions, also more likely to exhibit weaker party attachments? Second, it examines the relationship between Black Nationalist ideology and endorsement of a black third party.

Turning first to partisan strength, a measure is created in which strong partisans from either party are assigned the same score, moderate partisans are placed in a middle category, and independents are grouped together. In this party strength measure, a low score is assigned to those respondents who were self-reported independents, and a high score is assigned to strong partisans, almost all of whom were Democrats, of course. In relation to Black Nationalism, it is expected that Black Nationalists will exhibit weaker partisan strength. Party loyalty requires an implicit endorsement of the system as a whole. The previous OLS models are also employed here for comparison of predictive ability across multiple independent variables. The results, presented in table 6.4, indicate that numerous factors push respondents toward independence. The majority of these factors are conventional SES variables such as education levels, age, and gender. Additionally, religiosity and neighborhood context prove to be statistically significant. The index measuring Black Nationalism falls well short of statistical significance. Traditional liberalism-conservatism comes closer to significance, but it too falls far short.

These findings demonstrate the tendency for the least-educated participants in the sample to also exhibit the weakest attachment to the two main parties. Additionally, the youngest cohort (18–34) is more likely to self-report as independents rather than having strong or even moderate party attachments. This finding is not surprising given the fact that the youngest voters are also the least politically developed or entrenched in a party tradition. Women exhibit the strongest partisan ties. Black women have been found to be more politically participatory and knowledgeable than their male counterparts (Verba, Schlozman, and Brady 1995); in addition, black women turn out to vote at greater rates than black men. In 1996, the year the NBES was conducted, 50% of black women voted, as

TABLE 6.4
OLS Model of Partisan Strength

Variables	β	Standard Error	Significance
Education	**-.086**	**.032**	**.007***
Income	-.004	.020	.828
Age (18–34 Dummy = 1)	**-.188**	**.092**	**.042***
Gender (Female = 1)	**.194**	**.093**	**.037***
Region (South = 1)	.108	.096	.262
Black Nationalist Index	.005	.051	.922
Liberal/Conservative Ideology	-.035	.023	.125
Linked Fate	-.015	.042	.721
% Poverty	**-.010**	**.006**	**.083[b]**
% Black	.002	.001	.167
Feeling Thermometer: Blacks	-.0002	.002	.941
Feeling Thermometer: Whites	.001	.002	.545
Perceived Race of the Interviewer	-.105	.100	.295
Economic Position of Blacks vs. Whites	-.011	.036	.764
Will Blacks Ever Achieve Full Equality	.004	.049	.933
Religiosity	**-.167**	**.059**	**.005***
Political Church Attendance	.005	.042	.902
Constant	**3.044**	**.404**	**.000**
Adjusted R²	**.081**		
N	**283**		

Significant variables are in bold type.
** Indicates significance at $p < .01$ level.
* Indicates significance at $p < .05$ level.
[b] indicates significance at $p < .10$ level.

opposed to 42% of black men ("Voting Trends" 2000). In the 2008 primary election cycle, black women were courted because of their significant representation in state Democratic parties across the South (Sinclair and Price 2008). Respondents who reside in wealthier areas also boast more independent voters. Cohen and Dawson (1993) note that voter mobilization efforts play an important role in increasing turnout in poorer areas. The Democratic Party and its allies overwhelmingly support these efforts. Thus, it would make sense that the least educated, who also tend to be less wealthy, are inclined toward strong Democratic Party loyalty. Also, more educated people tend to be more aware of news and events and better able to critically scrutinize party rhetoric.[4] Consistent with other political attitudes and behaviors, the importance of religion to respondents significantly influences strength of party loyalty. People who see religion as important in their lives are more likely to support independent candidates and parties.

An additional way to examine individual perceptions of parties is through support for third parties. The structure of the American political system prevents the development of sustained third parties; however, during some periods in history, major parties become vulnerable and withered away, or new parties have developed to address crucial cleavages and gained popular support (Rosenstone, Behr, and Lazarus 1984). During the Civil Rights Movement, voting was viewed as the backbone of full citizenship and political influence, and there were efforts to change the nature of party politics in America. Organizations such as the Mississippi Freedom Democratic Party and the Black Democrats broke down the segregated delegate selection process. During the Black Power era, there were also attempts to form an independent third party (Johnson 2007). This effort led to more political influence for blacks in the Democratic Party because of Democratic desire to hold on to blacks as core members of their electoral coalition as a replacement for the loss of southern whites. In many ways, this expansion of black partisan influence was epitomized by the candidacies of Jesse Jackson in 1984 and 1988 (Reed 1986; Walters 1988; Tate 1991). Given the success of candidates in recent elections who have worked outside of the party system (often relying on personal funding as a campaign source) and the popularity of the Reform Party in the 1990s, third parties may seem a more viable avenue for influencing the political system.

Respondents were asked whether they supported the formation of a black third party. Those respondents who supported a third party were assigned a score of 1; those who did not were assigned a score of 0. One-third of respondents approved the formation of a black party, and two-thirds were opposed. Citizens who are least involved in politics and exhibit the least political experience should be more likely to take on new party attachments. Therefore, younger respondents should be more likely to endorse a black third party. Additionally, moderate Black Nationalists who support only partial withdrawal might prefer an independent third party because it invokes greater solidarity among blacks in general. Overall, Black Nationalists should be more likely to endorse the formation of a third party because it fosters black independence by breaking from traditional, majority-white parties. Having a strong sense of linked fate should lead individuals to endorse an all-black third party as well.

From the results in table 6.5, we get a clear sense of which groups support the formation of an independent black party. First, the measure of interest here, Black Nationalist subscription, leads to greater support for a black third party. Forming a separate party represents a move toward greater self-determination and independent influence on the political process; consequently, Black Nationalists should be more supportive of a separate black party. Like many arguments offered by moderate Black Nationalists in the focus groups, third-party strategies allow blacks to withdraw somewhat from the political process without forfeiting all stakes. This was demonstrated by efforts in the 1970s to formulate a cohesive black political agenda around which the black community could coalesce and leverage political benefits from the two major parties. The efforts to form a viable third party reached their pinnacle with the National Black Political Convention in Gary, Indiana, in 1972. This convention was composed of delegates from across the United States and included elected officials, artists, activists, and ordinary citizens. In that same year, Shirley Chisholm's bid for the Democratic presidential nomination also galvanized the African American community politically.[5] In recent years, political commentator Tavis Smiley has convened a series of town hall meetings to discuss important social and political struggles in the black community. In the best-sellers that developed directly out of those meetings, *The Covenant with Black America* (2006) and *The Covenant in Action* (2007), Smiley and a collection of scholars, policy makers, and activists have highlighted the issues they consider important to the black community and have worked toward developing an action plan for eliminating or diminishing the impact of various policies and practices that challenge black progress.[6]

Additionally, those respondents with less education are more supportive of a black third party. More highly educated blacks may be more knowledgeable about the nature of the political system and the lack of viability of most third parties; hence, it would follow that they are less likely to support efforts to create a third party. This could also be related to the fact that less-educated blacks demonstrate lower levels of attachment to the two traditional parties, which makes them ripe for cultivation by any new party. Like respondents with less education, the youngest respondents also have less attachment to political parties and are more supportive of

TABLE 6.5
OLS Model of Support for a Black Third Party

Variables	β	Standard Error	Significance
Education	**-.035**	**.019**	**.071**[b]
Income	-.018	.012	.136
Age (18–34 Dummy = 1)	**.166**	**.056**	**.003***
Gender (Female = 1)	.016	.056	.782
Region (South = 1)	**-.153**	**.057**	**.008***
Black Nationalist Index	**-.084**	**.031**	**.008***
Liberal/Conservative Ideology	.004	.014	.774
Linked Fate	-.035	.026	.171
% Poverty	**-.006**	**.003**	**.099**[b]
% Black	-.0005	.001	.598
Feeling Thermometer: Blacks	.002	.002	.181
Feeling Thermometer: Whites	-.0009	.001	.528
Perceived Race of the Interviewer	-.034	.059	.561
Economic Position of Blacks vs. Whites	**-.041**	**.022**	**.063**[b]
Will Blacks Ever Achieve Full Equality	-.011	.030	.710
Religiosity	-.009	.032	.786
Political Church Attendance	-.010	.026	.705
Constant	**1.211**	**.245**	**.000**
Adjusted R²	**.102**		
N	**281**		

Significant variables are in bold type.
** Indicates significance at $p < .01$ level.
* Indicates significance at $p < .05$ level.
[b] indicates significance at $p < .10$ level.

a black third party. Arguments about education resonate with younger respondents as well, since younger people are also often less politically knowledgeable and have had fewer opportunities to participate in ways that reinforce party loyalty. Nonsoutherners and residents of more afflu-ent communities are also more supportive of a black third party. Although the actual numbers of respondents who believe that blacks are better off economically than whites are small, those who do are also more likely to support a black third party.

Ideology and Political Participation

In the last few decades, there has been a general decline in levels of political participation in America. In his now famous thesis, Robert Putnam (1995a, 1995b, 2000) argues that political participation has waned because of a lack of civic engagement in organizations of any kind. According to Putnam, Americans choose to "bowl alone" rather than engage in activities that increase social capital and ultimately encourage political involvement.[7] Social capital is important because it helps citizens gain the skills and impetus required to become involved in politics. Since the 1960s, decreased civic voluntarism and party loyalties have been coupled with declining voter turnout. Americans simply do not go out to the voting booths as much as they did in the past. Abramson and Aldrich (1982) note, "The combined effect of the decline in partisan strength and the decline in beliefs about government responsiveness appears to account for between two-thirds and seven-tenths of the decline in presidential turnout" (519).

Although voting does not represent the only form of political participation, it is seen as especially important because it is viewed as a simple, low-cost, one-shot effort to participate. Thus, individuals should be more inclined to turn out to vote even if they do not engage in more high-cost political activities. Traditional SES variables go far in predicting turnout. However, Verba, Schlozman, and Brady (1995) note that while SES models do "an excellent job of predicting political participation, SES models fail to specify the mechanisms linking statuses to activities" (272). Those links could include psychological attachments such as ideology, economic outlook, and religiosity. Understanding why some people vote and others do not has become particularly important given the closeness of recent presidential elections and slim majorities in the U.S. Congress.

African Americans play a pivotal role in swaying elections. As other groups that have traditionally voted in blocs continue to disintegrate (e.g., unions), African Americans remain a core source of support for the Democratic Party. As for other groups, African American levels of participation have decreased. The Associated Press reported that "black turnout was just over 52 percent in 1964 and was just over 46 percent [in 1996]" ("Voting Trends" 2000). Timpone (1998) found that in the 1980s, controlling for other political factors such as partisanship and SES status, African Americans registered more but turned out less. Some factors that are important in explaining black political participation are different than for other racial or ethnic groups. The first, and most studied, is that of linked fate. Group closeness is a strong catalyst for political participation. In addition, Leighley and Vedlitz (1999) find that feelings of intergroup proximity are also important in determining whether blacks participate. Blacks who feel more distant from other races are less likely to participate. Bobo and Gilliam (1990) find that blacks participate at similar rates as whites from comparable backgrounds and more than their white counterparts when they are empowered.

Examining voting is a narrow and incomplete way of examining participation. This is especially true for African Americans, who have been barred from the voting process for the great majority of their time in the United States. Consequently, it is more fruitful to examine the role of ideology in predicting varied political participation. Respondents are asked whether they contacted a public official or agency, whether they signed a petition, whether they attended a protest meeting or demonstration, and whether they participated in picketing, a boycott, or a sit-in in the last five years.[8] Initially, it seemed that combining mainstream forms of political participation such as contacting a public official, low-effort political behavior such as signing a petition, and nontraditional forms of political participation such as picketing and sit-ins might be misguided because of the variation in the types of activities. Further analysis demonstrates that these items are related in important ways. Three decades ago, participating in sit-ins essentially revolutionized American politics and increased responsiveness to civil rights demands. In the current political climate of terrorism and biological warfare, however, these behaviors appear quite tame. Tarrow (1997) has suggested that we now live in a movement society, in which tactics and organizing principles once seen as radical are now commonplace. Given the changing definition of "acceptable or appropriate" political participation, it is still important to note that protest activities in the form of picketing, sit-ins, and boycotts consistently yielded the lowest correlation to the other items and the weakest loadings in the factor analysis. Table 6.6 examines the correlation between these factors. First, the items are both significantly and positively correlated with one another. As the propensity to participate in one of these activities increases, so does the propensity to engage in other activities.

Combining these items to create a reliable index allows us to speak to a broader range of political activities beyond turnout. The Chronbach alpha coefficient was .657, which means an additive index of these items represent a cohesive measure of one phenomenon—in this case, propensity to

TABLE 6.6
Correlation Matrix of Four Items Used in Political Participation Measure

	Contacted a Public official or Agency	Signed a Petition	Attended a Protest Meeting/ Demonstration	Picket, Boycott, sit-in
Contacted a Public Official	1.00			
Signed a Petition	.454**	1.00		
Attended a Protest Meeting/ Demonstration	.380**	.348**	1.00	
Picket, Boycott, sit-in	.239**	.231**	.284**	1.00

** Indicates significance at the $p < .01$ levels.

TABLE 6.7
Factor Analysis of Political Participation Index Items
(Extraction Method: Principal Component Method)

Scale Items	Principal Component
Contacted a Public Official or Agency	.765
Signed a Petition	.740
Attended a Protest Meeting/ Demonstration	.726
Picket, Boycott, Sit-in	.568
Variance Explained	**49.5%**

participate in politics. Last, these items were subjected to a factor analysis using principal component analysis and are reported in table 6.7. This analysis suggests one underlying factor accounts for 49.5% of the variance among these items.

So, it is justifiable to combine these items in a five-point, additive index ranging from 0 to 4. A score of 0 means the respondent performed none of these four political activities; alternatively, a score of 4 means the respondent performed all of these activities. Most respondents fall on the low end of this participation index. More than one-third (39.3%) of the respondents reported participating in none of these activities. At the other end of the spectrum, only 4.2% participated in all these activities. Now, returning to Black Nationalism, the goal is to understand the relationship between ideological adherence and political participation.

Since all these political activities involve making demands on and attempting to adjust the current structure of the political system, it is hypothesized that Non-Nationalists would be significantly more likely to engage in these behaviors. Conversely, Black Nationalists, who are more likely to reject the American political system and see it as inflexible and unfair, are significantly less likely to make political demands. Thus, the BNI measure should be both significantly and positively related to political participation. This model is very similar to ones used previously, and all variables are coded the same. The only new variable is a measure for respondents who reported attending a political church. A high score on this measure indicates that the respondents' church strongly encourages its members to get involved in political activity. Alternatively, a low score is indicative of a church that does not encourage political activity.[9] Rejecters of Black Nationalism believe demands can be made on the system that will result in change, and the full incorporation of blacks into the political system is optimal. Thus, Black Nationalists should be less engaged and politically active. The results of this model are reported in table 6.8.

The BNI measure is not statistically significant. The BNI coefficient moves in the expected direction, which demonstrates that as individuals become more supportive of Black Nationalism, their level of political activity decreases, but the relationship is not strong enough to be significant. Consistent with traditional findings related to political participation, both education and income are significantly related to the level of political participation. Respondents with more education and those in higher income brackets are more likely to engage in multiple and varied forms of political participation as measured by the Political Participation Index. Additionally, decreased belief in linked fate also diminishes political participation. Blacks who reside outside of the South are more politically active. Finally, respondents who attended places of worship that encourage political participation are significantly more likely to be politically active. All these findings are consistent with conventional wisdom about what factors impact individual decisions to become involved in politics.

The fact that the BNI is not significantly related to political participation is contrary to the theory posited here. Although black opinion is laced with various levels of support for Black Nationalist ideology, blacks do not use those tenets as primary justifications for deciding to engage

TABLE 6.8
OLS Model of the Impact of Black Nationalism on Political Participation

Variables	β	Standard Error	Significance
Education	**.223**	**.044**	**.000****
Income	**.005**	**.027**	**.050**
Age	.004	.005	.404
Gender	.003	.133	.796
Region	**-.249**	**.133**	**.061b**
Integrationist/Nationalist Index	.009	.071	.198
Linked Fate	**-.122**	**.059**	**.040***
% Poverty	-.009	.008	.908
% Black	-.003	.002	.892
Feeling Thermometer: Blacks	.005	.003	.174
Feeling Thermometer: Whites	-.005	.003	.152
Perceived Race of the Interviewer	-.172	.136	.209
Economic Position of Blacks vs. Whites	-.005	.050	.348
Will Blacks Ever Achieve Full Equality	-.002	.070	.750
Political Church Attendance	**.216**	**.059**	**.000****
Constant	-.008	.576	.883
Adjusted R²	**.206**		
N	318		

Significant variables are in bold type.
** Indicates significance at $p < .01$ level.
* Indicates significance at $p < .05$ level.
b indicates significance at $p < .10$ level.

in political activity. When asked directly, it is obvious that members of the focus groups struggle with these ideological constructs and with the ambivalence they feel toward the American government and their own community. In analysis of the NBES data, there was no way to ask these kinds of questions directly. An indirect measure was created, and individual respondents were assigned an ideological attachment based on their response to items used in the BNI. This measure forces individuals into ideological categories through indirect measurement. This demonstrates that blacks are similar to others Americans in that they do not make explicit connections between separate attitudes and broad ideologies. Thus, glimpses of individual ideological components can be detected, but there is very little sense that these components are constrained to consciously form strong ideological support. This lack of constraint then renders this measure, at least in its current formulation, unable to significantly move beyond association to actual prediction.

Conclusion

After extensive analysis of attitudes and behaviors, Black Nationalism as measured by the Black Nationalist Index proves to have a significant impact on some measures of public opinion and political behavior. Respondents who reject Black Nationalism trust the government to act in ways that benefit them and similar others. They also exhibit higher political efficacy. Conversely, Nationalists exhibit lower political efficacy and less political trust. On the surface, it appears Nationalists should then be less inclined to participate. What may be demonstrated here is the outward rejection of American politics or, less extreme, disinterest by respondents who see black interests as marginal to mainstream political institutions and representatives.

Another important finding is that Nationalists are more likely to endorse the formation of an all-black third party. It has been shown here and elsewhere (Brown and Shaw 2002; Dawson 2001) that blacks do not endorse complete withdrawal from the political system. However, moderate levels of withdrawal are acceptable, even preferable, to complete racial integration. By separating from the two main parties, blacks would wield an independent advantage in the form of vote giving and withholding. Some members of the focus groups rejected full separation because it seemed to lack viability. A third party might provide a more politically comfortable distance. Additionally, Tate (1993) has demonstrated that blacks were reporting increased alienation from the Democratic Party because of perceived unfair treatment of Jesse Jackson. In the absence of an alternative (and despite increased Republican attempts to court black votes), blacks may see the formation of a third party as politically smart and necessary. It is likely, yet still untested, that the election of Barack Obama as the first African American president of the United States has shored up black Democratic support for at least another generation. Unlike Jackson's 1988 campaign, which somewhat undermined Democratic support among blacks, Obama's victory potentially solidifies support among older blacks and crystallizes support among black youth and first-time voters.

7

Dreaming Blackness: Making Sense of Support or Rejection of Separatism

In chapter 2 I began with the opening exercise of the focus group discussion; here I move to the concluding exercise of those same discussions. This exercise, which I called "Dreaming Blackness," was a way to get participants to think about and focus on what it would mean if a self-determining black nation was actually achieved. They were probed to talk about an all-black America, which did not require the rejection of American democratic principles or traditions. Nor did it require participants to take a position on emigration or speculate about potential destinations. This diminished the potential for their disagreement with the formation of a separate nation on the basis of negative assessments of a particular destination. By leaving those kinds of considerations up to participants, I was attempting to create a space in which they could consider the notions of separation and self-determination. They merely had to talk about what it would mean if a political structure was led, governed, and inhabited solely by African Americans.

Ultimately, this exercise illuminated more than participants' views of separatism. While outlining their vision of this mythical black America, participants also provided insight into their current views of the African American community. In some ways, we get a sideways glance into the racial imagination of participants by asking them to create something new. They directly expressed sentiments about collective ability and about solutions to and prospects for future problems. Further, we learn more about participants' opinions about the current state of the American government and perceptions of where blacks fit in it.

Complete and total separation is, for some, the most difficult and most extreme measure blacks could take to solve race problems. Dawson (2001) found that only 14% of black respondents endorsed a separate black nation. In the course of these focus group discussions, no one ever actually proposed this as a potential strategy; this was also demonstrated by Brown and Shaw (2002). To get a sense of overall beliefs about separatism, participants were asked to complete an exercise. At the end of each session, each participant was asked to speak about his or her reactions to the idea of an all-black America. I asked participants to describe what such an America would look like or be like to them.

How responses were formulated was left up to the individual. Participants were able to take a utopian view of black America, a realistic view based on current conditions within the United States and the black community, or a fantastical view in which they could create a recipe of what their black America would look like. Of course, some participants were vehemently opposed to the idea, and some supported it wholeheartedly; the views of others were muddier. Through participants' words you can hear echoes of Maria Stewart, Marcus Garvey, and others who felt the push and pull effect created by black struggle. Also reverberating in these spaces were the arguments of Frederick Douglass and others who, like contemporary black citizens, sought to make good on "the promissory note to which all Americans was to fall heir" that King talked about in his "I Have a Dream Speech" in 1963.

Before asking focus group participants what an all-black America meant to them, it was hard to predict what they would say. As the moderator, I often made silent guesses about who would support the idea and who would reject it out of hand. These guesses were not always completely accurate; in fact, sometimes they were flat-out wrong. As an African American, I had my own views about the viability, necessity, and potential structure of my black America, though I tried not to let it influence the tenor of the group discussions. For the most part, this question intrigued participants, most of whom were surprisingly eager to speculate about it. Indeed, they were not only eager to offer their opinions, positive, negative, or cautious; they seemed to be equally fascinated by and attentive to the comments of their fellow group members.

These conversations are enlightening for several reasons. First, through these discussions we are able to get a clear sense of what African Americans think of separatism beyond an up or down vote in large surveys. We know that when African Americans are given the choice of simply yes or no, they consistently choose no. This is true in both opinion polls and their own actions. Large groups of blacks are not leaving the United

States en masse for any destination, though many now have the resources to do so. Periodically, there have been isolated cases of artists and writers expatriating; more recently, noted activist and TransAfrica founder, Randall Robinson, left the United States as a result of racial frustration and disillusionment (Robinson 2004). However, when they are allowed to develop and justify a position, fewer (though still a majority) offer an outright rejection. Instead, they offer conditions that reflect hope of what an all-black America could be and fear of what it might be, suggesting that, when probed, participants are thoughtfully considering the state of the black community, its relationship to broader America, and the proper social and political course for black people to take.

Because this was an unstructured exercise, evaluations of the black community used to justify answers were particularly telling. Participants took stock of their racial group members and, when they found them lacking, it was difficult to support withdrawal. But participants' decisions were based on more than just in-group difficulties; they rejected withdrawal as a strategy because they supported the goal and ultimate benefits of diversity. Whether it was the melting pot, the salad bowl, or spicy soup, they invoked metaphors of racial integration and prioritized it as the optimal social structure. Another reason these conversations were so informative was because the diagnosis of tribulations and triumphs signaled perceptions of current black problems, when matched with other opinions offered by individual respondents. The problems outlined by those who oppose an all-black America were based on specific problems that participants currently saw, especially the excessive divisions in the black community that would ultimately destroy this fictitious all-black America.

Instead of absolute rejection, other participants acknowledged contemporary issues and problematic histories and offered only conditional support for a black nation. Like those who completely rejected the notion, they saw past and present struggles and suggested that absent these experiences they probably would endorse a black America. In many ways they were making plain the concerns of Martin Delany, Henry Highland Garnet, Marcus Garvey, and others who believed blacks had been dealt a tremendous blow by slavery and the oppressive conditions following emancipation that relegated blacks to second-class status. Hence a significant amount of work needed to be done to eliminate or at least diminish the impact of past injustices; once this was accomplished, blacks could thrive on their own. Yet they did not, primarily, acknowledge the possibilities that these injustices could be repeated in this new homogeneous nation. Nor did they allow for the possibility that the psychological, social, economic, and political effects of injustice might be reversed by participating in a self-determining nation.

Interestingly, those participants who would be willing to live in an all-black America also acknowledged problems in the black community through two common threads. First, they were interested in this all-black America despite problems. They recognized problems but supported the idea that having an opportunity to try was still worthwhile, even if it was an ultimate failure. The second thread was particularly interesting because when respondents offered details of the structure of their all-black America, it was much like the current America, with blacks in power instead of whites. Rather than suggest a new system, they simply reversed the racial roles. Just as whites were in power in America, so would blacks be in an all-black America. None of them used this opportunity to speculate about changing governmental structures or removing hierarchies and standards that have been used to oppress African Americans. Later in this chapter, Delia's and Terrence's comments describe a structure that references and is very similar to existing majority-black cities where there are black mayors, businessmen, homeowners, and CEOs.

Melting Pots and Multiple Divisions: Opposition to a Black America

A high level of opposition to an all-black America is expected, given the survey results offered by Dawson's *Black Visions*. In a passage quoted in the introduction, Maria Stewart declared centuries ago that she would rather be pierced by a bayonet than be resettled in Africa or any "strange land." From the focus group evidence, we know that even the staunchest supporters of Black Nationalism supported mainstream forms of participation in the American political process like voting. All groups expressed distrust of the government, but no participants offered withdrawal from the American political system as an option. Those people who were strongly opposed to the idea of an all-black America gave three main reasons for their opposition: support for diversity, too many in-group problems, and the inability of blacks to create and sustain a nation.

First, some participants who rejected Black Nationalism were opposed to an all-black America because they truly endorsed diversity. They embraced the imagery of the great American melting pot and saw it as the optimal national character. They liked racial heterogeneity as a mechanism for diversity in thought. Neil offered an idea for what an all-black America would look like and in the end simply decided, "I think, too, I like the diversity and the melting pot aspect of America." Using a similar and oft-repeated food metaphor, Adrienne added, "It's like a pot of soup. The more stuff you put in it, the better it is. It's the spice of life—the differences. She cooks different from me. I cook different from her. We need all those things coming together." In addition, some felt the learning process that blacks and whites would undergo through continued integration was simply the way it was supposed to be. Paula offered:

> Personally I like the mix-up and with the racism and whatever is going on . . . to me, it's supposed to be happening. It's happening as it is supposed to be for a reason. It is not just by accident. It is for a learning, training, more creative process. I don't know. It is horrible. What happened to us is horrible. Racism is horrible, but for whatever reason, it is and it is for a reason. And so therefore . . . um . . . whatever experiences I have had and am having . . . I could have been raped, killed, whatever . . . apparently there is some purpose in that. And so to change the process . . . I don't know . . . I don't guess I want to be a part of that . . . I don't want to be a part of utopia. I want to be a part of this, and it's insane . . . but I know that within the insanity there is organization even though we don't see. And because we don't see it don't mean we don't participate.

It is certainly understandable that any view of a separate nation would be filtered through an American lens. After all, black Americans, in many ways, have more connection to their Americanness than to anything else. Severing those ties is obviously difficult to do. Moreover, imagining a new and different nation is a similarly difficult task. Somehow, for Paula and others, this new nation represented a "utopia." Unfortunately, they were not interested in a utopia; they were willing to remain in America despite its flaws and despite a belief that these flaws are entrenched and enduring.

A second reason for opposition to an all-black America was the belief that it would be unworkable because there are too many divisions within the black community. For these participants, racial unity is necessary for national success. Their opposition also signaled a belief that an all-black America, because of its divisions and problems, would be too similar to what currently exists in the United States to make it a viable alternative.

Melissa, who was pessimistic about the existence of any differences between current America and an all-black America, offered:

> I think it would backfire just because I have noticed from my interaction with certain black people that we are so. . . . I don't think we can prosper until we ourselves are a whole and are working toward the same thing. . . . We'd still be divided and you could send us all over and give us our own little continent [but] something's going to be wrong with it. There are still going to be the haves and have-nots. I don't think we would benefit from it at this point.

This was also echoed by Breanna, who supported the need for diversity as well but finally concluded that there is too much division and too many problems in the black community to even think about separating. For Breanna:

> There could not be a black America where we are all in unison. I just don't think that. There is too much . . . there is too much racial divide just in the black community alone. . . . There's a lot of black-on-black hate . . . just the mentality is just not there. They are not able to move forward. Like I said . . . I can organize it . . . help them go . . . not go myself.

The requirement of complete group unity would be difficult for any group or nation to meet. Indeed, a large portion of the focus group discussions emphasized group divisions of all ilks (e.g., racial, economic, geographic). One was left wondering, then, why did blacks have to achieve such high levels of cohesion? Was there a sense that other groups are more united? Were these expectations indicative of a collective sense of self-doubt? The answers to these questions were hard to determine, but it was clear that divisiveness was seen as a prevailing hindrance to black empowerment in America and in an all-black America.

As revealed by Breanna's earlier comment, some participants were passionate about the impossibility of an all-black America. For them blacks are not able to design and maintain a workable system. Again, unity became the culprit, but more than unity was at issue. A major claim posited by Black Nationalists was that blacks have succumbed to white supremacists' beliefs about black inferiority. Was this true of participants who viewed their racial group as incapable of self-governing? African American history was taken into consideration as participants took stock of the damage resulting from social and political subordination. In addition to liberating blacks from the oppressive American system, black self-hate must also be combated. Mae and other members of her group discussed this idea:

> MAE: It would be a war. I mean constant nicking and picking at folks try-
> ing to bring everybody down to your level and stuff. Everybody pulling in
> their separate ways. Doing what they best at.
> RHONDA: It would be how the beginning was. You know what I'm saying?
> MAE: I mean it would be hard . . .
> RHONDA: But knowing our record, our track record, far as being united, it
> wouldn't be a good thing at all.
> LENA: I will say this, it wouldn't last.

Whether Rhonda's and Mae's comments represented self-hate is open for debate. To be sure, they have a negative image of African Americans' interactions with one another. It is also clear that this negative perception led them to doubt the ability of blacks to self-govern. For opponents of an all-black America, there was a strong belief that, as a result of current community problems, blacks lack the tools necessary to implement and maintain a plan for nationhood. Disunity among blacks was seen as the largest obstacle, but allegiance to popular ideals that have been especially championed by multiculturalism also served as an important barrier to support for an independent black nation.

Moral Standards and Missing Histories: Conditional Support for a Black America

From the outset, respondents were allowed to imagine an all-black America in any manner they chose; however, many respondents who were open to the idea of living in such an America offered only conditional support, centered on the elimination of intraracial divisions, the ability to control who becomes a citizen, or the deletion of blacks' history of oppression. Given the current state of black people, they could not support the idea of black nationhood without ensuring that existing problems would not follow them into the new nation. Rather than dismissing the notion as entirely out of the question, like participants in the previous section, they explained how a black utopia could be created and how that utopia was shaped by their personal visions of the black community.

Given African Americans' troubled history in America, it is expected that some participants would base their endorsement of any new nation on conditional changes in the current political landscape. First, those conditions involved being able to rid this new system of any social ills that currently exist in the American political system. Shandra pointed out:

I mean, not that we are a homogeneous community, but it would be fantastic to see a community within our area that's our own. I want us to have political power. I want us to have economic power. I'm not saying . . . I mean I do agree with Henry and I disagree with Henry. There's a place for, you know, lower-class blacks, and I want to see a little bit of that. I don't mind people who are poor. I just don't want to see them bring the drugs, the guns, and the alcohol and the violence. There's always going to be guns. There's always going to be drugs. I just think that my view of black America, it should not be the predominant number of people in jail would be black people. And I think we need to find positive ways to lift our community up so that people find alternatives to all the illegal stuff. That's what my black America would look like.

Shandra set up clear moral standards and societal norms for her black America. African Americans currently engage in some undesirable behaviors that she would not want transferred to her new nation. In addition, participants offered conditions for support that were based on their ability to choose who would be able to participate in this all-black America. For instance, Nicole would support an all-black America if she "could have an all-black America that was as simple and perfect . . . well, not that my house is perfect, but as simple and noncomplex as my house, then that would be fine." This comment seemed to be another nod to the notion of unity laced throughout this exercise.

The last subset of participants who offered conditional endorsement believed that this hypothetical country would be a good idea if there were never a history of slavery and oppression. In a discussion of the impact of slavery on the viability of an all-black America, Cameron and Gina pointed to the greatest concerns. Cameron placed the blame for African America's inability to self-govern squarely on the shoulders of white supremacy and its correlate—black inferiority—embedded in the American political system. This group offered:

CAMERON: But in this country we were told or made to hate each other. We were made to hate what we represented. If you look in the mirror, that person was black. That person was negative. That person was a bad person. That kind of racism causes us to discount each other. It caused us to hate each other. It causes us to not be able to form a country where we are able to get something done. I don't think that necessarily happens in countries in Africa that didn't experience that same kind of racism. This is the worst racism, worst kind of slavery, that ever existed in the history of man.

GINA: Yeah, I think that's the difference . . . you have to make the statement . . . okay if this is an all-black country, would it be postslavery or would it be without a history of slavery, because I think a lot of our problems stem from slavery.

Making Memories and Managing Home: Supporting an All-Black America

Some participants offered enthusiastic support for the formation, possibility, or even notion of an all-black America. If nothing else, it provided an opportunity for blacks to create something new and distinctive that was free of the shortcomings participants saw in the current political system. Delia realistically thought that under current conditions things would not change, but her model of a black America would be different:

Because I think if the world was exactly the way it is now and everybody was black. I don't think that . . . not too much would change because, like Evelyn said, we have so many divisions because of the way we got to the United States has created a lot of identity crises. We don't have . . . there isn't just one black community. Now, ideally, it would be what it would it be. It would be, you know, black people in every position of power. I think it would look very much like Washington, D.C., where there's a black mayor, and people in the political positions are black, the chief of police is black, a lot of the teachers in the school are black, people wouldn't feel any fear of speaking up on an issue because, okay, is this going to be perceived as "Here's that black person again on that black issue." Or it's just going to be an issue that we need to deal with. People would be owning homes and taking responsibility for themselves and other people and other people's children. There would be economic diversity. I think it would be unique and diverse and peaceful.

Sasha, who would also eliminate undesirable societal traits and agreed with Delia's conditions, added:

> The youth of America I would love for them to be in a situation where they are around other people who are working toward a bigger goal, but I know that with the trappings of today's society it's not going to happen. It's too strong . . . it's like crack cocaine turning on the TV nowadays. You know people want that stuff . . . people think that this is what they should have in their lives . . . but if I was to have a black America it would not be about stuff like that . . . not for one moment, second, whatever . . . about just immediate gratification . . . looking good and being cool and bling-bling. No, those things wouldn't exist. We would be humanist working toward the goal of uplifting ourselves. And getting to the next level of, as far as I'm concerned, evolution because our bodies can change as much as possible, but it's our mind is what needs to change the most . . . to me it's about . . . to me . . . I would love to see it happen . . . but I know it wouldn't work. Maybe on the small scale, then it would grow and grow and grow.

Still other participants supported this all-black America because it would give blacks a chance to be in power and in important decision-making positions. Their black America was a mirror of the current America, with a role reversal. It would be an America in an alternative universe in which everything is topsy-turvy. In contrast, the alternative America would be free of racial oppression, but there was rarely any discussion of other forms of oppression. A black America as envisioned by Terrence would

> be an all-inclusive black America. Everything you see white now would be black. Black TV, black president, black bankers, black CEO . . . people would be progressive . . . black people doing what they need to do . . . you'd see us as role models all over the place . . . um . . . you know . . . black folks out here buying restaurants, running restaurants . . . everywhere you go you would see a black person in a leadership or entrepreneurial relationship . . . it would be something like that. We would be part of the game. We're not just a sideline trying to get . . . like a third-string quarterback or third-string receiver trying to get on the field to make a play. Let's not say make a play. Let's just say trying to get on the field and start at that. I just think it would be more inclusive . . . you'd be seeing more of us in these positions or more of us in the mainstream.

This sentiment resonated with Crystal, a middle-class student in her early twenties, who described her preferences as follows:

> If I could choose the way that black America was going to be, then I would definitely go, but . . . because I would love to see that . . . black ambitious, prosperous people with goals, but I know that will not happen. So I definitely would not go unless it was somewhere where I wanted to be. Well, I shouldn't say where I wanted to be, but the way that it should be. Or the way I am used to seeing things happen.

For Keesha, who consistently represented the Black Nationalist perspective, a black America would be a wonderful idea and something she endorsed. In true Black Nationalist fashion, she invoked a connection to the African Diaspora in her explanation for why and under what circumstances she would support an all-black America:

> Let me just say that when I went to Ghana, it was all black. I could have counted on my hand three white people in three weeks. That's how many white folks I saw, and it was absolutely wonderful. Even though there was corruption, and I mean there was corruption, but there was no racism. No racism. Now if you could have a mixture of everybody in the same pot with no racism, that would be wonderful. But to say all black, I could see that. If it could be that way, because then you don't deal with racism, you deal with flat-out corruption.

Keesha was the only participant who recognized the potential for political problems like the ones she witnessed in her travels to African countries, but she was willing to try it anyway. The presence or pervasiveness of corruption was acceptable as a part of the political process, but the absence of racism trumped all other problems.

Conclusion

In the early nineteenth century, David Walker wrote of a belief that blacks would at some point want "to govern themselves." At that time, the vast majority of blacks were legally designated as property, devoid of civil and human rights as well as many of the skills political scientists see as necessary for fostering strong democratic citizenry. In spite of the racial climate of Walker's era, there was still a healthy debate among black elites over the viability of black self-governance. Many of the early Black Nationalists would agree with assessments offered by these participants. They would say that the only national connection blacks know is their bond with America; therefore, without that bond, they would be stateless, cultureless, and occupants of liminal space—not quite African or American. Still others would agree that blacks (in their current state) are not prepared to be a self-determining nation. For them, black Americans lack resources, education, confidence, unity, and numerous other characteristics needed for nation-building. They might, however, as some participants did, conjure the ideals of Marcus Garvey, who was confident that despite the legacy of slavery and oppression, a free black nation could be accomplished. Despite an awareness of the past and concerns about the future, they still believe that blacks have a right (and to some extent an obligation) to try.

Today, the racial and political terrain is drastically different than during previous eras of heightened support for Black Nationalism. The Thirteenth, Fourteenth, and Fifteenth Amendments and the civil rights legislation of the 1960s have established that blacks are equal citizens under American law. There have been major gains in every area of American life, including a larger black middle class and more blacks in elective office. This has not resulted in the abatement of frustrations, disappointments, and ambivalence toward the American government. Nor has it swayed internal debates among blacks to a separatist position on the question of self-governance. It is a question that three centuries after its introduction still resonates, still animates, and still divides.

8

Conclusion

Black Nationalism at the
Post–Civil Rights Crossroads

On the eve of the third anniversary of Hurricane Katrina, Barack Obama, the presumptive Democratic nominee for president of the United States, took the stage for his official nomination at the Democratic National Convention in Denver. The inability of the federal government to help stranded black citizens in New Orleans after Hurricane Katrina led many blacks to question the gains made in the previous decades. To a large extent, the Katrina event and Obama's nomination and ultimate victory embody the paradox of blacks' relationship to the United States. Three years after a particularly low moment for the nation, and especially for African Americans, blacks were buoyed by the election of the first black president. These events demonstrate the push and pull factors that reinforce blacks' bond to America and underscore the fragility of that bond. These stark examples are also necessary to create space for Black Nationalism to take hold because they highlight the instability of blacks' access to full citizenship rights.

There is actually no need to position Hurricane Katrina and Obama's victory as presenting oppositional political cues for black Americans. Indeed, Obama's candidacy, especially during the primary season, provided enough evidence of the conflict African Americans experience. During this process the black community was portrayed as both complex and monolithic, black candidates were both patriots and subversives, black votes were both worthy of courting and disregard, and blackness was both American and other. The best path to African American political empowerment continues to present a puzzle for individuals in the African American community and for America writ large. In fact, the torrid relationship is still best characterized by W. E. B. DuBois, in words written more than a century earlier. DuBois (1903) sees the black American predicament as this double-consciousness, this sense of always looking at one's self through the eyes of others, of measuring one's soul by the tape of a world that looks on in amused contempt and pity. One ever feels his twoness,--an American, a Negro; two souls, two thoughts, two unreconciled strivings; two warring ideals in one dark body, whose dogged strength alone keeps it from being torn asunder. (3)

At the time of DuBois's writing, the distance between the two poles of that consciousness was much greater. During most historical periods, that "dogged strength" has been used to repeatedly petition America's government and conscience for full recognition. At times, however, those petitions have been replaced by demands for withdrawal from the American political process and increased focus on community-building and self-help. The separation between "black spaces" and "American spaces" has become murkier in the post–civil rights era, making it more difficult to maintain an intraracial transcript that is transmitted among and policed by African Americans, as demonstrated repeatedly throughout the 2008 primary. Whether it is controversial sermons offered by black preachers or comments made at a local NAACP dinner, the African American community in its entirety has been put under a microscope for everyone to dissect, and many aspects were either lost in translation or not well received. As once seemingly private spaces for African American discourse have become more integrated and accessible—churches, fraternal organizations, and other social spaces—how does the African American community integrate race and nation? Or does it seek to integrate it at all? At what point might blacks start ignoring that "tape of a world that looks on in amused contempt and pity," stop attempting to reconcile the "two souls," and heed the call of Black Nationalists to chart a more self-determining path?

The data from *Dreaming Blackness* can tell us something about the potential of a Black Nationalist revival. First, we know that there is widespread support for some, but by no means all, policies and behaviors that encourage community control of black institutions and social spaces. Though blacks are willing to support moderate withdrawal, the vast majority of focus group participants and NBES survey respondents do not subscribe fully to Black Nationalist principles. Blacks are willing to patronize black businesses over similar businesses; they are willing to give conditional support for black candidates; and when they discuss views about commitment to their racial community, they express beliefs that responsible members should be engaged in a collective struggle for community uplift. This is true for even those participants in the focus groups who were most opposed to Black Nationalism. When this moderate support for Black Nationalism is coupled with the high level of frustration and distrust focus group members experience because of their desire for unfettered pursuit of the American dream and the obstacles to that pursuit because of enduring racial tensions, blacks seem primed for increased support for Black Nationalism.

In fact, the events surrounding Hurricane Katrina seemed to reopen old wounds and increase support for more independent organization building. Interestingly, and expectedly, the storm also reinforced notions of linked fate and reiterated the need for blacks to coalesce around issues that adversely and uniquely impact their community. African American churches, fraternal organizations, and other black organizations set up benefits, collected clothes, and engaged in other efforts in the storm's aftermath. In black communities nationally, impromptu and often informal organizations formed to aid in hurricane relief efforts and to support arriving storm victims. One *Cleveland Plain Dealer* reporter noted, "In some cases these newly minted black activists were poor themselves, but they felt a kinship with Katrina victims" (Bernstein 2005, F1). Black philanthropic organizations reported a dramatic increase in giving, and there was growing criticism of mainstream relief organizations like the Red Cross and its ability (or desire) to adequately meet the needs of African American communities (Dobrzynski 2005). Additionally, the Black Entertainment Television (BET) channel and a group called the Saving Our Selves Coalition held a telethon that primarily featured young black entertainers, as well as more established African American celebrities.[1] The initial emotional and physical upheaval in the African American community has not resulted in enough political force to keep Katrina recovery at the top of the national agenda. Outside of the impacted area, there has been very little sustained organizational effort. Additionally, African Americans have coalesced around the Obama campaign, which represents a high point (even if only symbolic) for African American politics. Like Katrina, it continues to highlight the myriad ways in which African Americans and other groups view the world.

Beyond general support for more moderate forms of Black Nationalism, there is also a great deal of insight to be gleaned from the focus group data on linked fate. It seems to be a political truism that black Americans feel connected to each other socially, politically, and economically. That connection generally has been viewed in two primary ways—either fixed and neutral or fixed and positive. While there is evidence in this analysis to support both of these claims, there is also support for the need to rethink how black politics scholars measure and employ the idea of linked fate in their analysis. These focus group participants clearly see themselves as allied with other members of the black community; however, the nature of that alliance is far more complicated than our current conceptualizations suggest. These participants are making distinctions about who is a member of their "black community." These distinctions are made on the basis of social and economic class boundaries, and geographic boundaries, and, interestingly, on the basis of what they see as socially acceptable behavioral choices. So for many participants this connection is important and sometimes positive, but it always serves as a problematic rather than a constant.

As a typology of ideological support reveals itself in the data, the existence of some form of linked fate is taken as a constant; however, how individuals frame their identities, whether they express a collective or an individual outlook, who is assigned blame for black problems, and other factors also become important. Supporters of Black Nationalism see their political world predominantly through a racial lens. An important difference between strong and moderate supporters of Black Nationalism is that strong supporters reject the notion that the American political system is one in which racial equality and fairness can be achieved. They see the government and subsequently its white actors as intentionally hindering black progress. Direct experiences with racism or race prejudice also have a profound impact on support for withdrawal efforts inherent in Black Nationalist ideology, unlike for Non-Nationalists, who are likely to talk about racism as an artifact of the past or reference indirect experiences based on secondhand accounts and media reports. In all the focus groups, participants searched for reasons to explain problems experienced by African Americans within the political system. Why, given all the progress that blacks as a racial group have made, do they continue to lag behind whites and other groups along various social and economic indicators? For Black Nationalists the answer was unambiguous. In the American political system blacks are playing with a stacked deck; the rules and norms governing the political process are structured in ways that negatively impacts blacks' ability to win, which is defined as the ability to achieve desired political and economic goals. For those who reject Black Nationalism, the primary answer becomes black blame and individual failure.

For them the post–Civil Rights era represents a golden opportunity for African Americans to take advantage of new opportunities once closed to them through racially biased policies such as Jim Crow laws. So, in the absence of overtly hostile policies, blacks have only themselves and their poor choices to blame for persistent problems.

As the analysis moves from the focus group data to the National Black Election Study, understanding this ideology becomes somewhat more difficult because of the paucity of Black Nationalist adherents in the sample. Fewer than 15% of respondents in this sample endorse Black Nationalist principles. Later in the conclusion, I will identify some methodological issues that might partially account for the low number, but for now it is important to note that the race of the interviewer has a profound effect on the strength of support for Black Nationalism. When respondents believe they are speaking with white interviewers, they are less likely to support Black Nationalism than when they believe the interviewers are black. Despite the low number of Black Nationalists in the sample, there are statistically significant and substantially important differences between those respondents who support Black Nationalism and those who reject it. Black Nationalist appeals seem to resonate with the moderately educated and the polar ends of the age spectrum; this is also true for those respondents who self-identify as liberals. Increased conservatism and decreased connection to other blacks significantly predict the likelihood of Black Nationalist rejection. Finally, Black Nationalists consistently demonstrate negative white affect.

It is important to understand the determinants of support for a particular ideological viewpoint; however, for students of politics, it is also important to know the political ramifications of holding these views. To that end, the Black Nationalist Index is employed as an independent variable in a series of OLS regression models measuring political behavior and attitudes. Two important findings are noteworthy here. First, adherence to Black Nationalism has a negative impact on blacks' perceptions of governmental responsiveness and their ability to impact political change. Increased support for Black Nationalism decreases the likelihood that NBES respondents will believe that government officials are responsive to their preferences or that they can have an impact on political outcomes. Second, in conjunction with decreased efficacy, Black Nationalists are also more likely to support the formation of a black third party. We know from the focus group data that a key component of Black Nationalist subscription is being cognitively liberated from a sense of allegiance to the rules and norms of the American political system. The result for Black Nationalists is a clear understanding that the American government displays very little concern for the preferences of blacks and that attempts by blacks to change this reality are mostly futile. Just as there is generalized support for moderate withdrawal efforts in the black community, as support for abandoning both main political parties increases, so does support for Black Nationalism.

Though there is considerable evidence of popular support for modest withdrawal efforts, support for widespread emigration from the Unites States or the formation of a separate black nation is minuscule. Given the contentious relationship that blacks have had historically with both the state and other groups, it is important to understand the absence of greater support for complete separation. Because emigration has so little traction in the mass public, it is not surprising that no participants offer it as a viable (or even a nonviable) option for the black community. So, it seemed important to get a better sense of the conditions under which participants might support a separate black nation. From discussions about a separate black nation, an enormous amount of information is gained about why there is such little support, and we learn a great deal about how participants conceptualize important issues and what kinds of strategies are created for addressing those concerns. Issues related to leadership, crime and safety, education, and racial solidarity surface as the primary themes for participants' hypothetical black America. These topics emerge during the discussion of an all-black America because they are currently seen as problem areas in the black community, and various strategies and remedies are put forth. Additionally, participants make clear that the same kinds of boundaries they currently use to guide their relationships and interactions with members of their racial group dictate the structure of their "black America." Like other aspects of this analysis, this kind of information would be unavailable without using multiple approaches.

The empirical findings in this text provide increased understanding of opinion formation among blacks by investigating the underlying components of Black Nationalist support. Another component of understanding African American opinion that emerges as especially important is the role that methodology and, more important, the use of multiple methodologies play in understanding black opinion. In Walton's (1985) critique of the behavioral approach to studying black politics, he suggests, "Those studies of black political behavior that have generated theories and stratagems based on single, deterministic factors are bound to be of limited use because they have caught only a portion of black political reality, and many . . . have mistaken the shadow for reality" (7).

If we simply looked at the survey data, this would be a short story. There are very few Black Nationalists, and to the extent that they exist, they are not relying heavily on Black Nationalist principles to make decisions. But when survey findings are augmented by the focus group data, we get a different and, I would argue, more robust story.

Undeniably, the presence of white interviewers in the NBES serves to diminish the strength of support for Black Nationalism. Multiple arguments can be made for why this is the case. Perhaps blacks are hesitant to express ideas that may be perceived as antiwhite when they believe they are speaking with a white interviewer. Alternatively, blacks could be attempting to "keep it real" with other blacks by disparaging "the man" and his government to other blacks. Said differently, perhaps blacks' concern for positive self-presentation is tailored to specific audiences. Since Black Nationalism represents a clear and often scathing critique of the American government and whites, those respondents concerned with positive self-presentation will amplify Black Nationalist leanings when talking to other blacks and decrease support when talking to whites. I am not trying to suggest that one of these positions is more "authentic" than the other. Knowing that attitudes change in this way, to me, seems less a problem for opinion holders and more a challenge for scholars. If blacks continue to endorse participation in a multiracial society (and all the data here suggest that they do), then knowing how blacks express opinions within their racial group and across racial lines is extremely valuable. However, if we want to learn more about how intragroup ideological appeals resonate, then having more black interviewers is a methodological imperative.

Then there are the "shadows and realities" referenced by Hanes Walton. In the shadows of the NBES and other large data sets lies a robust narrative created by individuals to explain their political world. In those narratives, one is able to glean the cognitive calculus that serves as the precursor to the up or down choices that individuals are asked to give in closed-ended survey questions. The point here is not to advocate for a rash abandonment of survey research. To do so would be impractical and improbable, but it would also be shortsighted in terms of our ability to capture robust opinion holding. Instead, I am arguing for the inclusion of a new set of questions that grapple with the challenges raised in *Dreaming Blackness*. This is best demonstrated by three areas of analysis. The first is the way we, as scholars, currently measure linked fate. More questions must be developed that deconstruct the meaning of racial connectivity in the black community. It is difficult, without the appropriate data, to say that more would be learned by doing so, but unraveling the web of racial perceptions held by all Americans and particularly racial minorities is complex work. An initial step in this direction would be to simply ask African American respondents follow-up questions that involve attaching an affective orientation to existing questions about liked fate. For instance, after asking respondents if they strongly agree or disagree with the linked fate question, interviewers could ask them whether or not that has been a good thing or a bad thing in their lives. Additionally, including questions that explicitly discuss perceptions (both positive and negative) of an individual's racial group orientation could yield helpful insights.

The second area of analysis that deserves more attention in survey research would be to ask more explicit questions about class differences and blame assessment. In the pursuit of political clarity and a sense of understanding of the political and social terrain, African Americans are not focusing simply on issues they see as problematic within the community; they are evaluating those problems and assigning credit and blame. Which target receives the balance of credit or blame has a profound impact on whether African Americans continue to embrace core American values and wholeheartedly participate in the political process or instead choose to disengage from the process and forge other political futures. Intuitively, black politics scholars and interested citizens are keenly aware of the role of the concept of blame in the black community. Blaming the American political system is often viewed as more understandable, more politically expedient, and in many ways more acceptable in the black community than blaming blacks themselves. Black blame, however, is more difficult to deal with theoretically and methodologically because of its potential to create intellectual discomfort. Labels like "sellout" or "Uncle Tom" are extreme manifestations, but milder forms of intraracial blame are interwoven in the explanations provided by black respondents.[2] There is a space for understanding concerned critiques of community strategies by citizens who are invested in some way in the collective struggle of fellow African Americans. Surely, this can be analyzed and written about without painting African Americans with a broad pathological brush. How else are those of us who are interested in black opinion to work toward providing a more accurate assessment of the opinion landscape? Only when we trouble black politics with confounding issues like the concept of blame do we come closer to the reality toward which Walton points.

The third area surrounds the primary interest of this book, which focuses on ideological diversity within the African American community. Cathy Cohen's *Boundaries of Blackness* (1999) cautions us to do more work to assess the experiences of subgroups within the African American community and concludes: "This phenomenon of increasing stratification, and its resulting variation in interests, has affected the ability of marginal groups to define and pursue a unified political agenda. Moreover, this bifurcation in access has also promoted a process of secondary marginalization in these same communities" (342).

These black subgroups often have an intragroup experience that mirrors that of African Americans in the larger society. But even within this context of inter- and intragroup contestation, there is also room for political success, critical assessment, and political growth. However, we must consider how African Americans whose opinions are in opposition to majority black opinion and dominant narratives of community leadership fashion a political space within their own racial group. Additionally, this analysis must be augmented with questions related to the management of disagreements, prioritizing of policies and preferences, and perceptions of racial separatist arguments. In focus groups, we can ask questions that compel participants to discuss policies and preferences that are rarely asked in surveys. These discussion exercises also offer opportunities for researchers to understand preferences as a real-world dialectic, where individuals offer points and counterpoints in real time, which more closely resemble the way citizens actually engage in political discussion. In surveys, we can ask a whole host of questions within acceptable time constraints. Thus, we can create scales and other measures to assess a wider range of political questions than are available in the focus group format.

In the current political climate, where overt racial hostility is publicly denounced by even the most racially conservative sources and more subtle attempts at retreat from civil rights gains endure, the space for the resurgence of Black Nationalism is both fertile and fragile. It is fertile because, as this research indicates, there is a high level of distrust and dissatisfaction with current conditions for blacks. Many feel blacks should have progressed much further in the forty years since the height of the Civil Rights Movement. Additionally, as the focus of the federal government and federal dollars shifts from domestic policy to international concerns and war, those social programs that were created as remedies to racially biased policies and practices are more likely to come under attack, which is likely to further distance blacks from the federal government. It is simultaneously fragile because characteristics and conditions that foster intraracial ties between blacks seem to be weaker than in previous iterations of Black Nationalist prominence. To be sure, blacks still see their fate as tied to that of other blacks, but they are engaging in high degrees of black blame that lead to conditional rather than unwavering support for community empowerment efforts.

As the gap between the black poor and the black middle class continues to widen, the ability to opt out (albeit on a limited basis) of the black community is more attainable than ever before. In the absence of overt residential segregation and other policies that reinforce blacks' communal solidarity, some blacks may simply choose to withdraw entirely from the African American community. Unlike in the past, when the only avenue of retreat from racial hostility was further cloistering oneself in the black community, in the face of increased racial hostility and absent overtly racist policies, blacks now have more options in terms of racial coping strategies. This seems especially true among those who most vehemently reject Black Nationalism and are also more likely to frame policies around individual concerns rather than community or collective benefits.

Whether there will be a full recovery for displaced Katrina residents is difficult to tell. We know that Barack Obama will be the forty-fourth president of the United States. Still, it is likely that blacks will continue to support some level of racial group independence. If the pendulum shifts toward increased racial hostility and black frustration, then there should be increased support for Black Nationalism. The ability of this ideology to gain traction among ordinary citizens in the post–Civil Rights era is undermined by the diminished importance of racial group membership among younger African Americans. Without legal and social barriers that keep the African American community bounded, defining problems through a narrow group membership lens fails to account for real changes in the African American community that make it more diverse than in any other period. Understanding, negotiating, and accounting for in-group diversity are the tests of post–Civil Rights black politics. As a result, the effort to achieve political empowerment remains a collective one. Henderson (2000) notes:

> DuBois was quite prescient in his view that the problems of the twentieth century would be the problem of the color line. . . . Cruse was no less prescient; his pendulum thesis suggests that the challenge of the twenty-first century will be the challenge of the culture line—at home and abroad. (359)

Given how recent events are playing out and the findings in *Dreaming Blackness*, there is an important caveat that should be added to and DuBois's and Cruse's predictions—that the contours of the culture line will be contested within the boundaries of the African American community at the same time that African Americans will have to negotiate the culture line, nationally and globally.

Afterword

Black Power? A Note about Black Nationalism, Barack Obama, and the Future of Black Politics

The 2008 presidential election represents a watershed moment in American political development. The same nation that at its founding saw humans of African descent as chattel to be bought and sold like livestock elected a citizen of African descent to be its forty-fourth president. Barack Obama's importance as a racial signpost for American progress cannot be denied: whether that progress is symbolic or substantive is an open question. In light of Obama's victory, it is important to discuss the ways in which the findings of *Dreaming Blackness* can inform the impact of his election on the future of African American politics. I see four primary findings of this project that may shed some light on the development of Black Nationalism and black politics in the age of a black president: (1) the (in)ability of Black Nationalism to thrive in an era of such mainstream political success, (2) the conflict between group politics and deracialized campaigns, (3) the employment of black blame, and (4) the political constraints resulting from the protest/protection impulse.

On election day, the vast majority of African Americans turned out to endorse Obama's candidacy. In a near-unanimous voice, African Americans not only supported the Democratic candidate (as they had for decades) but also offered specific support for the first African American nominee from a major political party. National exit poll data reveal that 96% of blacks voted for Barack Obama. This was thirty percentage points more than any other racial group and more than John Kerry and Al Gore received in the two previous presidential elections.[1]

Some have argued that the election of Barack Obama represents, for the first time, the full integration of African Americans as U.S. citizens. At various times in history, there have been halfhearted attempts to decrease the level of marginalization experienced by blacks. For example, there was the passage of the Thirteenth, Fourteenth and Fifteenth Amendments, which (outside of the Reconstruction era) were not fully enforced until more than a century later. If Obama's victory truly represents a fully integrated black America, then the ability of Black Nationalists to mobilize a mass movement should be greatly diminished. Black Nationalism thrives in an environment of continued marginalization of blacks by a white power structure. Can blacks continue to make claims based on racial oppression and exclusion when one of their racial group members occupies the most powerful elected position in the country? The answer to the question is, obviously, yes. The election of one African American does not erase persistent inequalities or prejudices. One man's individual success (even of this magnitude) cannot account for centuries of marginalization or continued contemporary discrimination. Nor can one man's voice fully articulate the preferences of an entire group. In light of this, there will be an ongoing need for black activists to engage in more robust debate with each other and make race-based petitions to the federal government.

Barack Obama's candidacy was widely characterized as race-transcendent. According to news pundits, Obama's failure to rely on traditional civil rights tropes and whites' willingness to vote for a black candidate demonstrated that Americans had moved beyond past racial tensions. In fact, his campaign style represented an existing electoral strategy developed by black mayors called deracialization (Persons 1993). Candidates who run deracialized campaigns avoid discussing issues that are explicitly or implicitly racial such as welfare, crime, and so on. Instead, they emphasize a political agenda that can be viewed as race neutral. Recent African American elected officials such as Michael White (former mayor of Cleveland, Ohio), Corey Booker (mayor of Newark, New Jersey), and Deval Patrick (governor of Massachusetts) all exemplify this growing cadre of deracialized (or race-neutral) black politicians. This strategy has some relevance for understanding contemporary expressions of Black Nationalism, which are predicated on a sense of racial group consciousness. Black Nationalism relies on explicit and collective racial appeals that are less likely to be made in a race-transcendent or deracialized context. This means that any problem uniquely impacting African Americans has to either be couched in a universal narrative or abandoned. Black Nationalists do not support either of these strategies.

Though Obama never denies his African heritage and accepts that this makes him African American, throughout the campaign, he went out of his way to assure the public that it simply did not matter (or at least not in the same way it mattered in the past). The one moment in which Obama dealt directly with race was when he seemed to have no other political option.[2] Obama chose to give his sole speech directly addressing race in the aftermath of the controversy involving the Reverend Jeremiah Wright. In that speech, he offered two arguments that are antithetical to the Black Nationalist project and the rhetorical aims of black activists who mobilize using group-based appeals. First, he suggested that Wright and like-minded members of his generation are reacting to static events that happened in the past rather than an ongoing (and current) racial reality that can impact blacks of all ages. Second, he characterized white racial resentment and black oppression as experiential equals, in a way that legitimizes both perspectives and undermines the differential impact of white racism on blacks. Obama characterized the "anger" of Rev. Wright as a generational by-product of those who came of age at "a time when segregation was still the law of the land and opportunity was systematically constricted" or as a result of the residual feeling from "the memories of humiliation and doubt and fear." The racial picture Obama painted was one of overt racial hostility that existed only in previous generations; he did not acknowledge more subtle forms of racism and discrimination that continue to shape the lives of racial minorities. After defining racism as primarily time bound, Obama asserted that a "similar anger exists within segments of the white community." This anger, in Obama's reading of white resentment, is based largely on class interests, such as the impact of globalization on the white working class or the discriminatory impact of civil rights policies like busing and affirmative action. Obama correctly defined all these experiences as discrimination. He failed, however, to differentiate between discrimination based on notions of inferiority and discrimination based on redress for historic and continued injustices. When this difference is taken into account, Obama's comparison serves to undermine African American experiences in a U.S. political context.

In the context of the 2008 election, the cost of mainstream success seemed to be the shedding (or explicit distancing) of group loyalties. This was done quite subtly by Barack Obama and was accomplished using a tactic that I outline in great detail in *Dreaming Blackness*—black blame. My work examines the employment of black blame within homogeneous community spaces and how the target of blame varies in relation to individual ideological subscription. However, the consequences of black blame outside of racially homogeneous spaces arose as an interesting and troubling puzzle in the 2008 election. In the process of defining the problems facing the black community, participants in *Dreaming Blackness* also clearly outlined sources of blame for these problems. There were two main culprits in their analysis: poor choices on the part of individual community members (black blame) or discriminatory practices and policies of the government, its agents, and citizens who benefit from those policies (system blame). I find that African Americans across the ideological spectrum utilize black blame as an explanation for community problems, but they differ in the proportion of community problems attributed to black blame. Black Nationalists see biases built into the system (or system blame) as the primary reason for persistent racial inequalities. Black Nationalists invoke black blame less often and with less severity than those who reject this ideology. Black blame as a public political strategy, however, presents a more difficult question for politics scholars and members of the black community. What is the message conveyed to blacks and other racial groups when black politicians excoriate members of the black community using tropes of personal responsibility?

The most damaging impact of the use of black blame by mainstream black candidates is that it reinforces views of the black poor as pathological. The salience of this image is compounded by its endorsement from a "legitimate" source—the first black president of the United States— who makes these statements in seemingly homogeneous spaces. With the proliferation of videotape and other recording technologies, even black safe spaces such as churches are made visible in the public sphere. For example, Obama uses black blame in black churches that have long recorded their services for parishioners or campaign meetings that are also simultaneously broadcast on mainstream news outlets. In this way, an African American candidate who provides critiques of the black poor using a framework of pathology legitimizes it both intraracially and interracially. Moreover, Obama gave a speech to a predominantly black crowd in southeast Texas and told them,

> Turn off the TV set, put the video game away. Buy a little desk or put that child by the kitchen table. Watch them do their homework. If they don't know how to do it, give them help. If you don't know how to do it, call the teacher. Make them go to bed at a reasonable time. Keep them off the streets. Give 'em some breakfast. Come on. . . . You know I am right.[3]

It was very difficult for any parent or interested observer—black or white—to disagree. His prescription was one that makes for a successful student and healthy childhood. As he continued this speech and offered more "advice," his frame became less universal, more racially laden, and clearly pathological. He added:

> I know how hard it is to get kids to eat properly. But I also know that if folks letting our children drink eight sodas a day, which some parents do, or, you know, eat a bag of potato chips for lunch, or Popeyes for break-fast. Y'all have Popeyes out in Beaumont? I know some of y'all you got that cold Popeyes out for breakfast. I know. That's why y'all laughing. . . . You can't do that. Children have to have proper nutrition. That affects also how they study, how they learn in school.

A reporter from the *Chicago Sun-Times* noted that these statements re-ceived "raucous applause from the mostly black audience."

In this speech and others, there is little rancor because many blacks agree with his assessment and utilize black blame as an explanation for the current circumstance of some within the black community. Additionally, he is offer-ing the assessment as a racial insider who possesses the right and responsi-bility to call out community problems when he sees them.[4] Within the black community Obama is part of a long history of racial uplift efforts that both criticize and offer aid to the poorest black communities. *Dreaming Blackness* finds a class component to the invocation of black blame. When asked about obligations they may feel toward their community, focus group participants from middle-class backgrounds discussed a sense of responsibility that was limited by the bounds of their geographic or class community. Within these boundaries composed of responsible citizens, these participants expressed a strong sense of civic duty and community responsibility generally while feeling more detached from blacks with whom they share racial identifica-tion but who reside outside of neighborhood or class boundaries. Though I found the class component to be important in my research, I do not want to suggest that poorer blacks were not also citing black blame as the source of community problems. They do. However, they do not utilize black blame as a method of social distancing from other blacks.

Beyond the African American community, the invocation of black blame serves a different purpose. I argue that it demonstrates for non-black voters that black candidates have the appropriate level of distance and objectivity in relation to their racial community as well. Put simply, it shows that black candidates are not in the pocket of the black com-munity. American politics is shaped by group conflict and compromises.

Traditionally, when leaders of a particular group assume political office, it is expected that members of the leaders' group(s) will benefit. This is especially true of individuals from groups for whom authority, leadership, and objectivity are not naturally imbued. Thus a precursor to support for some candidates has to be an overt demonstration of a candidate's ability to evaluate members of his or her own group using prevailing social norms as criteria. The majority of Americans believe that blacks could get better results if they work harder. Hence, a black candidate who explains racial inequality using any other narrative than the need for hard work will be seen as making excuses for black failure.

The election of Barack Obama and its consequences for those who subscribe to and mobilize from a Black Nationalist perspective also has the potential to create a protest/protection impulse. This impulse represents a desire for African Americans to protect those members or segments of their community that they see as embodying the best of that community. This need to protect can be in direct conflict with the ability to critique or protest the actions of those they have lifted up. It is a category that is often reserved for those African Americans who have achieved financial, athletic, or academic success. Cathy Cohen (1999) points to internal tensions within the African American community between the impulse to protect the image (or at least counteract prevailing negative stereotypes) and the need to adequately address certain community problems. She demonstrates this through an examination of African America's response to the AIDS/HIV crisis. African American church officials and community activists on the front line of dealing with the AIDS/HIV crisis have had to grapple with fulfilling their role as service providers and coming to grips with the moral dilemmas created by their interactions with the populations most affected (i.e., gay men, sex workers, and IV drug users). It is likely that a similar tension will exist in an Obama administration.

While racial problems will continue to exist despite Obama's victory, there will be a strong desire among African Americans to preserve this historic moment by protecting Obama's image and refraining from making protest demands that may call for the upheaval of the status quo. This is particularly interesting given that much of the political progress made by African Americans has resulted directly from protest demands. The controversy during the campaign over Obama's pastor, Jeremiah Wright, again, illustrates this point. There were dueling problems surrounding this controversy. On one hand, African Americans were singed by what they saw as an overt attack on their most powerful community institution, the black church. Alternatively, they wanted to make sure that this problem did not tank Obama's candidacy. Obama's chances were in clear conflict with the need to defend this critical political and cultural institution of the black community. This kind of tension will only increase when Obama begins to govern and is forced to makes choices that potentially conflict with black preferences and needs.

Indeed, most critiques of Barack Obama—black, white, or other—were seen as problematic in African American circles. Notably, talk show host Tavis Smiley resigned his position on *The Tom Joyner Morning Show* as a result of the fallout he received from his criticism of Obama. He reported receiving massive amounts of negative mail and death threats from members of the African American community. The *Washington Post* reported, in the fall of 2008, that many African American commentators, protesters, and bloggers were chided by other blacks for their critiques of Obama (Holmes 2008, A7). One African American woman told the *Post* reporter, "'We can be black all day' after the election, said Griffith, the Houston executive. 'We've got to get there first.'" This woman suggest that there will be a future time when African Americans will be able to articulate their policy and opinion differences with Obama, but getting him elected (by not doing anything to embarrass him or call attention to his weaknesses) was a higher priority. It is unclear, in her assessment and others, when that time will come. Though she speaks of it as an eventuality, the date of its arrival is ambiguous at best. Will African Americans be more open to exploring political difference when Obama is firmly ensconced in the White House, or will it be even more difficult to debate President Obama? I think the latter will be true.

Now that Obama has "gotten there," will black Americans and their advocates choose to make highly visible and contentious demands (especially those that are in conflict with mainstream preferences) as they would with any other president, or will they sublimate those demands to ensure the success of an Obama administration? *Dreaming Blackness* suggests that many will place Obama within the bounds of their community and choose the latter option. All in all, there is much to be gleaned from *Dreaming Blackness* as it relates to the current political landscape. While the current political climate appears to be less fertile for Black Nationalist activism, the door remains open for resurgence in support for Black Nationalism as long as discrimination and inequality persist.

Appendix A
Focus Group Characteristics

I completed a series of five focus groups composed of six to eight adults who self-identified as black or African American. Participants were recruited either by flyers distributed across the Columbus, Ohio, area or by the hosts at a particular location. The groups included a total of thirty-two participants, three-quarters of whom reported voting regularly. The sample was 56% female. The largest income group (34%) earned between $50,000 and $75,000 annually; the rest were evenly distributed across lower income cohorts. The ages ranged between nineteen and fifty-five. Only two participants reported having absolutely no college at all. Clearly these participants are more educated and wealthier than most blacks; however, steps were taken to ensure participant diversity. Frequencies generated from the questionnaire are reported in appendix B to allow for sample comparisons. The following is a list of the dates of the sessions.[1]

Group	Location	Date
1	North Side Community Center	August 8, 2002
2	Ohio State University	August 8, 2002
3	Natural hair salon	August 16, 2002
4	Fairview Pines residence	August 19, 2002
5	Near East Side residence	August 20, 2002

The focus group script was semistructured, with a prepared list of questions. Space was allowed for new and unexpected topics to be fleshed out by the entire group.

Script for Focus Groups

Hello, and thank you for agreeing to participate in this discussion. My name is Melanye Price, and today we are about to participate in a discussion about the political opinions of African Americans under the guidance of Paul Beck, who is a professor in the Department of Political Science at Ohio State. I want to remind you that this is a voluntary process, and you are welcome to withdraw from the process at any time. All of your names have been placed in an envelope for a drawing for a grand prize of [WILL BE VARIOUS ITEMS IN THE FORM OF GIFT CERTIFICATES FROM LOCAL STORES AND RESTAURANTS] at the end our discussion.

This will be a political discussion, so there is a strong potential for disagreement. Understanding differences in beliefs is what I am trying to understand. Hence, I encourage you to speak your mind and lay out the steps you go through to make a conclusion. We want to hear from everybody and provide each person with a chance to speak. To that end, I ask that we try not to cut each other off and not to insult or discredit the beliefs of others. You can disagree as much as you like, but there are no wrong positions. Everyone and all opinions are valued.

Let's start the discussion by talking about the beliefs of other African Americans. (Participants are instructed to look at a picture of Martin Luther King Jr.)[2]

1. Who is this person?
2. What kinds of things did he believe?
3. What did he suggest was the relationship between blacks and the rest of American?
4. Do you think that he was right? How are your beliefs different from or similar to his?

Okay, let's look at another picture. (Participants are instructed to look at a picture of Malcolm X.) (Go through the same questions as before.)

How have things changed for the better since these men were alive? Why?

How have things changed for the worse? Explain.

Looking back on what you know about the status of blacks since the civil rights movement, which one of these positions is a better strategy? Why?

Are there other alternatives than the ones put forth by these two men? What are they?

Do the beliefs of these men impact how you make political decisions today? How?

Have these beliefs shifted over time?

How important is it to interact with whites and other races?

Do you think it's important to always vote for the black candidate?

Do you think black candidates have a special responsibility to the black community? Do they live up to that responsibility?

What responsibility, if any, do you think you have to the black community? Or to America at large?

Do you think it's important to be politically active? What kinds of political activities do you engage in?

How do your views about black political activity shape your opinion of the American government?

What would an all-black America look like, feel like to you?

Thank you for agreeing to participate in this discussion. You have all provided very important and helpful information about the nature of the political opinions of African Americans. Because of your willingness to participate in this effort, your name has been placed in a raffle. So right now we will draw a name from the envelope to award a grand prize. [NAME IS DRAWN AND GIFT IS GIVEN. GIFT WILL BE IN THE FORM OF GIFT CERTIFICATES FROM LOCAL STORES AND RESTAURANTS]

Once again, I want to thank you and remind you that this research is being conducted under the guidance of Paul A. Beck in the Department of Political Science at Ohio State University. You have left us your address, and we will send you both a thank-you letter and a copy of our preliminary findings. Should you have any questions after we leave today, you can reach Dr. Beck at XXX-XXXX or me at XXX-XXXX. Thank you, and you are free to go.

Appendix B

NBES Survey Questions and Descriptive Statistics

The survey data used in this book come from the 1996 National Black Election Study conducted by Katherine Tate. The sample was composed of 1,216 black respondents in the preelection survey and 854 respondents in the postelection survey who were all selected using random digit dialing. For this project, I used questions from both the preelection and postelection survey, so the N is around 800 for each question. As expected in any survey of African Americans, the respondents were overwhelmingly Democratic. Additionally, they were mostly middle and working class. This appendix includes questions, frequency tables, and other descriptive statistics for items discussed the text. All statistics were generated using data from the 1996 NBES and the debriefing questionnaire from the focus group sessions.

Black Nationalist Index Items (Measures Are Percentages)

AFROCENTRIC SCHOOLS. Blacks should attend Afrocentric schools.
NBES: strongly agree (8%), agree (16.3), neither agree nor disagree (n/a), disagree (42.9), strongly disagree (32.8); FOCUS GROUPS: strongly agree (9.7), agree (9.7), neither agree nor disagree (51.6), disagree (22.6), strongly disagree (6.5)

BLACK CANDIDATES SUPPORT. Blacks should always vote for black candidates when they run.
NBES: strongly agree (5.2%), agree (7.0), neither agree nor disagree (n/a), disagree (46.5), strongly disagree (41.4); FOCUS GROUPS: strongly agree (3.2), agree (0), neither agree nor disagree (16.1), disagree (38.7), strongly disagree (41.9)

Frequency for Items Used in Black Nationalist Index

Categories	Four Index Items (percentage points)			
	Attend Afrocentric Schools	Always Vote for Available Black Candidates	Shop in Black-Owned Stores	Have Nothing to Do with Whites
Nationalists	8.0	5.2	28.2	1.4
Moderate Nationalists	59.2	53.4	55.0	32.9
Nationalist Rejecters	32.8	41.4	16.7	65.7

TABLE A.2

Correlation Matrix of Items Used in the Black Nationalist Index

	Attend Afrocentric Schools	Always Vote for Black Candidates	Shop in Black-Owned Stores	Have Nothing to Do with Whites
Attend Afrocentric Schools	1.00			
Always Vote for Available Black Candidates	.40**	1.00		
Shop in Black- Owned Stores	.32**	.18**	1.00	
Have Nothing to Do with Whites	.37**	.47**	.11**	1.00

** Significant at $p < .01$ levels.

TABLE A.3

Factor Analysis of Black Nationalist Index Items
(Extraction Method: Principal Component Method)

Scale Items	Principal Component
Children Attending Afrocentric School	.768
Always Vote for Black Candidates	.772
Shop in Black- Owned Stores	.489
Have Nothing to Do with Whites	.729
Variance Explained	48.9 %

Extraction Method: Principal Component Method.

SHOPPING IN BLACK-OWNED STORES. Blacks should always shop in black-owned stores whenever possible.
NBES: strongly agree (28.2%), agree (33.4), neither agree nor disagree (n/a), disagree (21.6), strongly disagree (16.7); FOCUS GROUPS: strongly agree (48.4), agree (29.0), neither agree nor disagree (12.9), disagree (3.2), strongly disagree (6.5)

BLACKS HAVING NO ASSOCIATION WITH WHITES. Blacks should not have anything to do with whites if they can help it.
NBES: strongly agree (1.4%), agree (1.1), neither agree nor disagree (n/a), disagree (31.8), strongly disagree (65.7); FOCUS GROUPS: strongly agree (0), agree (3.2), neither agree nor disagree (12.9), disagree (35.5), strongly disagree (48.4)

A Note about the Black Nationalist Index

Admittedly, there are weaknesses in the measure constructed here. Several important points, however, bolster confidence in this measure beyond the alpha level. First, several versions of this index were tested before accepting the one presented here. For instance, I recoded the individual items into a dichotomous measure, with those strongly agreeing with Black Nationalist sentiments in one category and those who simply agreed, remained neutral, or disagreed in any form in another category. With the measure constructed in this way, the alpha coefficient increased; however, better statistical reliability results sacrificed substantive reliability.[1] Although it would be better methodologically to dichotomize each item for construction of the scale, any models that included items coded in this manner would be difficult, at best, to interpret. A category that includes respondents who both agree and disagree with a particular item is rendered meaningless and precludes straightforward interpretation. The current measure, therefore, is based on items coded into three categories. The first includes those respondents who strongly agreed with Black Nationalist sentiments; the second category is composed of those who reported that they did not know their position on a particular item or merely agreed with either ideology; the third category includes those respondents who strongly rejected Black Nationalist principles. These three categories allow us to clearly distinguish between those who firmly placed themselves within or outside of our ideological category of interest and those who placidly or inconsistently fell into either category.

Frequencies and Comparisons of Other Variables
Used in Analysis of Focus Groups and NBES

AGE DISTRIBUTION
NBES: 18–24 (15.7%), 25–34 (25.5), 35–44 (26.0), 45–54 (15.5), 55–64 (9.2), over 64 (8.0); FOCUS GROUPS: 18–24 (24.1%), 25–34 (20.7), 35–44 (13.8), 45–54 (37.9), 55–64 (3.4), over 64 (0)

GENDER DISTRIBUTION
NBES: Male (36.1%), Female (37.9); FOCUS GROUPS: Male (37.9), Female (62.1)

LIBERAL OR CONSERVATIVE IDEOLOGY
NBES: strong liberals (16.6%), liberals (12.2), moderates (46.7), conservatives (10.4), strong conservatives (14.1); FOCUS GROUPS: strong liberals (3.4%), liberals (37.9), moderates (48.3), conservatives (6.9), strong conservatives (0)

INCOME DISTRIBUTION (IN DOLLARS)
NBES: less than 10K (12.5%), 10K–29,999 (43.3), 30K–49,999 (23.9), 50K and up (20.3); FOCUS GROUPS: less than 10K (15.4%), 10K–29,999 (23.0), 30K–49,999 (19.2), 50K and up (42.3)

EDUCATION LEVEL
NBES: grade school or some high school (3.0%), high school diploma (9.5), some college or associate degree (28.1), bachelor's degree (38.5), more than bachelor's (20.9); FOCUS GROUPS: grade school or some high school (0%), high school diploma (6.9), some college or associate degree (58.6), bachelor's degree (24.1), more than bachelor's (10.3)

PERCEIVED RACE OF THE INTERVIEWER
NBES: black (41.8%), white (58.2); FOCUS GROUPS: black (100%)[2]

CHURCH ATTENDANCE. Would you say you go to church or place of worship every week, almost every week, once or twice a month, a few times a year, or never?
NBES: two or more times a week (2.2%), every week (31.8), almost every week (17.8), once or twice a month (23.4), a few times a year (19.7), never

(5.1); FOCUS GROUPS: two or more times a week (26.6%), every week (40.0), almost every week (3.3), once or twice a month (0), a few times a year (3.3), never (26.7)

POSSIBILITY OF FULL EQUALITY. Will blacks in this country *ever* achieve full social and economic equality?[3]
NBES: yes (38.7%), depends (9.4), no (51.9); FOCUS GROUPS: yes (43.5%), depends (21.7), no (34.8)

RELATIVE ECONOMIC POSITION OF BLACKS VERSUS WHITES. On the whole, would you say that the economic position of blacks is better, about the same, or worse than that of whites?[4]
NBES: better (9.8%), about the same (33.0), worse (57.3)

LINKED FATE. What happens to blacks in this country has a lot to do with what happens to me. Do you strongly agree, agree, disagree, or strongly disagree?
NBES: strongly agree (42.2%), somewhat agree (28.2), somewhat disagree (15.1), strongly disagree (14.6); FOCUS GROUPS: strongly agree (46.9%), somewhat agree (28.1), somewhat disagree (15.6), strongly disagree (9.4)

THINK ABOUT BEING BLACK. Would you say you think about being black a lot, fairly often, once in a while, or hardly ever?
NBES: hardly ever (40.6%), once in a while (26.5), fairly often (15.6), a lot (17.4)

POLITICAL BEHAVIOR INTRODUCTION:
Now, I'm going to read a list of things people have do to protest something they felt needed to be changed in the nation, their neighborhood, schools, or communities. Please tell me if you have done any of the following in the last five years.

Contacted a public official or agency? *NBES*: no (64.1%), yes (35.9)

Signed a petition in support of something or against something? *NBES*: no (47.1%), yes (52.9)

Attended a protest meeting or demonstration? *NBES*: No (81.8%), Yes (18.2)

Picketed, taken part in a sit-in, or boycotted a business or government agency? *NBES*: no (88.9%), yes (11.1)

POLITICAL CHURCH ATTENDANCE. Aggregate measure of political churches based on the following questions:

1. Do you think churches or places of worship should be involved in political matters?
2. Have you heard any announcements or talks about the presidential campaign at your church or place of worship so far this year?
3. Has your church or place of worship encouraged members to vote in this election?

NBES: no political activity (39.3%), one activity (24.4), two activities (19.9), three political activities/very politically active (16.3)

POLITICAL TRUST. How much of the time do you think you can trust the government to do what is right?
NBES: never (3.1%), only some of the time (71.2), most of the time (21.6), just about always (4.1)

POLITICAL RESPONSIVENESS. Public officials don't care what people like me think.
NBES: strongly agree (22.8%), somewhat agree (29.9), neither agree nor disagree (5.3), somewhat disagree (29.5), strongly disagree (12.4)

PERSONAL INFLUENCE. People like me don't have a say about what the government does.
NBES: strongly agree (19.1%), somewhat agree (22.1), neither agree nor disagree (1.5), somewhat disagree (26.4), strongly disagree (30.8)

VOTING. Did you vote in the recent presidential election?
NBES: no (23.6%), yes (76.4)

SUPPORT FOR A BLACK THIRD PARTY. Do you think that blacks should form their own third party?
NBES: no (66.3%), yes (33.7)

OPINION ON GOVERNMENT EFFORT SCALE. Some people feel the government in Washington should make every effort to improve the social and economic position of blacks. Suppose these people are at one end of the scale, at point 1. Others feel that the government should not make any special effort to help blacks because they should help themselves. Suppose these people are at the other end, at point 7. (And, of course, some other people have opinions somewhere in between, at points 2, 3, 4, 5, or 6.) Where would you place yourself on this scale, or haven't you thought much about this?

NBES: Government should make every effort to improve position of blacks (31.0%), point 2 (6.7), point 3 (12.5), point 4 (15.0), point 5 (15.6), point 6 (6.8), blacks should help themselves (12.4)

INTEGRATION JUSTIFIES BUSING. The racial integration of schools is so important that it justifies busing school children to schools outside of their neighborhood.
NBES: strongly agree (27.1%), somewhat agree (28.3), somewhat disagree (23.4), strongly disagree (21.4)

Notes

1. The terms "African American" and "black" are used interchangeably. To distinguish African Americans who are descendants of Africans enslaved in the United States from African Americans who are more recent immigrants from Africa and the Caribbean, I use "black American" and "black immigrants," respectively.

2. The terms "Black Nationalist" and "Black Nationalism" are capitalized throughout to denote a unique form of nationalism that was developed and is adhered to by members of the African Diaspora in the United States. This is also true of other race-specific ideologies such as Black Conservatism and Black Feminism.

3. Dawson (1994) refers to this as the "black utility heuristic," but it is largely the same concept. Dawson's concept has more to do with a shared history of oppression and the ability to determine what is the best for the individual by determining what is best for all black people. Both the black utility heuristic and linked fate have to do with an individual's view of the connectivity of the black community and individual African Americans who are bound together for social and political reasons.

4. These findings are developed further in Shingles 1981; Gurin, Hatchett, and Jackson 1989; and Simpson 1998. There is also a developing body of empirical work in which race consciousness is viewed as an important variable in explaining black political decision making (Allen, Dawson, and Brown 1989; Reese and Brown 1994).

5. Recently, much of this evidence has come in the form of black conservatives who seek to de-emphasize race and discuss the impact of negative perceptions of African Americans on their interactions with white counterparts. See Stephen Carter's *Reflections of an Affirmative Action Baby* (1991) and Ellis Cose's *Rage of a Privileged Class* (1993). For more discussion of this phenomenon, see Reuter 1995, 93–95.

6. The frequencies that follow were generated from the 1996 National Black Election Study.

7. The list includes Stephen Carter 1991; Ellis Cose 1993; and, more recently, John McWhorter's *Losing the Race* (2000). More broadly, the success of early

books spawned other authors (primarily journalists) to write similar books, though not necessarily discontented with the tendency to be so closely connected with other blacks. Examples include Jill Nelson's *Volunteer Slavery* (1993), Sam Fulwood's *Waking from the Dream* (1996), and Lorene Cary's *Black Ice* (1992).

8. In *The Ties That Bind,* Simpson connects Black Nationalism and black Republicanism. This is counterintuitive on the surface, but there are strong commonalities in terms of support for self-help and restrictive moral codes that position men at the head of households and communities. She also finds that members of the post–civil rights generation are more wedded to individualism than previous generations.

9. Tilly (1995) suggests that oppressed or excluded groups develop a toolbox of political strategies to use in an effort to empower themselves in spite of the state and its actors. We have traditionally looked monolithically at the empowerment tools blacks have used.

10. Cruse is referring to all areas of leadership, from politicians to artists.

11. Kinder and Sanders's *Divided by Color* (1996) and Sniderman and Piazza's *Scar of Race* (1993) outline the nature of the debate and provide a historical background of previous iterations.

12. The decrease in overt racial expressions does not mean that overt forms of racism and racial discrimination have diminished or disappeared. In fact, refraining from using socially unacceptable language is no indication of relief from structural and institutionalized forms of racism (Bonilla-Silva 2003; Ture and Hamilton 1992).

13. Unlike the American National Election Study (ANES), which has been conducted since the 1950s, the National Black Election Study has been conducted only three times—in 1984, 1988, and 1996. Additionally, one similar survey, called the National Black Political Study, was conducted in 1993. Because of the longevity of the ANES, principle investigators have been able to focus on particular topics during certain waves of the study (i.e., the 1986 ANES focuses specifically on racial politics). Thus far, this has not been possible for surveys targeted solely to black respondents.

14. See Gurin, Hatchett, and Jackson 1989 for a definitive project based on the earlier waves of the NBES. For a more general overview of survey research in black politics, see McClain and Garcia 1993.

15. Initially, this group was supposed to be solely composed of GED students; however, others who worked at or utilized the services of the center were included when some GED students were not available.

16. Despite making every effort to cast a wide net while recruiting participants and ensure a wide array of participants, we must still ask whether these participants are somehow different than the larger black population in ways that skew our results. To assess the comparability of this group to black respondents in the 1996 National Black Election Study, it is important to look at how they match up

across various measures. Strong similarities exist in terms of gender distribution, but there were differences in terms of income, age, and education. There was almost an equal number of males and female in both samples. The focus group and the 1996 NBES respondents had nearly equal percentages of participants who were in the age range of seventeen to thirty-four; however, the ages for the focus group sample peaked at fifty-five years, whereas the NBES sample reported respondents who were well into their eighties. The focus group sample was also somewhat more educated. Sixty percent of the NBES participants reported having taken some college courses or having received college degrees; in contrast, the vast majority (around 90%) of the focus group respondents reported the same. The focus group respondents also reported higher incomes than the NBES sample. It is important to reiterate here that steps were taken to ensure a good distribution across all these variables by contacting both community centers that catered to the poor and community groups in middle-class neighborhoods, as well as using a black beauty salon and a group of college students, which would yield a broader set of participants in relation to these variables.

NOTES TO CHAPTER 1

1. Italics added.

2. Rogers Smith (1993) argues that rather than simply relying on the republican and liberal tradition for its ideological foundations, the American political tradition should be seen as a set of multiple traditions. Smith notes that one of those traditions is a system of ascriptive hierarchy based on race and gender discrimination.

3. Italics added.

4. For more information on the politics surrounding the Republic of New Africa, see Davenport 2005.

5. More information can be found at http://www.oyotunjivillage.net/oyo2_006.htm (accessed May 5, 2006). At its height, the village boasted around 300 members; however, during the 1980s and with the end of the Black Power movement in the United States, those numbers diminished greatly. This group has been viewed quite suspiciously by its neighbors in South Carolina and other blacks. It has also been criticized for various reasons such as its practice of polygamy and polytheist religious traditions. The leader and others were suspected in several criminal cases for which they were never convicted (Frazier 1995).

6. For more information, see http://www.shrinebookstore.com/about.ihtml#church (accessed May 5, 2006).

7. The Fugitive Slave Act of 1850 allowed southern plantation owners unfettered ability to search for runaways. The act mandated that law enforcement officials across the nation arrest suspected runaways in their jurisdiction. Additionally, criminal consequences were attached to the act of aiding runaways in any

way. The entire act can be read at http://www.yale.edu/lawweb/avalon/fugitive. htm (accessed August 23, 2006).

8. This is true even though much of that focus has been on eastern African countries such as Kenya and languages such as Kiswahili, even though the vast majority of Africans enslaved in the American South were of West African descent.

9. After his journey to Mecca in 1964, Malcolm X changed his name to El-Hajj Malik El-Shabazz (Shabazz 1992 [1962]).

10. For a closer examination, see Carson's *In Struggle* (1981), Halberstam's *The Children* (1998), or Zinn's *SNCC: The New Abolitionists* (2002).

11. DuBois in his early career was an ardent Integrationist proponent and activist, serving as one of the founders of the NAACP. Ultimately, DuBois would adopt strong Black Nationalist beliefs, eventually emigrating from the United States to Ghana, West Africa, and relinquishing his American citizenship shortly before his death. Although his frustration did not rise to the level of relinquishing his citizenship or adopting Black Nationalist principles, Martin Luther King Jr. had come to see racism as entrenched and enduring in American life.

12. The following works provide more in-depth examinations of black political behavior that consider class distinctions: Hochschild 1995; Verba, Schlozman, and Brady 1995; Feagan and Sikes 1994; and Banner-Haley 1994.

NOTES TO CHAPTER 2

1. The American Council on Education found that while the number of black women attending college increased by 4% from 1990 to 2000, the number of black men decreased by 5 percentage points (Leonard 2002).

2. Watching the documentary was important to the analysis because it had been broadcast on the local PBS affiliate so close to the release of the movie.

3. For greater clarity, I use the word "group" solely to mean focus group. When discussing subsections of the focus group participants who held particular opinions, I use alternative words like "category," "subgroup," or "cluster."

4. For a detail discussion of the focus group process and the concluding survey, see appendix A.

5. The presence of black candidates is generally believed to have a strong impact on the attentiveness and turnout of African American voters, though there are some findings that suggest a lesser impact (Whitby 2007; Tate 1993; Guinier 1994).

6. All names provided are pseudonyms to ensure the privacy and anonymity promised in the informed consent process.

7. The *Columbus Dispatch* is the main newspaper in the central Ohio area of which Columbus is a part. It boasts between a quarter and a half million paid subscribers (www.dispatch.com).

8. The Schottensteins are a wealthy and influential family in Columbus, Ohio. They own several major retail chains and are philanthropic donors in the community.

9. This is interesting given Hochschild's (1995) finding that African Americans in higher income groups were extremely disillusioned with the American dream, whereas their poorer counterparts were extremely invested in the American dream and its potential benefits. Because our sample of poor African Americans is limited, it is difficult to say if this is reflected in the broader population of poorer African Americans.

10. Data taken from the trend table at the NES Web site, http://www.umich.edu/~nes/nesguide/toptable/tab5a_1.htm (accessed September 14, 2006).

11. This influx of whites was problematic for some participants who were residents of a rapidly gentrifying community. These white residents are mostly gay males, who are seen as a threat by black residents not only because of the changing demographics but also because they would be able to financially (and thus politically) outmaneuver residents who had "done their time" and weathered the economic downturn that had diminished the once-thriving African American middle-class community. The ongoing conflict between long-standing black residents and their new neighbors is portrayed in *Flag Wars*, a documentary that was aired nationally on PBS.

12. It is difficult to say whether Andrea, as a recent immigrant from the Caribbean and the only participant who was not a descendant of enslaved Africans from the American South, represents an attitudinal outlier. Presumably, the experiences of black immigrants in their native country and the United States are quite different than those of other black Americans. The only requirement to participate in this study was black or African American self-identification. For more information about the experiences of Afro-Caribbean immigrants and their descendants in the United States, as well as their relationship with black Americans, see Waters 1999; Vickerman 1999; and Rogers 2006.

13. This group expressed opposition to affirmative action despite the fact that all its participants were involved in a university affirmative action program at the time of their participation. This was not mentioned by members of this group, and I did not see it as my place as the author to insert it into the conversation.

14. The "DL" is an abbreviation for the colloquialism "down low." In this context, it means to keep something secret or quiet.

15. Interestingly, Evelyn was becoming more sensitized to racial issues because of her participation in a minority scholarship program that had been subjected to anti–affirmative action attacks.

16. I intentionally refrained from referring to it as the black community because I wanted the participants to define their community for themselves. I fully expected them to see that community as somewhat racially bounded, but I did not want to establish preset limits for them.

NOTES TO CHAPTER 4

1. Like Williams, Ira Katznelson's *When Affirmative Action Was White: An Untold History of Racial Inequality in Twentieth-Century America* (2005) examines the relationship between white skin privilege and the history of American entitlement programs. He highlights a legacy of exclusionary public policy that facilitated the burgeoning of the white middle class and denied blacks and other racial minorities the same opportunities.

2. This need to resist oppression on multiple fronts has been echoed by black feminist and womanist scholars and activists, who have successfully demonstrated how multiple forms of oppression serve to uniquely marginalize African American women and other women of color (Hill-Collins 2000; Hine, King, and Reed 1995; Crenshaw 1991; Hull, Scott, and Smith 1982).

3. Cosby's comments are excerpted on Dyson's Web site at http://www.michaelericdyson.com/cosby/index.html (accessed May 7, 2006).

4. The release of Herrnstein and Murray's controversial book, *The Bell Curve*, in the early 1990s sparked a new debate around the legitimacy and accuracy of, and the motivation behind, such claims. This spawned several academic retorts, in the form of edited volumes, to major findings of the book (Kincheloe, Steinberg, and Gresson 1996; Fraser 1995).

5. The Afrocentric School is a K-8 public school in the Columbus public school system. It is open to all races but is designed with the idea of putting African American history and the needs of African American children in the forefront (www.columbus.k12.oh.us/shcpro/).

NOTES TO CHAPTER 5

1. The total number of respondents for the Black Nationalist Index is 782.

2. See appendix B for question wording, coding scheme, and frequency distribution.

3. For more information, see appendix B.

4. For more information, see appendix B.

5. This index represents the best proxy for the ideology of interest in this project; however, it is not without weaknesses. The alpha coefficient is on the low end of the acceptability range. Although these items are significantly correlated, the relationship between the decision to shop in black-owned stores, voting for black candidates, and having nothing to do with whites is weakly correlated, and the relationship between shopping in black-owned stores and having nothing to do with whites has the lowest correlation coefficients. This may be related to the fact that support for these items requires the most extreme views or shifts away from the norm. The statistical significance of these relationships provides evidence and confidence that these measures can be

used to make further predictions, but the relationships are not as strong as desired.

6. This middle-range or neutral category is composed of respondents with conflicting views that place them in the Non-Nationalist and Black Nationalist camps. Additionally, it includes those persons who consistently place themselves into the category designated for respondents who offered "don't know" as a response. These categories represent two types of ambivalence. In the first category, respondents are torn between supporting oppositional views. The latter includes those respondents who were simply unsure of their positions. Although characterized by very different motivations, these two categories of respondents look similar methodologically.

7. For instance, there are no major black-owned grocery chains. Thus, African Americans, regardless of their desire to patronize black businesses, will be forced to use the same qualifications for patronage as other Americans such as proximity to home, price difference, selection, and so on. Additionally, poor blacks with limited incomes are forced to shop in the larger, more competitive national franchises because of their market dominance.

8. The National Association for the Advancement of Colored People was founded in 1909 by a multiracial coalition to push for equal treatment of African Americans under U.S. law. However, over the course of its history, the NAACP has expanded its efforts to address the needs of African Americans more comprehensively. Initial efforts of the NAACP revolved around voting rights and legal activism in which many suits were brought against governmental and other institutions that resulted in the expansion of legal and educational rights for blacks, other racial minorities, and poor whites. Since then, the NAACP has taken up more controversial and directly targeted efforts within the black community such as diversity in television programming, antiviolence efforts, and increased corporate diversity campaigns (www.naacp.org).

9. Although many, if not most, will agree that de jure segregation in the United States has been eliminated, discussions surrounding the elimination of de facto segregation are more divided. This is especially true given findings about the persistence of residential and social segregation across the United States and its subsequent impact on the creation of a black underclass (Massey and Denton 1993; Wilson 1978, 1999, 1997). More recently, researchers at the Brookings Institute found that although "Black/non-Black segregation levels are currently at their lowest point since roughly 1920," there are still a larger number of "'hypersegregated'" metropolitan areas (Glaeser and Vigdor 2001, 1). This suggests that even though racial segregation is on the decline, there are still problem areas throughout the country.

10. The largest age cohorts represented are 25–34 (25.5%) and 35–44 (26.0%).

11. A study by the Justice Policy Institute found that the number of black men behind bars is now greater than the number of black men who are enrolled in

institutions of higher learning. Recent statistics show that "the number of black men in jail or prison has grown fivefold in the past twenty years" (Butterfield 2002, 14). This trend is coupled with other alarming statistics. For instance, "Black males age 12 to 24 were 14 times more likely to be homicide victims than were the general population" (Bastian and Taylor 1994, 2).

12. Here racial resentment is measured using Kinder and Sanders's (1996) scale, which assesses attitudes based on whether respondents believe there should be special favors for blacks, whether discrimination continues to exist, and if blacks should try harder.

13. Religiosity in this analysis is measured by respondents' answer to a question asking how often they attended church. Incidentally, a cross-tabulation was also run of the Black Nationalist Index and how important religion is in the respondent's life. This also proved to be statistically insignificant.

14. See appendix B for descriptive statistics of each variable included in all models.

NOTES TO CHAPTER 6

1. Rather than calling this linked fate, Michael Dawson (1994) refers to it as the "black utility heuristic."

2. Aberbach and Walker define this belief system based on individual levels of favorability toward the Black Power slogan, support of black militant leaders, and support for the recent riots that had taken place in Detroit.

3. Concentration effects likely had the reverse effect before the 1960s and the Civil Rights Movement, when states that were the most densely populated with African Americans were also those with the most hostile racial policies and stringent efforts to disenfranchise blacks (Woodward 1957; Key 1949).

4. This is a generally accepted finding in political science scholarship; however, Sniderman and Piazza (2002, chap. 5) have found that support for certain forms of Black Nationalism, especially those based on Afrocentrism, leads even the most educated African Americans to accept popular conspiracy theories about the origin of AIDS, the planting of drugs in urban black communities, and other theories that travel through black communities. They refer to this as a "blunting of critical standards." According to Sniderman and Piazza, educated blacks, like other educated Americans, should be able to distinguish outlandish theories from actual fact. It is important to note that some scholars might question the outlandishness of some theories pointed to by Sniderman and Piazza.

5. Two documentaries provide interesting reports and analysis of these events: *Eyes on the Prize II* and *Chisholm 72: Unbought and Unbossed*.

6. More information about this covenant can be found at http://www.covenantwithblackamerica.com/ (accessed August 11, 2006).

7. An alternative perspective is presented by Ladd (1999), who argues that civic engagement is not diminishing. Indeed, he argues, it is stronger than ever.

8. See frequency distributions for each item in appendix B.

9. Descriptive statistics associated with each of these variables are reported in appendix B. Additionally, the items of major concern in this analysis are in bold print.

NOTES TO CHAPTER 8

1. The Saving Our Selves Coalition was an attempt to help hurricane victims by combining the efforts of the black community across the nation. Though not listed on its Web site, the group claims to work with 117 groups to help "low and moderate income people in rural communities"; http://www.sosafterkatrina.org/mission_statement.html (accessed August 23, 2006).

2. Orey's (2003, 2001) work has even applied racial resentment scales used in research on white racial attitudes with some success.

NOTES TO AFTERWORD

1. In 2004 Kerry got 88% of the African American vote, and in 2000 Gore got 90%. http://www.cnn.com/ELECTION/2008/results/president (accessed December 19, 2008).

2. The full text of Barack Obama's speech can be found at http://www.huffingtonpost.com/2008/03/18/obama-race-speech-read-th_n_92077.html (accessed December 12, 2008).

3. He also repeated this admonition against fried chicken for breakfast in his Father's Day address in an African American church in June 2008. Lynn Sweet of the *Chicago Sun-Times* offered this account of a February event. Sweet, "Obama Tells Blacks: Shape Up," *Chicago Sun-Times*, February 28, 2008

4. I use the expression "call out" to give credit to the most recent manifestation of this kind of tough talk that was initiated by comedian Bill Cosby. After his famous "pound cake speech," Cosby embarked on a speaking tour that he called call-outs, which were supposed to force black people to get real about the harm they are doing to themselves. These events were widely reported, with the basic arguments summarized in his recent book (coauthored with Alvin Poussaint), *Come On People: On the Path from Victims to Victors* (Nashville, TN: Thomas Nelson, 2007). For another account, see Ta-Nehisi Coates, "This Is How We Lost to the White Man," *Atlantic Monthly*, May 2008, http://ww.theatlantic.com/doc/200805/cosby (accessed December 20, 2008).

NOTES TO APPENDIX A

1. In the case of private residences used for this research, the owner's names are not listed because they were participants as well as hosts.

2. The order in which Malcolm X and Martin Luther King were discussed was varied across the groups.

NOTES TO APPENDIX B

1. The coefficient increased to .73, which falls squarely into the acceptable range.

2. A question about the perceived race of the interviewer is not applicable to the focus groups. All the group discussions were led by this author, who is African American.

3. The middle-range response for the focus group survey was "unsure" rather than "depends."

4. This question was not asked of the focus group participants.

References

Aberbach, Joel D., and Jack L. Walker. 1970a. "The Meanings of Black Power: A Comparison of White and Black Interpretations of a Political Slogan." *American Political Science Review* 64:367–388.

——. 1970b. "Political Trust and Racial Ideology." *American Political Science Review* 64:1199–1219.

Abramson, Paul R. 1972. "Political Efficacy and Political Trust among Black Schoolchildren: Two Explanations." *Journal of Politics* 34:1243–1275.

——. 1983. *Political Attitudes in America: Formation and Change.* San Francisco: Freeman.

Abramson, Paul R., and John H. Aldrich. 1982. "The Decline of Electoral Participation in America." *American Political Science Review* 76:502–521.

Abramson, Paul R., and William Claggett. 1984. "Race-Related Differences in Self-Reported and Validated Turnout." *Journal of Politics* 46:719–738.

Abron, Jo Nina. 1998. "'Serving the People': The Survival Programs of the Black Panther Party." In *The Black Panther Party [Reconsidered]*, edited by Charles E. Jones. Baltimore: Black Classics Press.

Adeleke, Tunde. 1998. *UnAfrican Americans: Nineteenth-Century Black Nationalism and the Civilizing Mission.* Lexington: University Press of Kentucky.

Akers, Rodney. 2005. "Calling Hurricane Victims 'Refugees' Is Insensitive." *Pittsburgh Post-Gazette*, September 7, A13.

Allen, Ernest, Jr.. 1998. "Minister Louis Farrakhan and the Continuing Evolution of the Nation of Islam." In *The Farrakhan Factor: African American Writers on Leadership, Nationhood, and Minister Louis Farrakhan*, edited by Amy Alexander. New York: Grove Press.

Allen, Richard L., Michael C. Dawson, and Ronald E. Brown. 1989. "A Schema-Based Approach to Modeling an African American Belief System." *American Political Science Review* 83:421–442.

Anderson, Barbara A., Brian D. Silver, and Paul R. Abramson. 1988a. "The Effect of Race of the Interviewer on Measures of Electoral Participation by Blacks in SRC National Election Studies." *Public Opinion Quarterly* 52:53–83.

——. 1988b. "The Effect of Race of the Interviewer on Race-Related Attitudes of Black Respondents in SRC/CPS National Election Studies." *Public Opinion Quarterly* 52:289–324.

Assante, Molefi Kete. 1988. *Afrocentricity*. Trenton, NJ: Africa World Press.

———. 1998. *The Afrocentric Idea*. Revised and expanded edition. Philadelphia: Temple University Press.

Bambara, Toni Cade. 1970. "The Pill: Genocide or Liberation." In *The Black Woman: An Anthology*, edited by Toni Cade Bambara. New York: Mentor.

Banner-Haley, Charles T. 1994. *The Fruits of Integration: Black Middle-Class Ideology and Culture, 1960–1990*. Jackson: University Press of Mississippi.

Barker, Lucius J., Mack H. Jones, and Katherine Tate. 1999. *African Americans and the American Political System*. 4th ed. Upper Saddle River, NJ: Prentice Hall.

Bastian, Lisa D., and Bruce M. Taylor. 1994. "Young Black Male Victims." *Crime Data Brief*. Bureau of Justice Statistics' National Crime Victimization Survey. December.

Beck, Paul Allen. 1997. *Party Politics in America*. 8th ed. New York: Longman.

Benedetto, Richard. 2000. "Poll: GOP Reached Out but Grabbed Few Black Votes." *USA Today*, August 8, sec. A.

Bernstein, Margaret. 2005. "Winds of Change; After Katrina, Spirit of Unity Stirs for Blacks." *Cleveland Plain-Dealer*, October 13, F1.

Blassingame, John W. 1979. *The Slave Community: Plantation Lift in the Antebellum South*. Revised and enlarged edition. New York: Oxford University Press.

Bobo, Lawrence, and Franklin D. Gilliam Jr. 1990. "Race, Sociopolitical Participation, and Black Empowerment." *American Political Science Review* 84:377–393.

Bonilla-Silva, Eduardo. 2003. *Racism without Racists: Color-Blind Racism and the Persistence of Racial Inequality in the United States*. New York: Rowman and Littlefield Publishers.

Bositis, David A. 2000. *The Black Vote in 2000: A Preliminary Analysis*. Washington, DC: Joint Center for Political and Economic Studies.

———. 2001. *Black Elected Officials: A Statistical Summary 2001*. Washington, DC: Joint Center for Political and Economic Studies.

Brady, Henry E., Sidney Verba, and Kay Lehman Schlozman. 1995. "Beyond SES: A Resource Model of Political Participation." *American Political Science Review* 89:271–294.

Brehm, John, and Wendy Rahn. 1997. "Individual-Level Evidence for the Causes and Consequences of Social Capital." *American Journal of Political Science* 41:999–1024.

Brooks, Roy L. 1996. *Integration or Separation: A Strategy for Racial Equality*. Cambridge, MA: Harvard University Press.

Brown, Elaine. 1992. *A Taste of Power: A Black Woman's Story*. New York: Pantheon Books.

Brown, Robert A., and Todd C. Shaw. 2002. "Separate Nations: Two Attitudinal Dimensions of Black Nationalism." *Journal of Politics* 64:22–44.

Browning, Rufus P., Dale Rogers Marshall, and David H. Tabb, eds. 1990. *Racial Politics in American Cities*. New York: Longman.

Bumiller, Elisabeth, and Anne E. Kornblut. 2005. "Black Leaders Say Storm Forced Bush to Confront Issues of Race and Poverty." *New York Times*, September 18, late edition–final, 21.

Burns, Nancy, Kay Lehman Schlozman, and Sidney Verba. 2001. *The Private Roots of Public Action: Gender, Equality, and Political Participation*. Cambridge, MA: Harvard University Press.

Butterfield, Fox. 2002. "Study Finds Big Increase in Black Men as Inmates since 1980." *New York Times*, August 28, A14.

Calhoun-Brown, Allison. 1996. "African American Churches and Political Mobilization: The Psychological Impact of Organizational Resources." *Journal of Politics* 58:935–953.

Carlisle, Rodney. 1975. *The Roots of Black Nationalism*. Port Washington, NY: Kennikat Press.

Carmines, Edward G., and James A. Stimson. 1989. *Issue Evolution: Race and the Transformation of American Politics*. Princeton, NJ: Princeton University Press.

Carmines, Edward G., and Richard A. Zeller. 1979. *Reliability and Validity Assessment*. Thousand Oaks, CA: Sage.

Carson, Clayborne. 1981. *In Struggle: SNCC and the Black Awakening of the 1960's*. Cambridge, MA: Harvard University Press.

Carter, Stephen L. 1991. *Reflections of an Affirmative Action Baby*. New York: Basic Books.

Cary, Lorene. 1992. *Black Ice*. New York: Vintage Books.

Citrin, Jack, Herbert McCloskey, J. Merrill Shanks, and Paul M. Sniderman. 1975. "Personal and Political Sources of Political Alienation." *British Journal of Political Science* 5:1–31.

Citrin, Jack, and Donald Philip Green. 1986. "Presidential Leadership and the Resurgence of Trust in Government." *British Journal of Political Science* 16:431–453.

Coates, Ta-Nehisî. 2008. "This Is How We Lost to the White Man." Atlantic Monthly, May.

Cohen, Cathy. 1999. *Boundaries of Blackness: AIDS and the Breakdown of Black Politics*. Chicago: University of Chicago Press.

Cohen, Cathy J., and Michael C. Dawson. 1993. "Neighborhood Poverty and African American Politics." *American Political Science Review* 87:286–302.

Converse, Philip E., 1964. "The Nature of Belief Systems in Mass Publics." In *Ideology and Discontent*, edited by David E. Apter. New York: Free Press.

Cooks, Carlos. 1997 [1955]. "Hair Cooking: Buy Black." In *Modern Black Nationalism from Marcus Garvey to Louis Farrakhan*, edited by William L. Van Deburg. New York: NYU Press.

Cosby, William H., and Alvin Poussaint. 2007. *Come on People: On the Path from Victims to Victors*. Nashville, TN: Thomas Nelson.

Cose, Ellis. 1993. *Rage of a Privileged Class*. New York: HarperCollins.

Craig, Stephen C. 1985. "The Decline of Partisanship in the United States: A Re-examination of the Neutrality Hypothesis." *Political Behavior* 7(1):57–78.

Crenshaw, Kimberle. 1991. "Mapping the Margins: Intersectionality, Identity Politics, and Violence against Women of Color." *Stanford Law Review* 43:1241–1299.

Cruse, Harold. 1967. *The Crisis of the Negro Intellectual: A Historical Analysis of the Failure of Black Leadership*. New York: Quill Press.

Davenport, Christian. 2005. "Understanding Covert Repressive Action: The Case of the US Government against the Republic of New Africa." *Journal of Conflict Resolution* 49:120–140.

Davis, Angela Yvonne. 1974. *Angela Davis: An Autobiography*. New York: Random House.

Davis, Darren W., and Ronald E. Brown. 2002. "The Antipathy of Black Nationalism: Behavioral and Attitudinal Implications of an African American Ideology." *American Journal of Political Science* 46:239–253.

Davis, Darren W., and Christian Davenport. 1997. "The Political and Social Relevancy of Malcolm X: The Stability of African American Attitudes." *Journal of Politics* 59:550–564.

Dawson, Michael C. 1994. *Behind the Mule: Race and Class in African American Politics*. Princeton, NJ: Princeton University Press.

———. 2001. *Black Visions: The Roots of Contemporary African-American Political Ideologies*. Chicago: University of Chicago Press.

Delany, Martin R. 1996 [1852]. "The Condition, Elevation, Emigration, and Destiny of the Colored People in the United States." In *Classical Black Nationalism: From the American Revolution to Marcus Garvey*, edited by Wilson Jeremiah Moses. New York: NYU Press.

———. 1996 [1861]. "Official Report of the Niger Valley Exploring Part." In *Classical Black Nationalism: From the American Revolution to Marcus Garvey*, edited by Wilson Jeremiah Moses. New York: NYU Press.

Dillard, Angela D. 2001. *Guess Who's Coming to Dinner Now? Multicultural Conservatism in America*. New York: NYU Press.

Dobrzynski, Judith H. 2005. "Shock of Katrina Pushes Black Charities to New Fund-Raising." *New York Times*, November 14, late edition–final, 22.

Donlan, Ann E. 2004. "Democratic National Convention; Beantown Blowout; Politics Aside, Reagan Pitches for Stem Cells." *Boston Herald*, July 28, C6.

Douglass, Frederick. 1996 [1894]. "The Lessons of the Hour." In *The Oxford Frederick Douglass Reader*, edited by William L. Andrews. New York: Oxford University Press.

DuBois, W. E. B. 1903. *Souls of Black Folks*. New York: Bantam Books.

———. 1995 [1922]. "Africa for the Africans." In *W. E. B. DuBois: A Reader*, edited by David Levering Lewis. New York: Holt.

———. 1995. "On Being Ashamed of Oneself." In *W. E. B. DuBois: A Reader*, edited by David Levering Lewis. New York: Holt.

Dyson, Michael Eric. 1995. "Malcolm X and the Revival of Black Nationalism." In *The Politics of Race: African Americans and the Political System*, edited by Theodore Reuters. Armonk, NY: Sharpe.

———. 2005. *Is Bill Cosby Right? Or Has the Black Middle Class Lost Its Mind?* New York: Basic Civitas Books.

Ellison, Michael. 2000. "Race for the White House: Ballots: Defiant Jackson Leads New Rainbow Protest: Legal Challenge to Poll after Voters Claimed They Were Misled." *Guardian*, November 12, 2.

Essien-Udom, E. U. 1962. *Black Nationalism: A Search for an Identity in America.* Chicago: University of Chicago Press.

Fanon, Franz. 1963. *The Wretched of the Earth*. New York: Grove Press.

———. 1982 (1967). *Black Skin, White Masks*. New York: Grove Press.

Feagan, Joe R., and Melvin P. Sikes. 1994. *Living with Racism: The Black Middle-Class Experience*. Boston: Beacon Press.

Fessenden, Ford. 2001. "Examining the Vote: The Patterns: Ballots Cast by Blacks and Older Voters Were Tossed in Far Greater Numbers." *New York Times*, November 12, A17.

Fields, Gary. 2000. "Election 2000: Civil-Rights Officials Are Sent to Florida to Probe Alleged Irregularities in Voting." *Wall Street Journal*, November 10, A8.

Fields, Robin. 2006. "The Nation; 'A Dispersion of New Minorities' to New Places; The Foreign-Born Are Increasingly Moving to the South and Midwest, US Census Data Suggest." *Los Angeles Times*, August 15, A12.

Flanigan, William H., and Nancy H. Zingale. 1998. *Political Behavior of the American Electorate*. 9th ed. Washington, DC: CQ Press.

Franklin, John Hope. 1956. "History of Racial Segregation in the United States." *Annals of the American Academy of Political and Social Science* 304:1–9.

Franklin, V. P. 1992. *Black Self-Determination: A Cultural History of African-American Resistance*. Brooklyn, NY: Lawrence Hill Books.

Fraser, Steven, ed. 1995. *The Bell Curve Wars: Race, Intelligence and the Future of America*. New York: Basic Books.

Frazier, E. Franklin. 1964. *The Negro Church in America*. Reprint. New York: Knopf.

Frazier, Eric. 1995. "African Village." *Post and Courier*, April 23, sec. E, 81.

Frymer, Paul. 1999. *Uneasy Alliances: Race and Party Competition in American.* Princeton, NJ: Princeton University Press.

Fulwood, Sam, III. 1996. *Waking from the Dream: My Life in the Black Middle Class*. New York: Anchor Books.

Gaines, Kevin. 1996. *Uplifting the Race: Black Leadership, Politics and Culture in the Twentieth Century.* Chapel Hill: University of North Carolina Press.

Gamson, William A. 1992. *Talking Politics.* New York: Cambridge University Press.

Garcia Bedolla, Lisa. 2005. *Fluid Borders: Latino Power, Identity, and Politics in Los Angeles.* Berkeley: University of California Press.

Garvey, Amy Jacques, ed. 1989. *The Philosophy and Opinions of Marcus Garvey: Or, Africa for the Africans.* Dover, MA: Majority Press.

Garvey, Marcus. 1997 [1920]. "Declaration of the Rights of Negro Peoples of the World." In *Modern Black Nationalism from Marcus Garvey to Louis Farrakhan,* edited by William L. Van Deburg. New York: NYU Press.

Gay, Claudine, and Katherine Tate. 1998. "Doubly Bound: The Impact of Gender and Race on the Politics of Black Women." *Political Psychology* 19(1):169–184.

Giddings, Paula. 1984. *When and Where I Enter: The Impact of Black Women on Race and Sex in America.* New York: Bantam Books.

Glaeser, Edward L., and Jacob L. Vigdor. 2001. *Racial Segregation in the 2000 Census: Promising News.* Washington, DC: Brookings Institution.

Gomez, Michael. 2005. *Black Crescent: The Experience and Legacy of African Muslims in the Americas.* New York: Cambridge University Press.

Goodman, Paul. 1998. *Of One Blood: Abolitionism and the Origins of Racial Equality.* Berkeley: University of California Press.

Granberg, Donald, and Soren Holmberg. 1992. "The Hawthorne Effect in Election Studies: The Impact of Survey Participation in Voting." *British Journal of Political Science* 22:240–247.

Guinier, Lani. 1994. *The Tyranny of the Majority: Fundamental Fairness in Representative Democracy.* New York: Free Press.

Gurin, Patricia, Shirley Hatchett, and James S. Jackson. 1989. *Hope and Independence: Blacks' Response to Electoral and Party Politics.* New York: Russell Sage Foundation.

Gurin, Patricia, Arthur Miller, and Gerald Gurin. 1980. "Stratum Identification and Consciousness." *Social Psychology Quarterly* 43:30–47.

Halberstam, David. 1998. *The Children.* New York: Random House.

Handlin, Oscar. 1965. "The Goals of Integration." In *The Negro American,* edited by Talcott Parsons and Kenneth B. Clark. Boston: Houghton Mifflin.

Harris, Fredrick. C. 1994. "Something Within: Religion as a Mobilizer of African-American Political Activism." *Journal of Politics* 56:42–68.

———. 1999. *Something Within: Religion in African American Political Activism.* New York: Oxford University Press.

Harris-Lacewell, Melissa V. 2004. *Barbershops, Bibles, and BET: Everyday Talk and Black Political Thought.* Princeton, NJ: Princeton University Press.

Hartz, Louis. 1983 [1955]. *The Liberal Tradition in America*. Orlando, FL: Harvest Books.

Haygood, Wil. 2005. "To Me, It Just Seems Like Black People Are Marked." *Washington Post*, September 2, final edition, A1.

Henderson, Errol. 1998. "War, Political Cycles, and the Pendulum Thesis: Explaining the Rise of Black Nationalism, 1840–1996." Paper presented at "The Crisis of the Negro Intellectual, Past, Present, and Future: A Conference in Tribute to Harold Cruse," Ann Arbor, MI, March 13.

Henderson, Errol. 2000. "War, Political Cycles and the Pendulum Thesis: Explaining the Rise of Black Nationalism, 1840–1996." In *Blacks and Multiracial Politics in America*, edited by Yvette Alex-Assensoh and Lawrence J. Hanks. New York: NYU Press.

Herrnstein, Richard J., and Charles Murray. 1994. *The Bell Curve: Intelligence and Class Structure in American Life*. New York: Free Press.

Hetherington, Marc J. 1998. "The Political Relevance of Political Trust." *American Political Science Review* 92:791–808.

Hill-Collins, Patricia. 2000. *Black Feminist Thought: Knowledge, Consciousness, and the Politics of Empowerment*. New York: Routledge.

Hine, Darlene Clark, Wilma King, and Linda Reed. 1995. *"We Specialize in the Wholly Impossible": A Reader in Black Women's History*. Brooklyn, NY: Carlson.

Hochschild, Jennifer L. 1981. *What's Fair? American Beliefs about Distributive Justice*. Cambridge, MA: Harvard University Press.

———. 1995. *Facing Up to the American Dream: Race, Class, and the Soul of the Nation*. Princeton, NJ: Princeton University Press.

Holmes, Steven A. 2008. "Blacks Forming a Rock-Solid Bloc behind Obama." *Washington Post*, October 1, A7.

Howell, Susan E., and Deborah Fagan. 1988. "Race and Trust in Government: Testing the Political Reality Model." *Public Opinion Quarterly* 52:343–350.

Huckfeldt, R. Robert. 1984. "Political Loyalties and Social Class Ties: The Mechanism of Contextual Influences." *American Journal of Political Science* 28:399–417.

Hull, Gloria T., Patricia Bell Scott, and Barbara Smith. 1982. *All the Women Are White, All the Men Are Black, but Some of Us Are Brave: Black Women's Studies*. Old Westbury, NY: Feminist Press.

Iyengar, Shanto. 1991. *Is Anyone Responsible? How Television Frames Political Issues*. Chicago: University of Chicago Press.

Jeffers Jr., Gromer. 2004. "Blacks Who Demanded Inclusion Honored; Tense Standoff an Enduring Memory of '64 Convention." *Seattle Times*, July 29, A14.

Jencks, Christopher, and Paul E. Peterson. 1991. *The Urban Underclass*. Washington, DC: Brookings Institution.

Jennings, M. Kent, and Gregory B. Markus. 1984. "Partisan Orientations over the Long Haul: Results from the Three-Wave Political Socialization Panel Study." *American Political Science Review* 78:1000–1018.

Johnson, Cedric. 2007. *Revolutionaries to Race Leaders: Black Power and the Makings of African American Politics*. Minneapolis: University of Minnesota Press.

Johnson, Janet Buttolph, and Richard A. Joslyn. 1991. *Political Science Research Methods*. 2nd ed. Washington, DC: Congressional Quarterly Press.

Jones, Charles E., and Judson L Jefferies. 1998. "'Don't Believe the Hype': Debunking the Panther Mythology." In *The Black Panther Party [Reconsidered]*, edited by Charles E. Jones. Baltimore: Black Classics Press.

Karenga, Maulana. 1993. *Introduction to Black Studies*. 2nd ed. Los Angeles: University of Sankore Press.

———. 1996. *Kwanzaa: A Celebration of Family, Community and Culture*. Los Angeles: University of Sankore Press.

Katznelson, Ira. 2005. *When Affirmative Action Was White: An Untold History of Racial Inequality in Twentieth-Century America*. New York: Norton.

Key, V. O. 1949. *Southern Politics in Nation and State*. New York: Knopf.

Kim, Jae-On, and Charles W. Mueller. 1978a. *Factor Analysis: Statistical Methods and Practical Issues*. Newbury Park, CA: Sage.

Kim, Jae-On, and Charles W. Mueller. 1978b. *Introduction to Factor Analysis: What It Is and How to Do It*. Newbury Park, CA: Sage.

Kincheloe, Joe L., Shirley R. Steinberg, and Aaron D. Gresson III. 1996. *Measured Lies: The Bell Curve Examined*. New York: St. Martin's Press.

Kinder, Donald R., and Lynn M. Sanders. 1996. *Divided by Color: Racial Politics and Democratic Ideals*. Chicago: University of Chicago Press.

King, Colbert I. 2004. "Fix It Brother." Editorial. *Washington Post*, May 22, A27.

King, Martin Luther, Jr.. 1986a. "The American Dream." In *A Testament of Hope: The Essential Writings and Speeches of Martin Luther King Jr.*, edited by James M. Washington. New York: HarperCollins.

———. 1986b. "The Current Crisis in Race Relations." In *A Testament of Hope: The Essential Writings and Speeches of Martin Luther King Jr.*, edited by James M. Washington. New York: HarperCollins.

———. 1986c. "The Ethical Demands for Integration." In *A Testament of Hope: The Essential Writings and Speeches of Martin Luther King Jr.*, edited by James M. Washington. New York: HarperCollins.

———. 1986d. "Our Struggle." In *A Testament of Hope: The Essential Writings and Speeches of Martin Luther King Jr.*, edited by James M. Washington. New York: HarperCollins.

Krugman, Paul. 2005. "Tragedy in Black and White." *New York Times*, September 19, A25.

Ladd, Everett Carll. 1999. *The Ladd Report*. New York: Free Press.

Landrine, Hope, and Elizabeth A. Klonoff. 1996. *African American Acculturation: Deconstructing Race and Reviving Culture.* Thousand Oaks, CA: Sage.

Lane, Robert E. 1962. *Political Ideology: Why the American Common Man Believes What He Does.* New York: Free Press of Glencoe.

Lee, Barbara. 2005. "Katrina Exposed Two Americas." *Herald News*, September 18, B11.

Leighley, Jan E., and Arnold Vedlitz. 1999. "Race, Ethnicity, and Political Participation: Competing Models and Contrasting Explanations." *Journal of Politics* 61:1092–1114.

Leonard, Mary. 2002. "Race, Gender Gaps Found in Colleges: Black Women Add to the Enrollment Lead over Black Men." *Boston Globe*, September 23, A3.

Levins, Harry, Ron Harris, and Clay Barbour. 2005. "Are Victims Refugees? Editors, Dictionaries, Readers Weigh-In, Post-Dispatch Plans to Reduce Word Use." *St. Louis Dispatch*, September 7, A13.

Lewis, Hylan, and Mozell Hill. 1956. "Desegregation, Integration, and the Negro Community." *Annals of Academy of the American Academy of Political and Social Science* 304:116–123.

Lincoln, C. Eric. 1974. *The Black Church since Frazier.* New York: Schocken Press.

Lincoln, C. Eric, and Lawrence H. Mamiya. 1990. *The Black Church in the African American Experience.* Durham, NC: Duke University Press.

Lipset, Seymour Martin, and William Schneider. 1987. "The Confidence Gap during the Reagan Years, 1981–1987." *Political Science Quarterly* 102:1–23.

Malcomson, Scott L. 2004. "An Appeal beyond Race." *New York Times*, August 1, sec. 4, 5.

Marable, Manning. 1985. *Black American Politics from the Washington Marches to Jesse Jackson.* New York: Verso.

Massey, Douglas S., and Nancy A. Denton. 1993. *American Apartheid: Segregation and the Making of the Underclass.* Cambridge, MA: Harvard University Press.

McAdam, Doug. 1982. *Political Process and the Development of Black Insurgency, 1930–1970.* Chicago: University of Chicago Press.

McClain, Paula D., and John A. Garcia. 1993. "Expanding Disciplinary Boundaries: Black, Latino, and Racial Minority Group Politics in Political Science." In *Political Science: The State of the Discipline II*, edited by Ada W. Finifter. Washington, DC: American Political Science Association.

McDaniel, Mike. 2005. "Katrina's Aftermath; Racial Bias Comes to the Forefront; Terms, Pictures Used by the Media Prompt Debate." *Houston Chronicle*, September 19, Star, 1.

McGary, Howard. 1999. "Douglass on Racial Assimilation and Racial Institutions." In *Frederick Douglass: A Critical Reader*, edited by Bill E. Lawson and Franklin M. Kirkland. Malden, MA: Blackwell.

McIver, John P., and Edward G. Carmines. 1981. *Unidimensional Scaling.* Thousand Oaks, CA: Sage.

McWhorter, John H. 2000. *Losing the Race: Self-Sabotage in Black America*. New York: Free Press.

Meier, August. 1991. *Negro Thought in America 1880–1915: Racial Ideologies in the Age of Booker T. Washington*. Ann Arbor: University of Michigan Press.

Mendelberg, Tali. 2001. *The Race Card: Campaign Strategy, Implicit Messages, and the Norm of Equality*. Princeton, NJ: Princeton University Press.

Miller, Arthur H. 1974. "Political Issues and Trust in Government: 1964–1970." *American Political Science Review* 68:951–972.

Miller, Arthur H., Patricia Gurin, Gerald Gurin, and Oksana Malanchuk. 1981. "Group Consciousness and Political Participation." *American Journal of Political Science* 25:494–511.

Morgan, David L. 1997. *Focus Groups as Qualitative Research*. 2nd ed. Thousand Oaks, CA: Sage.

Morris, Aldon D. 1984. *The Origins of the Civil Rights Movement: Black Communities Organizing for Change*. New York: Free Press.

Moses, Wilson Jeremiah, ed. 1996. *Classical Black Nationalism: From the American Revolution to Marcus Garvey*. New York: NYU Press.

Muhammad, Elijah. 1965. *Message to the Black Man in America*. Chicago: Final Call.

Myrdal, Gunnar. 1962. *An American Dilemma: The Negro Problem and Modern Democracy*. New York: Harper and Row.

The National Election Studies, Center for Political Studies, University of Michigan. The NES Guide to Public Opinion and Electoral Behavior. http://www.umich.edu/~nes/nesguide.htm. Ann Arbor: University of Michigan, Center for Political Studies [producer and distributor], 1995–2000.

Nelson, Jill. 1993. *Volunteer Slavery: My Authentic Negro Experience*. New York: Penguin Books.

Nelson, Thomas E., Zoe M. Oxley, and Rosalee A. Clawson. 1997. "Towards a Psychology of Framing Effects." *Political Behavior* 19(3):221–246.

Nelson, William E., and Phillip Meranto. 1977. *Electing Black Mayors: Political Action in the Black Community*. Columbus: Ohio State University Press.

Orey, Byron D'Andra. 2001. "A New Racial Threat in the New South? (A Conditional) Yes." *American Review of Politics* 22:233–256.

———. 2003. "The New Black Conservative: Rhetoric or Reality?" *African American Research Perspective*, Winter, 38–47.

Orey, Byron D'Andra, and Melanye T. Price. N.d. "A Note on Black Conservatives and Black Nationalists: Convergence or Divergence?" Typescript.

Parent, Wayne. 1985. "A Liberal Legacy: Blacks Blaming Themselves for Economic Failures." *Journal of Black Studies* 16:3–20.

Patillo-McCoy, Mary. 1999. *Black Picket Fences: Privilege and Peril among the Black Middle Class*. Chicago: University of Chicago Press.

Persons, Georgia, ed. 1993. *Dilemmas of Black Politics: Issues of Leadership and Strategy*. New York: HarperCollins.

Piven, Frances Fox, and Richard A. Cloward. 1979. *Poor People's Movements.* New York: Vintage Books.

Pollock, Philip H. 1983. "The Participatory Consequences of Internal and External Political Efficacy: A Research Note." *Western Political Quarterly* 36:400–409.

Powell, Stewart M. 2005. "Black Leaders Slam Response." *Times Union,* September 3, A6.

Price, Melanye T. 1998. "The Biographical Consequences of Radical Activism." Paper presented at "The Crisis of the Intellectual, Past, Present and Future: A Conference in Tribute to Harold Cruse." Ann Arbor, MI, March 13.

———. 1999. "An Examination of African American Ideology: Gender Differences in Adherence to Integrationism and Black Nationalism in the 1996 National Black Election Study." Paper presented at the annual meeting of the Southern Political Science Association, Savannah, GA, November 3–7.

———. 2008. "What Obama Means to Me." Commentary section. *Hartford Courant,* March 16 , 1.

Putnam, Robert D. 1995a. "Bowling Alone: America's Declining Social Capital." *Journal of Democracy* 6:65–78.

———. 1995b. "Tuning In, Tuning Out: The Strange Disappearance of Social Capital in America." *PS: Political Science and Politics* 28:664–683.

———. 2000. *Bowling Alone: The Collapse and Revival of American Community.* New York: Simon and Schuster.

Quarles, Benjamin. 1987. *The Negro in the Making of America.* New York: Collier Books.

Reed, Adolph. 1986. *The Jesse Jackson Phenomenon.* New Haven, CT: Yale University Press.

———. 2002. "The Study of Black Politics and the Practice of Black Politics: Their Historical Relation and Evolution." Paper presented at "Problems and Methods in the Study of Politics Conference," New Haven, CT, December 6–8.

Reese, Laura A., and Ronald E. Brown. 1994. "The Effects of Religious Messages on Racial Identity and System Blame among African Americans." *Journal of Politics* 56:24–43.

Reid, Ira De A. 1956. "Foreword." *Annals of the American Academy of Political and Social Science: Racial Desegregation and Integration* 304:ix–x.

Reuter, Theodore. 1995. "The New Black Conservatives." In *The Politics of Race: African Americans and the Political System,* edited by Theodore Reuter. Armonk, NY: Sharpe.

Rhodes, Jane. 2007. *Framing the Black Panthers: The Spectacular Rise of a Black Power Icon.* New York: New Press.

Richardson, Valerie. 2000. "Black Republicans Make Mark in U.S. Elections." *Washington Times,* November 10, sec. A.

Robinson, Randall. 2004. *Quitting America: The Departure of a Black Man from His Native Land*. New York: Plume.

Rogers, Reuel. 2006. *Afro-Caribbean Immigrants and the Politics of Incorporation: Ethnicity, Exception, or Exit*. New York: Cambridge University Press.

Rosenstone, Steven J., Roy L. Behr, and Edward H. Lazarus. 1984. *Third Parties in America: Citizen Response to Majority Party Failure*. Princeton, NJ: Princeton University Press.

Rupp, Leila J., and Verta Taylor. 1987. *Survival in the Doldrums: The American Women's Rights Movement, 1945 to the 1960s*. New York: Oxford University Press.

Schultz, Connie. 2005. "'Refugee' Tag Adds Insult to Injury." *Cleveland Plain-Dealer*, September 8, F1.

Sewell, Tony. 1990. *Garvey's Children: The Legacy of Marcus Garvey*. London: Macmillan.

Shabazz, El-Hajj Malik El- (Malcolm X). 1989a [1965]. "After the Bombing." In *Malcolm X Speaks: Selected Speeches and Statements*. New York: Pathfinder Press.

———. 1989b [1965]. "The Ballot or the Bullet." In *Malcolm X Speaks: Selected Speeches and Statements*. New York: Pathfinder Press.

———. 1992 [1962]. *The Autobiography of Malcolm X* (as told to Alex Haley). New York: Ballantine Books.

Shingles, Richard D. 1981. "Black Consciousness and Political Participation: The Missing Link." *American Political Science Review* 75:76–91.

Simpson, Andrea Y. 1998. *The Tie That Binds: Identity and Political Attitudes in the Post–Civil Rights Generation*. New York: NYU Press.

Sinclair-Chapman, Valeria, and Melanye Price. 2008. "Black Politics, the 2008 Election, and the (Im)possibility of Race Transcendence." *PS: Political Science and Politics* 61:739–745.

Smiley, Tavis, ed. 2006. *The Covenant with Black America*. Chicago: Third World Press.

———. 2007. *The Covenant in Action*. Carlsbad, CA: Hay House.

Smith, Robert C. 1995. *Racism in the Post–Civil Rights Era: Now You See It, Now You Don't*. Albany: State University of New York Press.

———. 1996. *We Have No Leaders: African Americans in the Post–Civil Rights Era*. Albany: State University of New York Press.

Smith, Rogers M. 1993. "Beyond Tocqueville, Myrdal, and Hartz: The Multiple Traditions in America." *American Political Science Review* 87:549–566.

Smooth, Wendy G., and Tamelyn Tucker. 1999. "Behind but Not Forgotten: Women and the Behind-the-Scenes Organizing of the Million Man March." In *Still Lifting, Still Climbing: African American Women's Contemporary Activism*, edited by Kimberly Springer. New York: NYU Press.

Sniderman, Paul M., and Thomas Piazza. 1993. *The Scar of Race*. Cambridge, MA: Harvard University Press.

———. 2002. *Black Pride and Black Prejudice*. Princeton, NJ: Princeton University Press.

Sniderman, Paul M., Thomas Piazza, Phillip E. Tetlock, and Ann Kendrick. 1991. "The New Racism." *American Journal of Political Science* 35:423–447.

Solomon, Deborah. 2005. "Bill Cosby's Not Funny." *New York Times Magazine*, March 27, 15.

Spector, Paul E. 1992. *Summated Rating Scale Construction: An Introduction*. Thousand Oaks, CA: Sage.

Stein, Judith. 1986. *The World of Marcus Garvey: Race and Class in Modern Society*. Baton Rouge: Louisiana State University Press.

Stewart, Maria. 1996 [1833]. "Address at the African Mason Hall." In *Classical Black Nationalism: From the American Revolution to Marcus Garvey*, edited by Wilson Jeremiah Moses. New York: NYU Press.

Sweet, Lynn. 2008. "Obama Tells Blacks: Shape Up." *Chicago Sun-Times*, Feb. 28, A1.

Sylvan, Donald A., and James F. Voss, eds. 1998. *Problem Representation in Foreign Policy Decision-Making*. New York: Cambridge University Press.

Tarrow, Sydney. 1997. "Towards a Movement Society." In *Social Movements: Perspectives and Issues*, edited by Steven M. Buechler and F. Kurt Cylke Jr. Mountain View, CA: Mayfield Press.

Tate, Katherine. 1991. "Black Political Participation in the 1984 and 1988 Presidential Elections." *American Political Science Review* 85:1159–1176.

———. 1993. *From Protest to Politics: The New Black Voters in American Elections*. Cambridge, MA: Harvard University Press.

———. 1996. "1996 National Black Election Study: Survey Respondents Report." Typescript.

Taylor, Verta. 1989. "Social Movement Continuity: The Women's Movement in Abeyance." *American Sociological Review* 54:761–775.

Tilly, Charles, ed. 1995. *Citizenship, Identity and Social History*. New York: Cambridge University Press.

Timpone, Richard J. 1998. "Structure, Behavior, and Voter Turnout in the United States." *American Political Science Review* 92:145–158.

Tucker, Cynthia. 2000. "The Republican National Convention: GOP Appeals to Minorities Can Work If They're More Than Just Skin Deep." *Atlanta Journal and Constitution*, August 6, B1.

———. 2004. "Bill Cosby's Speech: His Words Sting Because Truth Hurts." Editorial. *Atlanta Journal-Constitution*, May 26, 15A.

Ture, Kwame, and Charles V. Hamilton. 1992. *Black Power: The Politics of Liberation*. New York: Vintage Books.

Tyson, Timothy B. 1999. *Radio Free Dixie: Robert F. Williams and the Roots of Black Power*. Chapel Hill: University of North Carolina Press.

Vaca, Nicolas C. 2004. *The Presumed Alliance: The Unspoken Conflict be-tween Latinos and Blacks and What It Means for America*. New York: HarperCollins.

Verba, Sidney, Kay Lehman Schlozman, and Henry E. Brady. 1995. *Voice and Equality: Civic Volunteerism in American Politics*. Cambridge, MA: Harvard University Press.

Verba, Sidney, Kay Lehman Schlozman, Henry E. Brady, and Norman H. Nie. 1993. "Race, Ethnicity and Political Resources: Participation in the United States." *British Journal of Political Science* 23:453–497.

Vickerman, Milton. 1999. *Crosscurrents: West Indian Immigrants and Race*. New York: Oxford Press.

Violanti, Anthony. 2005. "Kanye West, Katrina Focus Spotlight on Race." *Buffalo News*, September 7, final edition, C1.

"Voting Trends in Presidential Elections." 2000. Associated Press. October 12.

"Wade in the Water." 1977. *The New National Baptist Hymnal*. Nashville TN: National Baptist Publishing Board.

Walker, David. 2000 [1785–1830.] *David Walker's Appeal to the Coloured Citizens of the World*. Edited by Peter P. Hinks. University Park: Pennsylvania State University Press.

Walters, Ronald W. 1988. *Black Presidential Politics in America*. Albany: State University of New York Press.

Walton, Hanes, Jr. 1985. *Invisible Politics: Black Political Behavior*. Albany: State University of New York Press.

———. 1997. *African American Power and Politics: The Political Context Variable*. New York: Columbia University Press.

Washington, Booker T. 1968. *The Future of the American Negro*. New York: Haskell House.

Waters, Mary C. 1999. *Black Identities: West Indian Immigrant Dreams and American Realities*. Cambridge, MA: Harvard University Press.

Wattenberg, Martin P. 1996. *The Decline of American Political Parties: 1952–1994*. Cambridge, MA: Harvard University Press.

Whitby, Kenny J. 2007. "The Effect of Black Descriptive Representation on Black Turnout in the 2004 Elections." *Social Science Quarterly* 88:1010–1023.

Williams, Linda Faye. 2003. *The Constraint of Race: Legacies of White Skin Privilege in America*. University Park: Pennsylvania State University Press.

Wilson, William J. 1978. *The Declining Significance of Race: Blacks and Changing American Institutions*. Chicago: University of Chicago Press.

———. 1997. *When Work Disappears: The World of the New Urban Poor*. New York: Knopf.

———. 1999. *The Bridge over the Racial Divide: Rising Inequality and Coalition Politics*. Berkeley: University of California Press.

Woodward, C. Vann. 1957. *The Strange Career of Jim Crow*. New York: Oxford University Press.Young, Alford A., Jr. 2004. *The Minds of Marginalized Black Men: Making Sense of Mobility, Opportunity and Future Life Changes*. Princeton, NJ: Princeton University Press.

Zewe, Charles. 2000. "Bush Seeks to Polish GOP Image among Black Voters: Some African Americans Wary of Texas Governor's Efforts." *CNN Online*, July 7.

Zinn, Howard. 2002. *SNCC: The New Abolitionists*. Boston: Beacon Press.

Index

Aberbach, Joel D., 129, 130
Abramson, Paul R., 121, 129, 144
activism, feminist, 11
affirmative action, 6, 48–49, 73–75
Africa, 24–25
Afristocracy, 86
Afrocentricism, 10, 25
"After the Bombing Speech," 25
age, 110. See also *Cross-tabulation of Age and the Black Nationalist Index;* generation gap
AIDS/HIV, 178
Aldrich, John H., 144
alienation, political, 127–128
American National Election Study (ANES), 194n15
"American spaces," 163
Anderson, Barbara A., 121
ANES. *See* American National Election Study
Appeal to Coloured Citizens of the World, 20
Asante, Molefi K., 25

black America, 150–151, 153, 166; benefits of, 159–160; conditions for, 156–157; political problems and, 160; racial unity and, 154–156; societal norms and, 157–159
black blame, 53, 76, 78, 80, 81, 83, 88, 118, 138, 169, 175–176; class

stratification and, 86–87; communities and, 94; frames and, 90–91; individual blame and, 88–89; opportunities and, 92–93; stereotypes and, 100–101
black communities, 55, 165. *See also* black America; education; income; real estate
Black Conservatives, 138
Black Democrats, 141
black empowerment, 3
Black Feminism, 9
black inferiority, 13
Black Marxism, 9
Black Nationalism: adherence, 104–106; black Republicanism and, 194n10; categories of, 19; classical period, 20; contemporary interpretations and, 108–110; Dawson's ideological category as, 9; focus groups and, 60–65; historical periods, 20; Malcolm X and, 19; modern era, 20; political participation and, 149; political world view as, 11; predictors for, 115–116; principles of, 3–4; racialized ideology and, 7–9, 136–138; revival and, 163–164; scholarship and, 11; Stewart and, 22; value systems and, 111; Wilson and, 20. See also *Frequency Distribution of Black Nationalism*

About the Author

MELANYE T. PRICE is Assistant Professor of Government at Wesleyan University.